ORIGINAL
LAND-ROVER
SERIES I

Other titles in the *Original* series available from Herridge & Sons are:

Original Austin Seven
by Rinsey Mills

Original Austin-Healey (100 & 3000)
by Anders Ditlev Clausager

Original Jaguar MkI/MkII
by Nigel Thorley

Original Honda CB750
by John Wyatt

Original Kawasaki Z1, Z900 & KZ900
by David Marsden

Original MGA
by Anders Ditlev Clausager

Original MGB
by Anders Ditlev Clausager

Original MG T Series
by Anders Ditlev Clausager

Original Mini Cooper & Cooper S
by John Parnell

Original Morris Minor
by Ray Newell

Original Range Rover
by James Taylor

Original Rolls-Royce & Bentley 1946-65
by James Taylor

Original Sprite & Midget
by Terry Horler

Original Vincent Motorcycle
by J P Bickerstaff

Original VW Bus
by Laurence Meredith

ORIGINAL
LAND-ROVER
SERIES I

by James Taylor

Photography by Rowan Isaac
Edited by Mark Hughes

H&S

FRONT COVER
A superb 80-inch model from early 1951, owned by
Graham Medlicott.

HALF-TITLE PAGE
Another 1951 80-inch version, but this is a highly original
Australian-assembled vehicle owned by Sue Combridge.

TITLE PAGE
A contrasting 1950 80-inch pair – British Army version and
Station Wagon – owned by Ken Wheelwright.

BACK COVER
David Viewing's 1953 80-inch Fire Engine is used as a water
tender for his steam traction engine, seen in the background.

First published in 1996 by Bay View Books Ltd
This edition published in 2009 by Herridge & Sons Ltd,
Lower Forda, Shebbear, Beaworthy, Devon EX21 5SY

Reprinted 2011, 2015

ISBN 978-1-906133-15-3
Printed in China

CONTENTS

INTRODUCTION

For very many years, the Series I Land-Rovers were just old light commercial vehicles, of very little interest to anyone unless in a condition to continue earning their keep. Then, all of a sudden, enthusiasts began to take an interest. Just as the classic car movement began to gather momentum in Britain, the first painstaking restorations of early Land-Rovers to pristine, ex-factory condition were undertaken. One of the 1948 prototypes, R.04, was rebuilt by Tony Hutchings in 1974; and, quite independently, Brian Carvey that year restored his 1950 production model EDP 999, affectionately known as 'Bessie'.

Land-Rovers nevertheless remained a minority interest among old vehicle enthusiasts for another decade, but by the middle of the 1980s the bug had bitten hard. 4x4s of all types had effectively replaced the sports car (and, in its turn, the hot hatch) as the fashionable vehicle to have – and old Land-Rovers suddenly became interesting to a large number of people. *Land Rover Owner* magazine, launched in 1987, rode the crest of this wave of interest and took the message far and wide across the globe. By 1995, there was a waiting market for a book like this one.

Even so, I have to admit that I swallowed hard at least twice when I was asked if I would consider writing it. As a Land-Rover enthusiast for many years, I was only too well aware of the heated debates among devotees of the early vehicles about tiny details of the specification. I was also only too well aware that some details have not been resolved satisfactorily and probably never will be.

Nevertheless, challenges make life interesting, so I agreed to do the job. Right from the beginning, it seemed to me that I was really doing little more than co-ordinating information which for the most part was already available somewhere; although I must say I was surprised to find how many gaps there appeared to be in that information. Rover's own service literature for the early Land-Rovers was surprisingly little help in many cases, and the hard nuggets of information came from a number of well-respected figures in the Land-Rover movement who willingly volunteered material which they have researched over the years. My sincere thanks therefore go to Michael Burn, Brian Carvey, Andrew Cross, Peter Galilee, Peter Hughes, Richard Hughes, Rob Ivins, Richard Lines and John Smith, all of whom saw at least part of the manuscript in its original draft form and offered constructive criticism. I hope they feel that their advice and guidance have been put to good use.

Many enthusiasts also kindly agreed to make their vehicles available for photographer Rowan Isaac, whose excellent pictures help to illustrate some of the myriad points of detail to which the text refers. So on that score, I am also extremely grateful to the following: Ray Adams (86-inch standard), John Banham (86-inch military), Brian Bashall (80-inch chassis), Brian Carvey (80-inch early production), Sue Combridge (80-inch 2-litre and 80-inch Australian CKD), David Davies (80-inch truck cab), Keith Gott (88-inch diesel), Andrew Ings (81-inch military, 80-inch Station Wagon under restoration, Brockhouse trailer and 86-inch fire tender), Rob Ivins (88-inch 4×2 and 107-inch standard), Richard Lines (80-inch welder), Graham Medlicott (80-inch standard), John Smith (80-inch pre-production), Andrew Stevens (80-inch canvas cab), John Taylor (86-inch station wagon, 107-inch station wagon and 88-inch fire tender), David Viewing (80-inch fire tender), Ken Wheelwright (80-inch pre-production, 80-inch early production, 80-inch station wagon and 80-inch military), the Automobile Association (80-inch patrol vehicle) and the Haynes Motor Museum (State Review vehicle, loaned from the Heritage Motor Centre).

As a 'belt and braces' exercise, all photographs were kindly vetted for accuracy and originality during a one-day session with a panel of experts comprising Brian Bashall, Michael Burn, Anders Ditlev Clausager (archivist at the BMIHT), Andrew Cross, Peter Hughes, John Smith, John Taylor and Ken Wheelwright. Among the locations used for photography, special thanks are due to the University of Manchester's Nuffield Radio Astronomy Laboratories, Jodrell Bank, Cheshire.

Restoration of an elderly vehicle of any kind can often be a lonely occupation, and all of those who worked on this book hope that it provides a few grains of help when all else seems lost. But we would also like to offer a little advice (if it is not already too late for some of those reading this). The advice is that if you want to embark on the restoration of a Series I Land-Rover of any type, please go into the job with your eyes wide open.

The Series I Land-Rovers were always primarily working vehicles rather than the car substitutes which so many modern 4×4s are. That meant that if they failed to work, they had no value at all. Consequently, many were modified in service, either to do a specific job or with non-standard parts to keep them running. Often it is almost impossible to determine whether some parts which look wrong belong on the vehicle or not. The best advice is to take them off the vehicle if you suspect their authenticity, but to store them rather than throw them away. Several rare and even prototype Land-Rover parts have been lost over the years because restorers did not recognise what they were and simply discarded them.

It is also very important to recognise that in these early years, the Rover Company was turning out Land-Rovers as fast as it possibly could. As a result, changes made on the production line sometimes went unrecorded or were wrongly recorded – as anyone who has tried to work with a Parts Catalogue

John Smith's 1948 pre-production vehicle, R.11, is representative of the pilot batch of 48 vehicles.

for these early Land-Rovers will know. It is also probably true to say that the serial numbers associated with specification changeover points for minor items should be treated with considerable caution, particularly during 80-inch production. It is only too easy to imagine a specification change being made on the assembly lines and appropriately recorded for service literature, and then another box of old-specification parts being found and used up. This kind of thing certainly happened in other British car factories in the early 1950s, and the anomalies found on some 80-inch Land-Rovers make clear that it happened at the Rover plant in Solihull as well!

Before you get into the real meat of this book, let me say that all those involved in its production would like it to be definitive, but all of us know that it cannot be. There is still plenty of work to be done before everything is known about these early Land-Rovers. We all hope that this book will provide a basis for further research. Lastly, if you want to restore your Land-Rover correctly down to the last little detail, then we hope this book will help and we wish you the best of luck. If, on the other hand, you simply want to own a good example of a Series I and have no intention of spending years searching for the 'correct' parts, then put this book on your bedside table and just enjoy browsing through it.

James Taylor
Woodcote, Oxfordshire, April 1996

The following points are understood throughout this book:

1. The Rover model year began in September and ended in August; thus, for example, 1949 models are those built between September 1948 and August 1949.
2. References to the left-hand and right-hand sides of the vehicle are taken from the viewpoint of someone sitting in the driving seat and facing forwards.
3. Most nuts and bolts used on Series I Land-Rovers are BSF sizes.

LAND-ROVER PAST & PRESENT

Andrew Stevens' 1949 model displays the light green paint used on early production vehicles and the optional canvas cab.

When Rover started building Land-Rovers at its Solihull factory in 1948, the company certainly had no idea that these vehicles would be the first in a line which would carry on for half a century. The Land-Rover was nothing more than an emergency measure, designed to keep the Rover production lines ticking over until the car market recovered from the turmoil into which the 1939-45 war had thrown it.

Rover's problem was simple. The company had built a formidable reputation with solidly-engineered and durable cars for the professional classes during the 1930s, but in the difficult economic climate which followed the war, such cars were not what the buying public wanted. Cars for the home market were in any case strictly rationed by Government decree, because all motor manufacturers were encouraged to export the vast majority of their products in order to earn revenue to rebuild Britain's war-torn economy. Rover, who had never taken overseas markets very seriously and who had been too busy on war work to have any new models ready, had neither the infrastructure nor the products to meet overseas demand.

While the company struggled to set up an overseas distribution network, its engineers began to look at new products. They had two in mind. The first was totally unlike the company's traditional products, and was a small car of advanced design called the M-type. Managing Director Spencer Wilks had initiated this project in 1945, believing that the economic climate after the war would lead to a demand for smaller and cheaper cars – just as it had led to the cyclecar boom after the 1914-18 war. However, it rapidly became clear that small cars were not what the public wanted, and so the M-type was abandoned, probably in the first months of 1947.

The second new product was a radically updated version of the company's pre-war saloons, known as the P3 model. That would be ready to enter production in 1948, but slow sales of the existing Rover saloons (revived pre-war models generally known as P2s) suggested that another car of this type was not going to provide the answer either.

A metal truck cab became available during 1952 and could be retro-fitted to earlier vehicles, such as this 1949 model owned by Dave Davies.

One of the first Land-Rovers ever to be restored was 'Bessie', Brian Carvey's 1950 model.

The original Station Wagon on the 80-inch wheelbase was too expensive to sell well. This 1950 example belongs to Ken Wheelwright.

Government policies only made things worse for Rover. Sheet steel was in short supply and had to be rationed, and the Government used this rationing as an incentive to force car makers to build for export. Rations were allocated strictly according to a maker's export performance, and (in theory at least) a maker which failed to export would be starved of the steel it needed to make any cars at all. The combination of poor sales and limited supplies of raw materials meant that Rover production had to be cut back, and on 1 May 1947 the Board of Directors was officially informed that the company was working for only four days on alternate weeks.

Fortunately, things were already in hand to save the day. Rover's Chief Engineer, Spencer Wilks' younger brother Maurice, had come up with the idea of building a multi-purpose agricultural vehicle which he believed would sell well overseas. His original inspiration had been a demobbed Willys Jeep, which he had bought from an Army Surplus dump early in 1947 for private use. Ex-military Jeeps were then in demand world-wide for agricultural use, and Willys itself had started to make a civilianised version for exactly those purposes. In April 1947, during a family holiday in Anglesey, Maurice Wilks conceived the idea of a Rover 'jeep', no doubt imagining that it would sell well in those areas of the Commonwealth where Willys had no market presence.

The great advantage of Wilks' idea was that the vehicle could be got into production very quickly, using mechanical components from the forthcoming P3 saloon cars. The chassis could be a very simple construction and the body could be simple enough to make by hand. These factors would mean that Rover would need neither to spend huge sums of money on new press tools nor to wait for those press tools to be made. While steel would be necessary for the chassis, the bodies could be made from aircraft aluminium, which was in plentiful supply after the war (even though it cost three times as much as steel) and was easy to work by hand. Moreover, that alu-

Land-Rovers were also shipped abroad in kit form for overseas assembly. This 1951 example belonging to Sue Combridge was assembled in Australia and has certain features not found on UK-assembled Land-Rovers. By this stage, the headlamps had emerged from behind the mesh grille.

Even Royalty used Land-Rovers. This one was built as a ceremonial review vehicle on the 86-inch chassis.

minium would resist corrosion better than steel and would thus be ideal for a vehicle which was going to spend much of its time out of doors.

A feasibility prototype was built in the late summer and early autumn of 1947. To save time, Rover built it on a Jeep chassis. They added a 1389cc engine from the current Rover 10hp (the larger P3 saloon engine they wanted was not yet in production and probably no prototypes could be spared), fitted Rover axles and a Rover gearbox, and hastily put together a transfer gearbox to give an extra range of low gears and four-wheel drive. As the vehicle would be going to some territories where left-hand drive was expected as well as to others where right-hand drive was the norm, the Rover engineers compromised by putting the prototype's steering wheel in the middle. As it was intended to do some of the work of a tractor, which also had its driver centrally placed, Rover must also have reasoned that many customers would find this quite acceptable.

This prototype had not even been completed before the Rover Board agreed that what they initially called the Landrover (all one word) should go forward to production. The historic decision was taken on 4 September 1947. Over the next few months, the centre-steer prototype was tested on farmland around the Rover factory, at Maurice Wilks' home, and probably also at his holiday home on Anglesey. A great deal of redesign work was done, and by March the company was ready to begin assembly of a pilot-production batch, this time using its own design of chassis and the P3 saloon car engine which had entered production just a few weeks earlier.

As the Land-Rover was intended to appeal primarily to overseas customers, Rover would have liked to announce it at the prestigious Geneva international motor show in March – the first show since the war and therefore one which would be an ideal showcase for their new vehicle. However, the pilot-production models were simply not ready in time, and so Rover chose instead to announce the Land-Rover at the next show in the calendar, the rather less prestigious one at Amsterdam. Even then, the schedule was tight, but two vehicles were at the show, which opened on 30 April.

The pilot-production vehicles were built over the period of four months from March to June 1948, and the specification continued to evolve during this period. Of the 50 sanctioned for production, only 48 were actually built – probably because a viable production specification had been established by that stage and Rover was keen to get the vehicle into production as soon as possible. The huge interest generated by the Amsterdam show must have prompted this to a certain extent. Orders flooded in from all over the world, and Rover immediately found demand vastly exceeding the supply available as Land-Rover production slowly built up.

By 21 July – some six weeks after the Amsterdam

introduction – Rover had received enquiries or firm orders for no fewer than 8000 Land-Rovers. And by the end of the year Rover's Chairman was telling the company's shareholders of indications that 'this vehicle will be something very much more than an additional source of production. It may yet equal – and even exceed – our car output in quantity.'

His prediction was correct. By 1950 Rover was building twice as many Land-Rovers as it was cars, and over the ensuing years the Land-Rover completely changed the face of the company. Rover was slow to acknowledge this, always preferring to think of itself as a genteel car manufacturer which made light utility vehicles as a sideline. The truth of the matter, however, was that Rover had become a maker of light utilities for whom cars were a profitable sideline. Without profits from the Land-Rover, in fact, the company might have ceased to exist altogether in the 1950s.

The enormous demand for the Land-Rover in the late 1940s and early 1950s actually proved a constant headache for Rover. While the company could congratulate itself that Maurice Wilks' idea had been a winner, it also had to cope with the fact that the Land-Rover had been rushed into production and that it had been conceived as a short-term stop-gap with much lower production volumes. Minor specification details had to be changed on countless occasions as customers reported problems or suggested improvements which had not been apparent during the 1947-48 development phase. And the absence of proper production tooling slowed down assembly and gave rise to dozens of further modifications as the assembly line workers devised simpler and quicker ways of building the Land-Rover.

Yet Rover was not slow to exploit its success. By October 1948, just five months after production had started, the company was ready with Station Wagon and Mobile Welder derivatives. Neither sold very strongly – the Station Wagon because its coachbuilt body made it too expensive – and Rover learned an important lesson. This was that it should stick to building the Land-Rover as a basic platform, and let customers and specialist suppliers deal with low-volume conversions and adaptations.

By the early part of 1950, Rover was sufficiently confident of continuing Land-Rover sales to start looking at developing the vehicle further. Running in parallel with a programme to bore out the 2.1-litre six-cylinder saloon engine to 2.6 litres, the Solihull engineers looked at a similar development of the 1.6-litre four-cylinder Land-Rover engine to give 2

Companion model to the 86-inch Land-Rover was the 107-inch model, initially available only as a pick-up with truck cab. This 1954 example belongs to Rob Ivins.

The Station Wagon on the 86-inch chassis was very much more successful than the original coachbuilt 80-inch type. This left-hand-drive example belongs to John Taylor.

litres. A prototype batch of 50 had been built by the summer, and the vehicles were used for testing and evaluation of the new engine over the next year.

Meanwhile, there were also plans to make the Land-Rover more versatile by making it bigger. The first move was to stretch the wheelbase by six inches in order to give more room in the body, and by June 1950 a very early (possibly the earliest) 86-inch chassis had been fitted with an experimental closed body and fitted out as an Army Staff Car. Not long after that, Rover also started to look at a very much larger Land-Rover to compete in the pick-up market. Apparently designing the vehicle around a load bed which was a full six feet long, the company had come up with the first prototype of the 107-inch Land-Rover by the end of August 1950.

However, these developments took time to filter through to production. Rover's problem in the early 1950s was that it was trying to mass-produce a vehicle which had originally been designed for low-volume production, and the top priority whenever capital was available was to streamline the existing production processes. The original press tools sometimes failed under the strain; that for the bulkhead, for example, gave trouble on several occasions between 1949 and 1952. So it was that modifications and improvements had to be introduced one at a time, and a completely new Land-Rover had to wait its turn.

The first of the major changes came in the summer of 1951, when the 2-litre engine replaced the original 1.6-litre type on the 1952-season Land-Rovers. At the same time, the slow-selling Tickford Station Wagon was dropped from the range. It would then be two more years before Solihull could cope, logistically and financially, with the introduction of the enlarged 86-inch and 107-inch models.

The new models were made available in the autumn of 1953 for the 1954 season. Anticipating much larger production volumes than had ever been envisaged for the original 80-inch models, Solihull had this time geared up properly with production tooling. In consequence, there would be far fewer changes in the three years and nearly 77,000 vehicles of 86-inch and 107-inch production than there had been in the rather haphazard five years and around 78,000 vehicles of 80-inch production. Perhaps the most major was the change in autumn 1954 to a different design of 2-litre engine – and that was dictated by developments in Rover saloons rather than by any pressing need on the Land-Rover side.

As those production figures show, the Land-

A Station Wagon became available on the 107-inch chassis during 1956. This 1958 example belongs to John Taylor.

Rover's popularity just went on increasing during the 1953-56 period. This time, Solihull's problem was not with turning a low-volume vehicle into a mass-production type, but with finding room at the works to build enough vehicles to meet demand. It was not surprising that the numbers of CKD Land-Rovers – vehicles assembled abroad from Completely Knocked Down kits of parts shipped out from Solihull – multiplied greatly during this period.

The great advantage of the 86 and 107 models over their predecessors lay in their vastly increased load-space. The 86 offered 25% more room than the superseded 80, although its payload remained unchanged at 1000lb. The 107, meanwhile, offered a huge load-bed even though its payload was just 50% greater at 1500lb. From the beginning, the 86 came with the same body configurations as the superseded 2-litre 80, plus a new seven-seater Station Wagon body – this time built at Solihull following standard Land-Rover construction principles. The 107 was always sold in pick-up form in its first years, although a ten-seater Station Wagon did become available in June 1956. By this time, however, the days of the 86 and 107 versions were already numbered.

In fact, the 86s lasted just a few more months in production, and the 107 pick-up models disappeared with them in the autumn of 1956. Their replacements were the third-generation Land-Rovers, each of them with an additional two inches in the wheelbase. The new 88 and 109 models remained in production alongside the 107 Station Wagon until the whole range was replaced in April 1958 – exactly ten years after the Land-Rover's first public appearance – by the considerably revised Series II models.

When the 88s and 109s were introduced, it was very far from clear to the customers why their wheelbases had been stretched. With the 86s and 107s, the extra length in the wheelbase had contributed directly to increases in the size of the load-bed; but the extra two inches in the 88s and 109s had been added, apparently uselessly, by moving the front axle forwards in the chassis. There were no new body styles to suggest an explanation, and it was not until April 1957 that the reason became clear.

The Land-Rover's popularity as a runabout in commercial vehicle fleets had led as early as 1953 to enquiries about a diesel-engined version, and in fact that year an aftermarket conversion to diesel had been introduced by Turner Engineering of Wolverhampton. This company offered two different engines, a 40bhp two-cylinder and a 60bhp three-cylinder, in each case supercharged and built under licence from the Austrian Jenbach company. Neither proved very popular, probably because the public mistrusted any engine with fewer than four cylinders, but the Rover engineers were well aware of the potential sales of a diesel-engined Land-Rover.

By 1955, they had started work on a new small diesel engine, and as soon as they were able to find factory space to build this they put it into production. The engine was a 2-litre overhead valve design, with a robust block which made it physically larger than the 2-litre inlet-over-exhaust petrol engine. To

This 88-inch military Land-Rover, owned by John Banham, has been restored with the colours and insignia from its time in service with British forces in the Middle East.

LAND-ROVER SALES, 1949-58

1949	8000
1950	16085
1951	17360
1952	19591
1953	18570
1954	20135
1955	28882
1956	28365
1957	25775
1958	28656

Note These figures were provided by Land Rover Ltd and are based on financial years. Thus, '1949' represents the period from April 1948 to April 1949. However there were no sales in '1948' as only prototypes were made.

accommodate it within the engine bay of the Land-Rover, the engineers had needed to insert those extra two inches between bulkhead and front axle. It was designed to have similar speed range and power output to the petrol engine, so that the same transmission components could be used.

The first diesel Land-Rovers were all sold on the home market and proved to be troublesome. However, once Rover had sorted out a weakness in the cylinder head, which was prone to cracking, the diesel became available for overseas markets as well. Around 19% of 88s and 109s built in the 1958 model year were diesel-powered, and this percentage would continue to increase after the introduction of the Series II models in April 1958.

The question of what to call these Land-Rovers built between 1948-58 is sometimes debated, and there is no single answer to please everybody. Some people, for example, do not accept the name 'Series I' at all, arguing that the vehicles were never called that when they were in production, and pointing out that there are so many different varieties of 'Series I' that it is misleading to use a single generic title for all of them.

The plain facts of the matter are that the name by which these vehicles were known kept on changing over that first decade. The 1948-51 models were just Land-Rovers, pure and simple, during their production lifetime. The only exception was the Station Wagon which, not surprisingly, was known as a Land-Rover Station Wagon. The first change to the status quo came in 1951, when the 2-litre engine replaced the original 1.6-litre type. To Rover, the new models were still Land-Rovers – nothing more and nothing less – but users and garage mechanics quite reasonably started to call them 2-litre Land-Rovers as a way of distinguishing them.

The next change came in 1953, when the 86-inch model replaced the original Land-Rover, and the 107-inch companion model was introduced. Sales literature always called the 86 a Land-Rover, usually adding '86-inch wheelbase' in brackets; most people settled for calling it an 86-inch Land-Rover, to distinguish it from the earlier types which were now unofficially known as 80-inch types. The 107 was briefly a Land-Rover 4-Wheel Drive Pick-Up Truck in sales literature and later a Land-Rover 4-Wheel Drive Long Wheelbase. Neither name caught on, not least because both were far too complicated. Instead, the 107 was known as a Long-Wheelbase Land-Rover.

Things became even more complicated with the introduction of the 88-inch and 109-inch models in 1956. Rover christened them the Regular and Long Land-Rovers respectively, but these names also failed to register. The rest of the world started to call them by their wheelbase lengths, and by extension to do that with the 80, 86 and 107 models as well. When Rover decided to give the 'Series II' name to the restyled and revitalised Land-Rovers introduced in April 1958, the preceding models quite naturally became Series Is. And so they have remained ever since, the name being given legitimacy in Rover service literature from quite early on.

PILOT-PRODUCTION VEHICLES

R.19, the 19th of the pilot-production Land-Rovers, has been meticulously restored by Ken Wheelwright. It is seen here with sidescreens installed and canvas top erect.

No book dealing with the Series I Land-Rovers would be complete without at least a passing reference to that Holy Grail of the early Land-Rover enthusiast – the pre-production batch. These were built in the early months of 1948, and incorporated a number of design improvements which experience with the original centre-steer prototype had suggested. In most respects, they closely anticipated the specification of the production vehicles, assembly of which began in June 1948 (more than a month after the Land-Rover had been announced at the Amsterdam Motor Show at the end of April).

It is clear from surviving records that the Rover engineers originally planned to make what Board meeting minutes dated 16 October 1947 call 'a pre-production batch of fifty' Land-Rovers. In fact, only 48 were built between March and May 1948, for reasons that are both unclear and hotly debated in enthusiast circles. Several of these vehicles survive.

Restoration of a pre-production Land-Rover is, however, little short of a nightmare. There are three major problems. First of all, the specification was still evolving as these vehicles were being built, with the result that there are many differences between vehicles. As no detailed records have been found (and such records may never have been kept), it is impossible to establish the 'correct' or 'original' specification for any individual vehicle.

The second problem is that many of these vehicles were used for development trials, and would therefore have been modified at Rover. It is almost impossible to distinguish between an assembly line modification and a development modification made while the vehicle was on test. And thirdly, as prototype components failed in later years, so they were replaced by production specification items – which in many cases were different. Thus the irreplaceable originals were lost forever.

Nowhere is this latter problem more clearly illustrated than in the case of R.01 – the first of the pre-production batch. This vehicle was bought back by Rover in the mid-1950s and was rebuilt to as-new condition. As the correct, original specification, parts were no longer available, worn or damaged items were replaced with their production specifica-

R.11 is now owned by John Smith, and in this picture shows off the chassis number stencilled on both front and rear cross-members. The rear cross-member, of course, is galvanised, like the rest of the chassis, and there is no guard under the fuel tank. Note also the simple seat backs – no more than a lightly padded strip.

tion equivalents. As a result, the vehicle which the Heritage Motor Centre at Gaydon now proudly displays as 'the first Land-Rover' looks very different from the way it must have done on the day it left the assembly line.

Nevertheless, there were certain features that were common to the pre-production Land-Rovers, and it is worth examining these in order to understand better why the first production vehicles were as they were.

The centrally placed steering wheel of the Jeep-based prototype probably proved impractical in use, and all the pre-production vehicles had conventional left-hand or right-hand steering. It appears that 26 were built with right-hand drive and 22 with left-hand drive, but at least seven of these were later converted to right-hand drive by Rover.

The 1389cc engine of the centre-steer prototype was also not carried over. It had in any case been scheduled to go out of production, and the pre-production Land-Rovers all had a detuned version of the company's brand-new 1595cc four-cylinder petrol engine. This had been designed for the Rover 60 (P3) saloons that entered production in February 1948, just before the Land-Rover.

The first pre-production vehicles had a simple and ingenious permanent four-wheel drive transmission. This used a modified four-speed Rover car gearbox, with a specially designed two-speed transfer gearbox that drove both the front and rear axles and offered reduction gearing for difficult cross-country work. To avoid the problem of transmission wind-up (which occurs when road conditions cause the front and rear axles to rotate at slightly different speeds), there was a freewheel in the front drive-line. This could be locked to give maximum traction off-road. The freewheel was yet another item borrowed from the Rover saloons, where it had been a feature for many years, enabling clutch-free gearchanges and allowing the engine to idle at cruising speeds along level roads.

This permanent four-wheel drive, however, was not fitted to all the pre-production batch. Several were either built with, or perhaps modified to have, selectable four-wheel drive. The first examples with this system had rod-type selector controls that ran through the bulkhead and were sited just below and to the right of the centrally placed instrument cluster. These were probably not fitted after the 20th vehicle had been built; subsequent pilot-production models had the production type of controls.

The pre-production models all had an enormously strong box-section chassis, the main rails of which were made very simply by welding four flat strips of steel together. This crude manufacturing method – introduced to save the cost of purpose-built chassis stamping machinery – was actually used on some Land-Rover chassis for the next 35 years! These chassis were also galvanised, although, contrary to popular myth, the chassis of the production Land-Rovers were never galvanised as standard. They also had their front bumpers welded on as an integral part of the chassis frame. As a result, minor bumper damage involved expensive welding and straightening repairs. This was clearly unsatisfactory, so the integral bumper was abandoned, and production models had a bumper bolted to the front of the chassis for easy replacement.

The exhaust system on the earliest examples was unique, having a short front downpipe leading to a long tubular silencer (probably the Rover P3 saloon item) outside the left-hand chassis rail. This in turn led to a pipe that discharged below the rear cross-member on the left-hand side. Later examples, however, had the production type system that crosses the chassis to emerge on the right-hand side.

The bodies of the pre-production models were designed to be hand-made, again so that Rover did not have to invest capital in production tooling or wait for such tooling to be manufactured before starting series assembly of Land-Rovers. As a result, they had simpler front wings than had been made for the centre-steer prototype. The outer body panels were made from Duralumin, a hard aluminium alloy (although Birmabright would be chosen for the production vehicles), and strength was provided by steel cappings that were galvanised to resist corrosion. Steel was also used for the bulkhead, which was folded up by hand; where local reinforcement was needed, in the area of the steering box, additional steel plate was simply welded in place.

As assembly of the pre-production batch progressed, so certain minor changes were made. Rover found that the wing-mounted mirror reflected light from the bulkhead-mounted sidelight at night, and so the mirror was repositioned on the windscreen frame. The sidescreens which Rover planned to offer as optional weather protection were found to need a hinge support at their leading edges, so one was welded to each side of the windscreen frame.

Protecting the wing from damage by fitting a rubber buffer to the door (which had no check-strap) must have proved unsatisfactory, because Rover relocated the buffer on the front wing. The

Characteristic of the first pilot-production vehicles was a bumper welded to the chassis frame. This is the one on R.19.

R.11 shows off the shield-shaped flap covering its fuel filler. The flat seat cushions are correct, but it is debatable whether both they and the seat backs would originally have been upholstered in green rather than black.

The 'square' bellhousing cover fitted to the pilot-production models and to the first 1500 production vehicles is visible in this picture of R.19. The ring-pull control for the freewheel is not recessed into the floor panel as on production and other pilot-build vehicles, which suggests that R.19 may originally have been built with rod-type transmission controls in the bulkhead. The heater is a later fitment.

The chassis number of R.19 is stamped into the left-hand engine bearer.

Many parts were hand-fabricated on the pilot-production models. They included the bronze pedals (pictured on R.11, right) and the steering wheel support bracket (pictured on R.19, far right) with obvious weld lines.

The pilot-production vehicles differed one from another. R.19 had wooden packing pieces between body and chassis at the rear (right), although R.11 did not. There was no drip-moulding on the bulkhead of the pilot-production models, and the coil was therefore protected by a shield, seen here (far right) on R.19.

The galvanised cappings on R.11 were matched by a painted tailgate latch bracket, although this bracket was galvanised on other pilot-production models. Note the correct original D-lamps. The red reflector was not an original fitment but was added later to comply with road traffic regulations.

The original badges were cast in brass. Opinion differs on whether they were originally unpainted or were finished in red with black lettering.

original design of door handle, with a T-shaped grip projecting above the top of the door, probably proved too fragile, and so it was changed for the more robust type later carried over for production. After about 40 vehicles had been built, Rover decided against continuing with the light-coloured aircraft Cockpit Green paint, of which supplies must have been plentiful after the war. Instead, they started to use the so-called 'No.2 Green', a rather darker colour already in use on the 1948-model Rover saloons.

Several items planned or proposed as optional extras were also tried out on the pre-production Land-Rovers. These included the canvas 'three-seater' cab, the full-length canvas tilt (commonly known as the 'seven-seater' type), and various items intended for use with the vehicle's power take-offs. Among these were a capstan winch mounted on the front bumper, a similar winch at the rear, and a rear drum suitable for driving the belt-driven farm machinery that was common in the late 1940s.

Finally, some of the pre-production vehicles were used for more radical developments. Two of them were converted into Station Wagons, as prototypes for the model that would be introduced in October 1948. One became a prototype for the Mobile Welder, on which the generator was permanently mounted in the vehicle's body and driven from the centre power take-off. Another became the prototype Land-Rover Fire Engine.

Two vehicles were evaluated by the Ministry of Supply, the purchasing agency for Britain's armed forces, leading to the first of a series of major orders. Five were lent to the East Africa Ground Nuts Scheme, an overseas aid project in what was then Tanzania; two more were evaluated by the National Institute of Agricultural Engineering; four were temporarily exported to Europe; and three went further afield to Rover's overseas representatives.

These, then, were the 48 pre-production vehicles that not only proved the soundness and versatility of the Land-Rover design, but also promoted Rover's new product both at home and abroad. Shortly after the last one was built, work began on the first production examples of the vehicle that would quickly become a world-wide success.

80-INCH MODELS

'Tommy' (TMY 157) is a 1949 model with chassis number 86-2363. It belongs to the Rev. Andrew Stevens.

Rover was desperate to get its new products on to the market in 1948. The new P3 model saloons (the four-cylinder 60 and the six-cylinder 75) were announced in February, and the Land-Rover followed in April. In an ideal world, this new vehicle, which was aimed particularly at overseas markets, would have been announced at the prestigious Geneva Motor Show in March. However, build of the pre-production batch had only just begun, and Rover knew that there was no chance of having completed vehicles ready in time. So the announcement was deferred: Rover's dealers were notified on 19 April, a public announcement appeared in *The Times* the following day, and potential customers first laid eyes on the new vehicle at the next motor show in the international calendar – the one in Amsterdam which opened on 30 April. Even then, only a handful of pre-production vehicles had been completed.

The Land-Rover was an immediate success, both overseas and at home, where it was displayed at a number of agricultural shows over the next few months. Orders and enquiries came flooding in as production began slowly in June, and before the end of July the Rover Board were considering whether to increase production from the 100 Land-Rovers a week which they had initially planned to 500 vehicles a week, simply to meet demand.

CHASSIS

One consistent thread runs right through the design of the Land-Rover. As Rover planned from the beginning to make it only for a few years, until the car market in which the company had always operated returned to normal, the vehicle had to be cheap and easy to make. There was therefore no question of using advanced technology in its design; this vehicle needed to have traditional 'blacksmith' construction, with separate chassis and body. Both elements were so designed that they could be built up by hand, avoiding the need to commit large amounts of capital to tooling.

CHASSIS FRAME AND BUMPER

The chassis frame of the 80-inch Land Rover is a steel ladder-frame type, with box-section side rails and five box-section cross-members. The front, fourth and rear cross-members all have large circular apertures to allow the shafts used with the power

Another 1949 model, this one was the first Land-Rover to be bought by the Automobile Association for its breakdown patrols. It was restored to original condition on behalf of the AA by Ken Wheelwright.

Graham Medlicott's early 1951 model displays the dark green paint of the later models. This vehicle has chassis number 1610-0120.

RTW 837 again, this time with tilt erect. The later 'through-the-grille' headlamps are obvious in this view.

take-off drives to pass through. The second cross-member (below the engine) and the third one (below the gearbox) have no aperture.

There are two outriggers, which support the body, welded outboard of the side-members on each side. One is just ahead of the third (gearbox) cross-member, the other alongside the fourth. Support for the rear of the body is provided by the rear cross-member, which extends beyond the side-members by the same amount as the outriggers.

The chassis frame is made of 14swg steel, and each box-section element is assembled from four flat pieces of metal, seam-welded along their edges. It is a common misconception that the frame was galvanised on early production vehicles; in fact, it was galvanised only on the pilot-production models. However, galvanised reproduction chassis have been made and are a sensible buy if durability is more important than originality in a restoration.

Several brackets are welded to the chassis. Underneath each side-member are four spring-hanger brackets, two for each front spring and two for each rear spring. On the rear cross-member are four vertical brackets to which the body is bolted, and the fourth cross-member carries two more. Between the second and third cross-members on the right-hand side is an additional outrigger, which serves as the front mounting for the fuel tank. Still on the right-hand side, there is a flat battery support platform on four 'legs' just above the front cross-member. Early chassis (before 06103840, 06200091 and 06300021) have 'fishplate' bumper support brackets welded to the front of the side-members; these brackets should be painted the same colour as the main chassis frame.

Several items are also bolted to the chassis frame. The front bumper is the largest of these, and comes in three main types. On models built before about September 1949, the bumper is drilled to accept bolts from the fishplate support brackets attached to the chassis; the earliest of these bumpers have open backs along their full length, while later ones have their ends boxed in. The third type of bumper (from 0610-3841, 0620-0092 and 0630-0022) has support brackets welded to it, and these bolt directly to the chassis. All three types of front bumper should be hot-spray galvanised, as should the integral support brackets on the third type.

A battery casing and air cleaner support are bolted to the frame at the front. There are two different types of battery casing: the earlier one has deep walls and a detachable side-plate held in place by wing nuts. This side-plate grips the battery with two sponge strips. An air cleaner support plate is attached to the main battery casing and has three toggle clamps to hold the air cleaner in place. The later battery casing has shallow sides, with an upper battery support attached to vertical rods by three brass wing nuts. A clamp runs from the air cleaner support plate over the top of the air cleaner. The change in the battery casing was made during 1951, shortly before the 2-litre engine replaced the 1.6-litre type, and the first vehicle with the later components was 1610-

By the time Sue Combridge's 1953 2-litre model (3610-1808) was built, the sidelights had moved to the wings and the doors had gained external handles. The amber indicators in the front wings are a later addition.

0603. Both types of battery casing and air cleaner support should be painted semi-gloss black.

A draw bar is welded to the rear cross-member on basic vehicles up to 0610-3840, Station Wagons up to 0620-0091 and Welders up to 0630-0021. This is a step-like structure with ten holes drilled in its lower face. It was changed for a detachable item, probably to meet military requirements, at the same time as the front bumper was given integral support brackets; however, bolt-on draw bars appear to have been fitted throughout 1950-season (0610-) production. These later draw bars have only eight holes, and are secured to the cross-member by four bolts with nuts and lock washers and by three set bolts with a tapped plate.

The rear cross-member on all 80-inch Land-Rovers carries a lifting handle on either side. Each one is bolted through the cross-member with four bolts. Earlier types have a flat section between the curved handle and its fixing bracket which is absent from later types, and both types should have a dull grey hot-spray galvanised finish.

There is also a U-shaped check-strap on each side, bolted to threaded plates welded to the chassis side-members above the rear axle. These check-straps are made of khaki-coloured webbing, and each end is retained by a rectangular steel plate through which the two set bolts pass. The check straps are shorter on vehicles fitted with the 'short-nose' differential (see *Axles*, pages 25-26) and are accompanied by bump-stops under the chassis frame.

CHASSIS PAINT AND COLOURS

The earliest chassis frames were painted matt silver, and probably used on the first 4500 vehicles (up to 866-4500). The chassis colour then changed to Light Green to match the body colour, and remained so until 866-6000 in June 1949 approximately. Thereafter, the colour became Bronze Green, to match the new body colour introduced at that stage. Most experts believe that the new darker colour was introduced when the vehicles for the first major British military order were being built; to simplify production Rover painted both civilian and military vehicles in the darker colour required by the military.

The change-over points for these colours may not be precise, and so restorers of early vehicles would be well advised to check their chassis thoroughly before repainting. There will usually be some traces of the original colour lurking under the paint, underseal and general encrustation of dirt which have accumulated over the years since the chassis was new.

SPRINGS AND DAMPERS

Three different types of front road spring are used on 80-inch Land-Rovers. Springs are interchangeable from one side of the vehicle to the other, but one type of spring is not interchangeable with another. All types have nine leaves, and all have a black heat-treated finish.

The major change in the 80's front road springs came in the summer of 1950, when the original 'narrow' 1¾-inch springs with swinging shackles at

All Land-Rovers were built on a sturdy chassis. This is the rolling chassis of R86-0416 (above), a 1948 model owned by Brian Bashall. The frame is painted silver, although the petrol tank is black. The front panel supports, of course, are not a standard feature. Note the split-rim wheels. Rear view (far left) shows the sturdy cross-members, the layout of the exhaust system and the handles and draw bar on the rear cross-member. This chassis is fitted with a rear power take-off and rare capstan winch, and the black shaft carries drive from gearbox to rear power take-off. A 1953 chassis seen from underneath (left), looking towards the rear. The dents in the gearbox cross-member are not standard! Note the brake pipe (fitted rather vulnerably across the face of the second cross-member), gearbox mounting rubbers and exhaust with its bolt-on heat shield.

the front were replaced by 'wide' 2½-inch springs with shackles at the rear. The repositioned shackles helped to eliminate the front-end shimmy to which earlier Land-Rovers had been prone.

Two types of 'narrow' spring are fitted. On the earlier type, found on vehicles up to and including chassis number 86-2114, the second leaf has a square section where it is wrapped around the spring eye and back on top of the first leaf. There are also minor variations in the depth of the spring leaves themselves. These springs tended to flatten in use, so Rover introduced a stronger type. This is fitted to basic vehicles between chassis numbers 86-2115 and 0611-3529, to all Station Wagons up to 062-00419, and to all Welders up to 063-00030. On this second type of 'narrow' spring, the second leaf curves around the spring eye and back onto the top leaf. As with the first type of 'narrow' spring, there are minor variations in the depths of the spring leaves.

When new, it is probable that all the first type of springs had clamps with a bolt running across the top of the spring, while the second type had clamps which were simply bent over the spring at the top. However, replacement springs may have either type of clamp, so the clamps are not an infallible indicator of spring type. The 'wide' type of spring, which is

Detail of the rear cross-member with its body fixing brackets and draw bar, seen on Brian Carvey's 1950 model, 0610-7098. Rear spring shackle (far right) on an early vehicle. The vehicle is in fact a pilot-production model, R.11, with a galvanised chassis.

The front suspension and steering layout of a later 'green-chassis' vehicle, in fact Graham Medlicott's 1951 model, 1610-0120. Note also the fishplates attached to the bumper which bolt underneath the front dumb irons.

This early 1950-season Station Wagon must have been one of the last vehicles to be built with the front bumper fishplates attached to the chassis.

Sue Combridge's 1953 2-litre model has the third type of bumper, with fishplates attached to the bumper itself and bolted to the chassis dumb irons.

easily identified by measuring, is fitted to basic 80s from 061-13530, to Station Wagons from 062-00420, and to Welders from 063-00030.

The rear road springs on 80-inch Land-Rovers are 'handed', so they must not be fitted to the wrong side of the vehicle. There are two types, the standard one having nine leaves and the heavy-duty type having ten. At chassis number 86-2293, the camber of the offside rear spring was changed, and at 866-4115 the camber of both rear springs was changed. The length of these springs is 42 inches, and they should have the same black finish as the front road springs.

Two types of front damper are fitted, the first type on vehicles up to and including 86-2114 (the point at which the 'narrow' front road spring was strengthened) and the second on all subsequent 80s. Rear dampers are the same throughout 80-inch production. All original dampers were made by Woodhead.

AXLES

Throughout 80-inch Land-Rover production, both front and rear axle casings were finished in black, except on fire engines and some military vehicles (see pages 108-115 and 116-125 respectively). Axles built before approximately September 1948 have 4.88:1 crown wheel and pinion sets from the 1946-47 Rover saloons, while all subsequent axles have the 4.7:1 gearing used on the 1948-49 P3 saloons. In theory, the last axle with 4.88:1 gearing was 86-1319, but there appear to have been some anomalies.

All the 4.88:1 gear sets are contained in so-called 'long-nose' differential casings. There are minor casting differences in the rim which bolts to the axle casing: on later examples the rim is reinforced at intervals with a thicker section. Most of the 4.7:1 gear sets are contained in 'short-nose' differential casings, which are visibly shorter and were introduced because of problems with prop shaft operating angles. However, a small number of transitional types were built in which the later 4.7:1 gearing is combined with the earlier 'long-nose' differential casing.

The early 'short-nose' differential casings are essentially the P3 saloon car type, and have a circular driving flange; later ones have the square driving flange associated with the P4 saloons introduced in October 1949.

The P4 differentials are fitted from axles numbered 0610-6001 and later, and both their crown wheel and pinion assemblies and their drive flanges differ from those in earlier 4.7:1 axles. All 1951 and later axles (ie, 161-, 261- and 361- prefix types) also have spring washers on the ten bolts which hold the differential casing to the axle casing. These washers are absent from the earlier 86- and 061- prefix types.

The rear axle casing is the same on all 80-inch Land-Rovers, but there are two types of half-shaft. The earlier ones have a flat end (visible through the wheel centre) and the later ones have a dished end, but it is not clear when the change-over took place. In both cases, the visible ends should have a black chemical finish, and it is important not to use ordinary paint during restoration. Paint blocks the three drilled holes that allow oil to drain onto the wheel's nave plate if an oil seal fails, and if oil cannot escape through these holes it drains on to the brakes.

There are also two types of front axle casing, and these are not interchangeable. The first type has spring seats to suit the 1¾-inch wide springs used until approximately July 1950, and the later type has spring seats for the 2½-inch wide springs used on subsequent vehicles. Front axles numbered with the 86-prefix and all 061-prefix axles up to 061-14000 are suitable for 1¾-inch springs; axles numbered from 061-14001 are for the 2½-inch type.

At each end of the front axle casing is bolted a swivel pin bearing housing, which looks like a large chromed ball. Its outer end is partially covered by the swivel pin housing, which is the element that actually turns with the steering. On top of this second housing is the upper swivel pin, which is in unit with the steering lever; the bottom swivel pin is fixed. Inside the swivel pin bearing housing, the axle drive-shaft on each side is divided into two by a Tracta joint (which may have been replaced in service by the later Hardy Spicer type). The drive is taken from the drive-shaft to a hub assembly, and the road wheel is bolted to this.

All the elements of these assemblies are common to all 80-inch Land-Rovers, with just two exceptions. The first of these is the top swivel pin, which has a taper bearing with shim adjustment at the top and bottom on axles numbered up to and including 061-13204 (RHD) and 061-13115 (LHD). On later axles, the bottom still has a taper bearing but the top is splined and has a spring and case assembly. The second exception is the steering lock stop bolt, which may be either adjustable or fixed. It seems likely that all early vehicles had the adjustable type but that the cheaper fixed type was fitted to later examples. However, the adjustable type was also fitted to later vehicles which were supplied with the optional wider 7.00 × 16 tyres.

Views of rear axle and suspension on a 1953 2-litre model. Yes, that is an oil leak from the nose of the differential! Note that one spring has the bolted type of clamps (left) while the other has the 'bent over' type (below left)!

A rear axle check strap, seen on a Station Wagon undergoing restoration.

WHEELS AND TYRES

The standard wheels on the 80-inch Land Rover are 16-inch well-base pressed steel discs with a rim width of 5 inches. They have five holes for stud fixings and are painted to match the body colour.

The wheels were modified quite soon after production started. The original types have the hole for the tyre valve in one of the gaps between the 'spokes' of the wheel. The later and much more common wheels have the tyre valve hole in one of the 'spokes' and have a raised flange around the central hole in the wheel; no doubt the intention of both modifications was to make the wheel stronger. From early 1949, wheels have stamped into their rims a date of manufacture expressed as a month and year, such as 11.49 (November 1949).

From the beginning it was possible to order split-rim wheels as an alternative, although these are not common except on military vehicles. They have the same 16-inch diameter and 5-inch rim width as the standard wheels, and their inner and outer sections are held together by eight bolts. Split-rim wheels should also have a rubber gaiter around their rims (inside the tyre) to prevent chafing causing a puncture in the inner tube. Naturally, these wheels were ordered in sets, and standard discs should not be mixed with split-rim wheels on any vehicle.

The first 1000 or so Land-Rovers were supplied with Avon 6.00 × 16 Traction tyres, and a 7.00 × 16 Super Traction tractor-tread type was available as an alternative. Both types are directional and must be

Early wheels have the tyre valve in one of the gaps around the rim (right), while later ones, as on this fire engine, have the valve in one of the 'spokes' (below right).

The handbrake is more properly called a transmission brake, because it operates on the transmission rear output shaft. The drum should be painted black. The additional propshaft to the left is for a rear power take-off.

fitted with the V in the central part of the tread facing the front of the vehicle. This can, of course, be impractical when the spare wheel has to be fitted: sometimes, the tyre has to be turned round on the rim first!

Thereafter, all factory-supplied tyres were of Dunlop manufacture. The standard 6.00 × 16 tyres were Dunlop Trakgrip T28s, and the 7.00 × 16 type were Trakgrip T25s. Dunlop also made two types of sand tyre for optional fitting on the Land-Rover. The primary type was the Dunlop Fort 7.00 × 16, but Dunlop Standard 7.00 × 16 tyres were available for desert use. The 2-litre models could also be supplied with Dunlop Fort tyres in a 6.00 × 16 size.

BRAKES

All 80-inch Land Rovers have a Girling braking system which consists of hydraulically operated drum brakes on all four wheels and a mechanically operated drum brake (used only as the parking brake) on the transfer box output shaft. It is worth noting that owners sometimes changed the wheel brake components to Series II Land-Rover items when the original type of brakes became hard to find as the vehicles got older.

The drums of the wheel brakes are 10-inch in diameter, with leading and trailing shoes having a width of 1½ inches. The visible parts of these brakes – back plate and drum – should be painted semi-gloss black.

All 1948 models and those built early in the 1949 model year have Girling Hydrastatic brakes. From chassis number 866-7721, however, the brakes are Girling Semi-Hydrastatic. The drums of the two types are identical, but the later brakes have different back plate pressings to accommodate an extra spring between the primary shoe and a post on the back plate, together with a snail cam adjuster. It was possible to buy a kit to convert the early Hydrastatic brakes to the adjustable Semi-Hydrastatic type.

The brake fluid reservoir is the same metal cylinder with a screw top (with both parts finished in black) on 80s of all ages. There should be a blue decal on the tank, with orange lettering reading 'Use only Genuine Girling Brake Fluid'. On the first 1000 vehicles, the tank is in a very inaccessible position on the engine side of the bulkhead. However, from chassis number 86-1001 it is bolted to a bracket welded to the chassis, either inboard of the fuel tank (RHD) or in the equivalent position on the left-hand chassis rail (LHD). The same master cylinder, a Girling type CB with an unpolished bare metal finish, is also found on all 80s.

Steel brake pipes are clipped to the chassis frame, and there are flexible rubber hoses at each front wheel and between the main brake pipe on the chassis and the T-piece attached to the centre of the rear axle. The pipes should have a bare metal finish, the clips should have a yellowish plated finish, and the hoses should be made of black rubber.

The transmission brake is a 9-inch diameter drum, with the same back plate on 80-inch Land-Rovers of all ages. Rover parts catalogues suggest that 2-litre models had a different drum from the 1.6-litre types, but in practice there appears to be no difference. As with the wheel brakes, the visible parts of the transmission brake should be painted black.

STEERING

The steering gear on an 80-inch Land-Rover is a Burman Douglas worm and nut type with a 15:1 ratio, giving 2.4 turns of the steering wheel from lock to lock. The bulkhead-mounted steering box transmits movement through a drop arm to a longitudinal rod running above the chassis side rail to a relay on the front cross-member. This in turn operates a lever which moves a drag link connected to the wheel on the opposite side of the vehicle. The two front wheels are kept parallel by an adjustable track rod which runs between them. All connections are made by ball joints.

Early steering boxes are cast iron, with an oil filler on the down tube. Later aluminium alloy boxes have the oil filler on the casting, but there are also a few 'transitional' aluminium boxes which have a filler on both down tube and casting! The main shaft on early boxes has a bronze nut with a steel insert, but Burman changed this to a steel nut with a coarser thread when the steel insert was found to pull out in service; the earlier steering boxes could be modified to take this steel nut. Steering boxes should remain unpainted (although some experts believe some of the early steering boxes may have had a black finish). Some steering boxes are fitted with a packing plate to ensure correct alignment on the bulkhead.

The steering relay, all steering rods and the steering column should be painted black, but the ball joints have a black chemical finish. The steering column should have a large black rubber shroud around it where it enters the bulkhead to prevent fumes from reaching the driving compartment.

ENGINE

Two different engines were fitted to the 80-inch Land-Rovers. Before the middle of 1951, there was a 1.6-litre (1595cc) four-cylinder, similar to that used in the Rover P3 60 saloon cars of 1948-49. Subsequent vehicles – the ones Rover called their 1952 and 1953 models – had a larger-bore 2-litre (1997cc) version of the same design that was not shared with any other production vehicles. An early version of the 2-litre engine was fitted to a batch of 50 prototype 2-litre models during 1950.

Rover ceased to supply service exchange 1.6-litre engines in March 1953, from that date providing only the 2-litre. As a result, a few early Land-Rovers have a factory-supplied 'wrong' engine.

BLOCK, HEAD AND SUMP (1.6-LITRE)

The 1595cc engine has a cast iron block and cylinder head, with a water-heated inlet manifold made of aluminium alloy. It was an advanced design for its day, having a wedge-shaped combustion chamber which was ideally suited to the low-octane fuels available in the early post-war years.

A detail of the steering linkages on the 1948 rolling chassis. The tyre is a Dunlop Trakgrip T28.

This wedge-shaped chamber is achieved by a sloping top to the cylinder block and a matching angled face on the head. The piston crowns are carefully shaped to suit, and the valves are arranged to give optimum gas flow, with the inlets above the pistons in the cylinder head, and the exhausts in the side of the block. This inlet-over-exhaust configuration was used during the 1930s by Coventry Climax and in the 1940s and 1950s also by Rolls-Royce. The inlet valves are operated by pushrods, while the exhaust valves are operated directly by the camshaft, which in turn is driven by a duplex roller chain from a pulley on the nose of the crankshaft.

The Land-Rover version of this engine has a slightly lower compression ratio than the P3 saloon version (6.8:1 instead of 7:1) and a different camshaft. Using the same carburettor as the saloon engine, it develops only 50bhp instead of 60bhp, but offers a valuable increase in the low-speed torque so important in a working vehicle.

There are several variations of the 1.6-litre Land-Rover engine. Most obvious perhaps are the two types of cylinder block, the earlier type having two black plates bolted to its right-hand side and the later type having unpainted core plugs in circular holes. The change-over occurred some time around the spring or early summer of 1949, but was not a clean one: Land-Rovers continued to have the 'side-plate' engine after the 'core-plug' type had arrived and until supplies of the earlier engine ran out.

There are also two types of sump, the earlier type being 'stepped' at the front and the later reinforced type having a gentle curvature from front to rear. Both types of sump should be painted black.

The 'stepped' sump is the type designed for the P3 saloon, and was so shaped to clear the car's steering gear. The later sump was introduced at engine numbers 1610-2272 and 1613-1649 towards the end of 1.6-litre production in 1951, and is identical to the type fitted to 2-litre engines. The oil pump also differs from that on earlier engines, and the dipstick fitted with this sump is not the same as earlier types. There were in fact three different types of dipstick: the first had no locking spring, the second (on engines from 86-5713) had a locking spring to

The 1.6-litre engine (above) in the restored 1949 AA vehicle shows how the earliest examples looked; normally, all the body panels would have been green, of course! The clip alongside the exhaust pipe is for the bonnet prop rod. Note the correct type of clamp on the water hoses, and the colour of the engine block. An early 'side-plate' engine (right) in a Station Wagon under restoration by Andrew Ings; the plates are correctly finished in black. The dipstick is the first type, with no locking spring. The two red plates on the rocker cover of a 1.6-litre engine (below right) – this one is in Brian Carvey's 1950 model – carry information about settings and patents. Note that the plate on the left is printed alloy, while that on the right is painted brass.

improve dust sealing, and the third (associated with the 2-litre sump) had a longer guide tube.

There are also variations in the thermostat housing. Those on 1948 and early 1949 engines have two BSP-threaded plugs that are absent from later examples. However, this type of thermostat housing continued to be fitted when a heater was specified, as the heater connections tapped into it. Thermostat housings fitted to engines up to 061-12000 in mid-1950 also have bolts with special threaded heads to accept the bracket for the optional engine governor. These same engines have a double fan pulley to take the drive belt for the governor.

Both cylinder block and cylinder head were spray-painted before machining, with the result that their machined surfaces are unpainted but the remaining surfaces bear paint. On the earliest engines the paint is a dark blue-green, but most engines should have a blue-grey finish. This can be matched by mixing two parts of Humbrol no.96 to one part of Humbrol no.149. The original colour of even the dirtiest cylinder block can usually be found somewhere on it with a little persistence. The light alloy front cover of the engine should remain unpainted, as should the inlet manifold and the top rocker cover, which has nickel-plated brass securing nuts. None of these alloy components should be polished, although their finish should be smooth.

Several engine parts are also painted black. These include the engine mounting brackets, the pulleys, the long curved inlet pipe on the water pump, the cooling fan, and the side plates (on engines which have them). Other black items are the side rocker cover on the left of the engine and the oil filler pipe bracket, but the filler pipe and its screw-on cap, which has a securing chain on all but the very first vehicles, are unpainted alloy. The three brass securing nuts on the side rocker cover are nickel-plated.

Other colours are also found on the engine. The oil filter canister is most commonly finished in silver, but light green and orange examples also exist; the colour depends on which of three suppliers provided the filter. With all three colours, the oil pipes are unpainted steel, the unions are unpainted brass, and the bracket which holds the filter to the engine is black. The exhaust manifold, usually rusty after years of neglect, should have an unpainted cast iron finish which can be recreated quite successfully with modern heat-resistant paints.

FUEL SYSTEM (1.6-LITRE)

The carburettor fitted to the 1.6-litre engines is a Solex type 32 PBI-2. It is fed with fuel by an SU type AUA 58L electric pump mounted to a bracket on the bulkhead. This in turn draws fuel through an AC sediment filter with a glass bowl, located on a bracket lower down the bulkhead. The 10-gallon fuel tank is mounted below the right-hand seat box on both RHD and LHD vehicles, and is bolted to the chassis outriggers with an undershield (which is absent from very early vehicles). There is also an AC oil-bath air filter with an additional centrifugal filter.

The carburettor may be fitted with an Iso-Speedic governor for use with power take-offs. This takes the form of a steel box with a black chemical finish, attached to the engine thermostat housing by a bracket. On the top of the governor is an identification plate (brass on early examples, alloy on later ones), and on the front of it is a black pulley, with a belt which goes to the forward pulley on the nose of the water pump. The governor is operated by a rod running from a quadrant fitted below the instrument panel in the cab. The first and rarest type of governor does not have the cam and spring fitted to later types. Rover literature suggests that this first type of governor was fitted only on engines up to 86-1871, but dealers and owners may well have fitted it to many later engines.

On engines up to 061-12000, there are three bolt heads in the thermostat housing over which the governor mounting bracket fits. However, relatively slow sales of the governor persuaded Rover not to pre-prepare the engine for it in this way. As a result, these bolts are absent from engines numbered 061-12001 and above, and when a governor is fitted to one of these later engines it has stud fixings on the mounting bracket. In addition, the fan pulley is different and has a distance washer.

The carburettor elbow and associated rubber hose are seen here on the 1.6-litre engine in Graham Medlicott's 1951 vehicle.

On engines numbered up to and including 86-1871, a different carburettor bell crank assembly and accelerator pump control rod were used when an engine governor was fitted. On subsequent engines, the 'governed' type with its cranked instead of straight control rod was standardised, mainly because it helped to eliminate the acceleration flat spots sometimes associated with the earlier type. Fitting the later type was a Rover-approved service modification, and the original accelerator pump with its straight control rod is therefore probably quite rare.

There are also two types of sediment filter fitted with the 1.6-litre engines. The filter on early engines always has a long threaded pipe at the top and a round knob on the tap. This filter is found on later engines, interchangeably with a filter which has a short threaded pipe at the top and a rectangular metal tap grip with turned-up edges; probably Rover had started to buy in from two suppliers to meet increased production volumes, but it is not clear when the first vehicles were fitted with the second type of tap. The metal body of the sediment filter should be unpainted, and the bracket holding it to the bulkhead should have a black chemical finish.

The carburettor, of course, is unpainted. The fuel pump body should have a dull black chemical finish, but its rear mounting flange should be unpainted. There are two types of fuel pump mounting bracket, the early one of black-painted steel and the later one of unpainted alloy. The body of the air cleaner and the dome-type centrifugal filter should also be black, and there should be a black rubber pipe running between the air cleaner elbow and the crankcase breather on top of the engine rocker cover.

The earliest fuel tanks were plated with Manchester plate, a form of tinplate, and their undershields were painted body colour. As the plating proved unsuccessful, later tanks were painted silver like the chassis, and the undershield was painted to match. When silver chassis gave way to green ones, the tank and undershield were both painted black. On early 80s the screw-off filler cap was painted a semi-gloss black; on later examples it was nickel-plated.

The engine in Sue Combridge's 1953 vehicle is a 2-litre, readily recognisable in this view by the breather filter (with its correct lettering) at the front of the rocker cover. This engine is in original, unrestored condition, but a washer bottle has been added on the bulkhead to meet road traffic regulations. The red turnwheel at the front of the engine is the valve for the optional heater, which is plumbed into the cooling system at the thermostat housing.

2-Litre Prototype Engines

During the first half of 1950 Rover built an evaluation batch of 50 right-hand drive Land-Rovers with prototype 2-litre engines. These were given their own special chassis numbering sequence and were either used by the factory or lent to carefully selected contacts. These Land-Rovers were identical in every respect to the contemporary 1.6-litre models except for their engines.

The engines are visually similar to the contemporary 1.6-litre types with stepped sumps, but they can be recognised by an access plate for the water gallery bolted to the top rear of the cylinder block, and by their 0710-series serial numbers.

The last 1.6-litre engines and all production 2-litre types had a curved sump (right). This one is on the 1953 2-litre engine.

Block, Head and Sump (2-Litre)

The 1997cc engine is only slightly more powerful than the 1595cc type, with 52bhp at the same 4000rpm as the earlier engine's 50bhp is developed. However, it gives considerably more torque, and at lower revs: the 2-litre produces 101lb ft at only 1500rpm, as compared to the 80lb ft at 2000rpm of the 1.6-litre type.

The block and head of the 2-litre engines look generally similar to their 1.6-litre predecessors, and should be painted the same blue-grey colour. All engines have the circular core plugs in the block, together with the curved, black-painted sump.

Several features, however, are unique to the 2-litre engine. The top rocker cover has a breather at the front, with a transfer on its cover which reads, in white print on black, 'AC Air Cleaner. Wash thoroughly in petrol every 5000 miles. Re-oil gauze with engine oil.' The oil filler tube is a steel tube integral with the side rocker cover, and similarly painted black; it also has a large breather cap, without a transfer. There is an access plate to the water gallery at the top rear of the cylinder block, and the 2-litre engines are not equipped with the closed-circuit crankcase fume recycling system found on the 1.6-litre types.

FUEL SYSTEM (2-LITRE)

The 2-litre engines have the same Solex 32 PBI-2 carburettor as the 1.6-litre, but fitted with different jets and venturi. The fuel pump and fuel tank are also unchanged. However, there are minor differences associated with the air cleaner and sediment filter.

Three types of sediment filter are fitted with the 2-litre engines. These may be either of the types fitted to the 1.6-litre engines, or a third type distinguished by a 'hooked' tubular tap grip. The air cleaner is essentially the same as the 1.6-litre type, but there is no tube running between the air cleaner elbow and the crankcase breather on the engine.

When fitted, the engine governor is the same as the final type fitted to 1.6-litre models.

COOLING SYSTEM (ALL MODELS)

Both 1.6-litre and 2-litre versions of the 80-inch Land-Rover have a pressurised cooling system operating at 4lb psi. A centrifugal water pump mounted at the front of the engine is driven by a belt from the crankshaft pulley (the same belt also drives the dynamo). There is also a thermostat in an alloy housing at the front of the cylinder head above the water pump casing, to which it is connected by a short tube and a rubber joint ring. The radiator is mounted to the grille panel and has a cowl to improve the efficiency of the cooling fan mounted on the nose of the water pump.

The radiator and cowl should both have a black finish. The cowl is slightly larger on early 80s than on later examples. Original radiators were made by Serck and have a maker's name tag and batch number tag soldered to their header tanks. The very first ones had a honeycomb core, but by 1950 the slatted-core type was being fitted. The radiator filler cap is unpainted and should be held to the filler neck by a short chain which runs to a T-piece inside the neck.

Except on the earliest vehicles, a plate listing recommended oils is held to the horizontal top face of the front panel by four drive screws. This plate is made of brass on early vehicles and of alloy on later examples; the brass ones were probably originally finished in nickel silver and black, and would have looked similar to the later black-printed alloy type. The water hoses should all have screw-adjustable wire clips rather than the worm-drive ('Jubilee') clips used on more modern vehicles.

EXHAUST SYSTEM (ALL MODELS)

The exhaust system consists of two parts – a long front pipe which runs from the manifold and a silencer box fitted transversely within the rear of the chassis frame. Although there were several different versions of this system, the principle remained the same throughout. It is easiest to understand the changes by looking at the front and rear sections individually.

Early exhaust heat shields were detachable, as on this 1951 model.

The rear exhaust saddle-clamp and its supporting bracket on Graham Medlicott's 1951 80-inch.

The earliest type of front pipe is fitted to 1948 and '49 models up to and including chassis number 866-5603. It is quite different from later types because there are no heat shields welded to it. This early front pipe should be supported in two places, although few early Land-Rovers survive with the original front exhaust mounting intact. This front mounting is a wire bracket attached to the bulkhead cross-member, and it supports a rubber 'cotton-reel' bush. Through this bush is inserted a cranked rod, which in turn is bolted through a welded bracket on the exhaust pipe. The rear support is a triangular bracket at the rear end of the pipe, which contains an eye for another rubber 'cotton-reel' bush. A long bolt with a nut and two washers of different sizes then secures this to the chassis frame.

This pipe was changed for a second type with effect from chassis number 866-5604, most probably as the result of a report on two pre-production Land-Rovers produced in August 1949 by the National Institute of Agricultural Engineering. This second type of front pipe is not supported under the bulkhead cross-member, and it has two heat shields welded to it (very early examples had them attached by clamps, nuts and bolts). This type of front pipe is found on all subsequent 80s, and was used as a service replacement for the original type – which explains why the original front mounting so rarely survives.

The second element of the two-part system is the rear silencer, which incorporates the tailpipe. All vehicles built before approximately October 1950 and all later right-hand drive vehicles have the same silencer with the tailpipe emerging below the rear cross-member on the right-hand side. Later left-hand drive models have a different silencer, a 'handed' type with inlet and exhaust pipes at the same end of the expansion box so that the tailpipe emerges on the left-hand side of the vehicle.

All types of rear silencer are bolted to the front exhaust pipe through a conventional three-bolt flange, and all tailpipes are supported by a saddle-type clamp bracket. On right-hand drive models up to and including 0611-1063 (0620-0286 for Station Wagons and 0630-0029 for Welders), this clamp bracket has a rubber 'cotton-reel' bush at its top end, which is bolted over a threaded support rod on the chassis. This rod passes right through the chassis rail and its other end is used as the mounting pin for the left-hand rear damper. These same arrangements are used on rear silencers fitted to left-hand drive models up to and including chassis numbers 1613-1573, 1623-0080, 1633-0001 and 1663-0024.

Later right-hand drive chassis have no support rod, a bolt instead passing through the 'cotton-reel' bush and into the chassis. The Rover parts catalogue states that a stronger tailpipe bracket was fitted to chassis from 0611-1383, and that this was clamped to the pipe rather than welded to it as on earlier exhausts. In practice, the brackets vary considerably, and it is doubtful whether aftermarket exhausts followed the factory-fit pattern exactly, especially if there was a cheaper alternative!

The later left-hand drive models with a 'handed' tailpipe have different mountings again. Their rear silencers are supported in two places: firstly by a bracket welded to the tailpipe, and secondly by a saddle-type clamp on the pipe. Both are bolted to the chassis frame. These clamps and brackets are of course handed to suit the left-hand drive installation and are not interchangeable with their equivalents for right-hand drive models.

TRANSMISSION

The 80-inch Land-Rover has a 9-inch single dry-plate clutch and a four-speed primary gearbox with synchromesh on third and fourth gears only. This gearbox is generally similar to the contemporary Rover car gearbox. To its rear right-hand side is bolted a two-speed transfer gearbox. Propeller shafts run from the front of the transfer box to the front axle and from its rear to the rear axle. The parking brake is incorporated in a drum on the transfer box rear output shaft.

Vehicles built before October 1950 (ie, 1948, '49 and '50 models) have permanent four-wheel drive, with a freewheel device incorporated in the front drive-line to allow the front and rear axles to rotate at different speeds. Later examples have selectable four-wheel drive, with an additional control lever on the transfer box which operates a dog clutch and disconnects the drive to the front axle. A metal plate on the cab side of the bulkhead explains which type of transmission is fitted: those for the freewheel transmission are red, and those for the selectable four-wheel drive are black.

CLUTCH AND BELLHOUSING

The same bellhousing is used on all 80-inch Land-Rovers, but from gearbox number 261-00201 the dust sealing arrangements differ slightly. All bellhousings, of course, should be unpainted.

Two types of clutch are found. All 1948 and 1949 engines, and 1950 engines up to and including engine number 0610-0200 (built in approximately August 1949), have the so-called Rover clutch – actually made by Newton – with a Borg and Beck plate. On later models, the whole clutch assembly is by Borg and Beck. A different engine flywheel is also fitted with these later clutches. Early Borg and Beck clutches (fitted with gearboxes up to 0610-6828) have coarse splines on the cross-shaft, and later ones have fine splines.

PRIMARY GEARBOX AND CONTROLS

The primary gearbox fitted to Land-Rovers approximately to the end of 1949 is the P3 saloon type. Subsequent vehicles have the P4 saloon type, with a

The transmission in Brian Bashall's 1948 rolling chassis. The freewheel housing is just visible on the far side in this view, to the left. In the foreground is the optional power take-off with its control lever and propshaft running to the rear of the vehicle. The propshaft to the rear wheels is visible behind it, and the drum of the transmission brake is directly behind the power take-off control lever.

higher third gear ratio. However, the unpainted casing of the gearbox, with a brass drain plug in its underside, remained unchanged throughout 80-inch production. From gearbox number 0610-6001, built during the 1950 model year, a different speedometer drive pinion is fitted; the later types have a special retaining plate. A different rear output shaft is fitted on gearboxes numbered from 1610-2314 (RHD) and 1613-1688 (LHD). This coincides with the change from permanent four-wheel drive to selectable four-wheel drive and the loss of the freewheel.

Two different types of gear lever are found on the 80-inch models, and each is cranked differently to suit LHD and RHD vehicles. The first type, mounted to the transmission tunnel, is fitted to all chassis up to and including 86-1500. The second type, mounted to the gearbox itself, is fitted to all subsequent vehicles. All types of gear lever are painted black, with the same black knob with white-painted characters indented in its top face to identify the gear positions.

Transfer Box and Controls

The major change to the transfer box during 80-inch production occurred in August 1950, when the original permanent four-wheel drive system with freewheel was changed for a selectable four-wheel drive system without a freewheel, at gearbox numbers 1610-2314 (RHD) and 1613-1688 (LHD). The most obvious difference between the two types lies at the front of the transfer box: an additional housing is sandwiched between transfer box and front output shaft housing when the freewheel is fitted. Early transfer box casings were sand-cast, but later types were die-cast. In all cases, the transfer box casing and front output housing should be unpainted.

The 1948-50 transfer boxes were built with an oil capacity of six pints, which proved to be too great and led to leaks. So Rover reduced the capacity to four pints on later boxes, and introduced a service modification for the original boxes. This involved tapping a new level plug into the side of the transfer box about ⅞ inch below the original plug; as a result, some early transfer boxes have two level plugs.

One running change was made during production of the early type of transfer box. Those fitted to gearboxes up to and including 86-2380 had set screws to hold down the transfer lever cover plate on the top right of the casing. Those fitted to subsequent gearboxes had set bolts and spring washers to retain this cover plate.

The later transfer boxes used with selectable four-wheel drive have a different speedometer drive housing. This was further modified from gearbox numbers 2610-1454 and 2613-0447 by the addition of a mudshield to the rear face of the housing. In addition, the later transfer boxes have a much smaller oil level plug than the early type, although some

The later transmission in a Station Wagon (above) under restoration by Ken Wheelwright has no power take-off. Nor, of course, does it have a freewheel; instead there is a four-wheel drive selector lever just visible on the far side.

Two views of Brian Carvey's 1950 Land-Rover show the front output housing on the transfer gearbox (above left) and the transmission brake and gearbox sump with its brass drain plug (left).

The optional power take-off is seen here from underneath on a 1953 2-litre model.

early transfer boxes (probably those built just before the change-over) came with the small plug and an adapter.

The transfer box is operated by a red-knobbed rod alongside the main gear lever. This rod selects high ratio in the forward position, neutral (for the power take-off) in the middle, and low ratio in the rearward position. On models with selectable four-wheel drive, a second lever with a yellow knob disengages drive to the front axle when pushed down. The shafts of both rods should be painted black.

Note that on 1950-51 models equipped with a freewheel and permanent four-wheel drive, the yellow-knobbed selector does not disengage drive to the front axle, but rather locks and unlocks the freewheel.

Freewheel and Controls

The freewheel is fitted only on gearboxes numbered up to and including 1610-2313 (RHD) and 1613-2687 (LHD). Although similar in principle to the freewheels fitted to Rover saloon cars, the Land-Rover type actually shares only a small number of minor components with them. The only visible part of the freewheel is its housing, which should be left unpainted, like the transfer gearbox and transfer shaft housing to which it is bolted.

The freewheel can be manually locked to improve traction, especially over rough terrain, and there are two types of locking control. On gearboxes up to and including 0610-4014 (in late 1949), a simple ring-pull on the floor of the vehicle is connected to a wire cable which operates the freewheel selector lever. On later gearboxes, the freewheel is operated by a rod selector mounted to the right of the main gear lever. This rod is painted black and its knob is made of a yellow plastic material.

Two different types of freewheel, in fact, are fitted. Some of the pilot-production Land-Rovers were equipped with selectable four-wheel drive as well as a freewheel, and production gearboxes numbered up to and including 86-1988 incorporate the locking dog for this selectable system – although it is permanently locked by a steel spacer ring in the selector mechanism and there is no means of disengaging it! From gearbox number 86-1989, a simpler freewheel was fitted, without this locking dog. Early freewheel housing castings have a boss on either side, while later ones have one only on one side. However, the change of internal components did not coincide with this revised external appearance.

Propeller Shafts

The front and rear prop shafts have a splined sliding joint and are always finished in black. There are two primary types of each for the 80-inch Land-Rovers: short prop shafts are used with the earlier 'long-nose' differential, and longer ones with the later 'short-nose' type.

Very early prop shafts for use with the original 'long-nose' differential are made of thinner-gauge metal than later examples, but the two are interchangeable and later types were certainly fitted to earlier vehicles as service replacements. There are also two different types of prop shaft used with the later 'short-nose' differential. The earlier type is fitted with the P3 saloon car gearbox, up to and including gearbox number 0610-6001 (in theory, the change took place with axles numbered 0610-6001 as well). The later type of prop shaft is fitted with the P4 gearbox, and has different fixings between its yokes and the drive flanges on gearbox output shaft and axle differential.

Cover plates were available by July 1950 for the universal joints on both prop shafts, but were a rarely specified option.

Electrical Components

The electrical system on the 80-inch Land-Rovers is a positive earth 12-volt type, incorporating a constant voltage control for the charging system. Original batteries had black rubber casings, and the wiring harness carried clamp-type terminal connections to them. The earthing strap is a braided wire type with no outer sheath.

The wiring harness itself has an outer casing of black cotton braid, with a green and brown fleck stripe running through it; this stripe will almost cer-

The Lucas RF95/2 L2 control box on this early 1951 Land-Rover carries two spare fuses in a clip on the cover. Note the correct braided covers for the individual wires.

The later RB106/1 control box with separate fuse box seen on a 1953 2-litre model. Note also the fuel pump, with the yellow tape around its end cap, which reads 'Guaranteed Factory Replacement Unit'.

tainly be invisible on an elderly harness! The cables inside are braided and lacquered. There are minor variations in the detail of the harness, depending on the electrical equipment fitted, and in fact five different types exist. US export examples and military vehicles, for example, have special harnesses to suit their unique lighting arrangements.

Three different types of Lucas voltage control box are fitted. The first type (RF96/2 L13) is found on 1948, '49 and '50 vehicles up to and including 0610-6034, 0620-0139 and 0630-0030. This is accompanied by a separate Lucas fuse box (SF5/2) containing a single 25-amp fuse. Control box and fuse box are mounted on a metal plate bolted to the bulkhead. The second type of control box (RF95/2 L2) is found on subsequent 1950 vehicles and on '51 models up to and including 1610-3898, 1613-6865, 1616-3017, 1623-0080, 1626-0020, 1630-0004, 1633-0007, 1636-0009, 1663-0078 and 1666-2022. It incorporates two 35-amp fuses in a clip on the cover, no separate fuse box is fitted, and the control box is mounted to a smaller plate on the bulkhead. The third type of control box (RB106/1), found on later 1.6-litre and all 2-litre models, comes with a separate fuse box, the two once again mounted on a large plate bolted to the bulkhead. The fuse box incorporates a 35-amp fuse (1.6-litre) or 25-amp fuse (2-litre).

There are three types of Lucas dynamo. The first (C39P), with solid end plates and a plain pulley, lasted until approximately mid-1949. The second (C39PV), with ventilated ends and fan blades incorporated in the pulley, survived until well into the 1953 model year. The third (C39P2LO), again ventilated but this time with a slightly higher output, was introduced with engines numbered 3610-8386 and 3613-7385.

All dynamos have black bodies, although the ventilated ends of later types are unpainted alloy. The rear end of the early type is also unpainted, but the front is black. The dynamo mounting flange, rear clamp, top bracket and adjustment bracket should all be unpainted.

There are two types of Lucas starter motor, the earlier being M418G/76 and the later M418G/C. The Rover parts catalogue states that the later type was first fitted to engine number 86-2235, but the earlier one was certainly fitted to engines later than this. Once again the body is black, but the exposed end, the clamp ring and the circular housing which bolts to the flywheel housing are unpainted. Nevertheless, some examples have been found with black clamp rings.

The ignition system incorporates a Lucas DVXH4A distributor on both 1.6-litre and 2-litre engines. This has an unpainted body and a brown or black Bakelite cap with the ignition wires emerging horizontally from its top. Very early vehicles have

The black-painted starter is tucked inaccessibly away on the left-hand side of the engine block beside the bulkhead. Above it are the oil pressure switch and its adapter.

The DVX4HA 'side-entry' distributor seen on a 1950 model. The light green of the engine block indicates an engine delivered to the British Army.

Bakelite knobs on the threaded terminals of the Lucas B12 coil, but most 80-inch models have nut fastenings; the same coil is found on both 1.6-litre and 2-litre models, and should be fitted with its top towards the centre of the vehicle. The factory-issue spark plugs were Lodge HLNR until March 1952, and thereafter Lodge CLN; both types should have conical black plastic shrouds with a sealing ring at the cylinder head end and a knurled plastic nut at the top securing the plug lead. When the optional black Bakelite suppressers are fitted, these screw in between the plug lead nut and the shroud. All the ignition leads should have a dull black coating.

A single horn is bolted to the grille panel, but two types are found. The early type, a Lucas HF1235 with an offset adjuster, is fitted to all 1.6-litre models and the first 2-litres. The type fitted to later 2-litres has a central adjuster, the first home market model with it being 2610-4737.

Only one windscreen wiper was standard on the 80-inch models, and its Lucas CW1 motor, with a crackle-black finish and unpainted control levers, is bolted to the inside of the windscreen frame on the driver's side. A second motor could be fitted to the passenger side windscreen as an optional extra, operating independently of the first. The wiper motor cable is armoured and exposed outside the bulkhead on all 80s up to and including 0611-1546 in 1950; thereafter, the unarmoured cable is re-routed inside the bulkhead.

The Lucas CW1 wiper motor has a crackle-black finish. The braided green cable visible here is for semaphore trafficators.

The headlamp on the left is the early 5-inch Lucas type, fitted to models with headlamps behind the grille. On the right is an early example of the 7-inch F700, with 'cat's-eye' lens pattern.

The correct lenses for the bulkhead-mounted sidelights have a 'frosted' appearance, seen here (near right) on a 1950 model. The Lucas 'D'-lamp fitted to Brian Carvey's 1950 Land-Rover (far right) is correct for the vehicle. Lighting regulations in most countries have since demanded red reflectors at the rear; these items were not fitted as original equipment.

Lucas SE62 semaphore indicators were an optional extra. The wiring would normally be encased in armoured sheathing and clipped to the windscreen frame.

LIGHTING

The lighting system went through several permutations on the 80-inch Land-Rovers. On the first vehicles the headlamps were protected behind the grille and the sidelamps were located on the bulkhead. In May 1950, beginning with chassis numbers 0611-1547 and 0621-0311, the grille was modified so that the headlamps – now larger and more powerful – could protrude through it. At this stage, the sidelamps remained on the bulkhead. A third configuration arrived in summer 1951, when the sidelights moved from the bulkhead to the wing fronts; although the inverted-T grille which accompanied this change gave a very different appearance to the front of the vehicle, the headlamps in fact remained unchanged.

The original headlamps, fitted behind the grille, were quite different from later types. They are Lucas 5-inch units, type L-HI-O, with fluted glass and an output of 36 watts. Their large spherical bodies have a mounting bolt on top, and their metal parts are painted black. The later lamps, on exposed-headlamp models, are Lucas F700s of 7-inch diameter, screwed to the grille panel through their rims. The earliest examples have an elliptical or 'cat's-eye' lens pattern, and later ones have block-pattern lenses. Their outer rims should be chromed, although on military vehicles they will have been painted over. There are different specifications for RHD and LHD, and further variations from country to country; Land-Rovers sold in France, for example, had a special version with yellow bulbs.

There are three different types of sidelamp, one of them for vehicles exported to North America (see page 60). Those fitted to the bulkhead are Lucas 451, while the wing-mounted type used from summer 1951 are Lucas 52139. D-shaped Lucas ST51/1 lamps at the rear were specified on all except North American models.

Lighting is a problematic area for restorers because of changes in regulations over the years. In Britain, for example, the headlamp wiring on all vehicles up to 0611-2000 appears to have been arranged so that the offside lamp was extinguished on dipped beam. However, this system has now been illegal for many years, and vehicles must conform to the double-dipping standard, under which both lamps remain lit when they are dipped. Similarly, direction indicators – whether semaphore trafficators or flashers – were not fitted as standard to Land-Rovers of this vintage, but are now necessary in Britain, where the law insists that all vehicles built since 1936 must have them, whether originally fitted or not. The 1953 Road Transport Lighting Act also called for two red reflectors to be fitted to the rear of all cars after 1 October 1954, and earlier vehicles must of course comply.

Electrically-operated Lucas SE62 semaphore trafficators were an optional extra from the beginning of Land-Rover production. The very first examples were bolted directly to the windscreen frame, but Rover soon began to supply a bracket to hold them slightly away from the frame. The wiring for the trafficators should be protected by armoured cable and held to the windscreen frame by clips on each side. The control switch is fitted to a bracket on the lower edge of the windscreen frame (see *Dashboard, Instruments and Controls*, pages 48-50). This bracket was standard on vehicles after chassis number 86-0730; before that it was supplied as part of the semaphore trafficator kit and had to be fitted individually.

BODY

BULKHEAD AND WINDSCREEN

The key component of the body on 80-inch models is the bulkhead, which is bolted to outriggers on the chassis just ahead of the gearbox cross-member.

There are three main types. The first type is fabricated, and found on the first 1500 vehicles only. The second type is pressed and was introduced during 1948 with vehicle 86-1501, remaining in production until about May 1951. Both of these types carry the vehicle's sidelights. The third type, again pressed but now without sidelight mountings, then took over with effect from chassis numbers 1610-3899, 1613-6866, 1616-3018, 1623-0081, 1626-0021, 1630-0005, 1633-0008, 1636-0010, 1663-0079 and 1666-2023.

Small numbers of vehicles are fitted with bulkheads made of aluminium alloy over angle iron instead of the normal steel. These bulkheads are significantly different in several respects from the standard steel types, and there exist examples both with and without sidelight mountings. They were made by hand to keep the assembly lines moving when the press tool for the steel bulkheads failed, which seems to have occurred once in 1949, again some time in 1952, and possibly on other occasions. It is not possible to give a list of vehicles to which they were fitted, as no records exist. The issue would in any case be further complicated by the fact that some examples were supplied as service replacements to the military, and possibly also to Land-Rover dealers.

The first type of bulkhead is made of folded steel and has a detachable centre panel. The cut-out for the bellhousing in this centre panel has straight edges. An oval mounting box for the instrument panel is welded to the upper portion of the bulkhead, to which a full-width grab rail is also bolted. Land-Rovers built before the late summer of 1948 do not have this grab rail. There are also two catches for the windscreen fasteners bolted to the inner face of the bulkhead. Both these and the grab rail should have a dull grey galvanised finish.

The second type of bulkhead is pressed from sheet steel and weighs rather less than the first type. It has the same instrument panel mounting box and grab rail, but there are important differences. The centre panel is not detachable, and has a curved cut-out to clear the bellhousing. In addition, a sealing rubber is attached to the top of the bulkhead; with the earlier bulkhead, the screen-to-bulkhead seal is on the windscreen frame.

The third type of bulkhead is also pressed from steel sheet, but is once again different. It is generally associated with the 2-litre models introduced for the 1952 model year but, as the chassis numbers given above show, it was actually introduced right at the end of 1951-model 1.6-litre Land-Rover production. It is broadly similar to the 1948-51 type, but it differs in several details. The most obvious difference is in the lower housings for the door hinges, which are shorter than on earlier bulkheads, but there are also other recognition features, such as the position of some of the holes for the controls.

The windscreen frame remained the same throughout 80-inch production, always being made of galvanised steel and containing two panes of glass. Welded to the top rail of the frame are the 'shark's teeth' over which the eyes of the soft top are hooked, while the base of the frame has a Birmabright filler panel retained by drive screws and pop rivets. From about the middle of 1949, a full-width ventilator flap

The first 1500 vehicles have a bulkhead with a distinctively angular shape around the flywheel housing and gearbox cover. This one is actually on a pre-production vehicle.

could be ordered at extra cost to replace this panel; it was probably standard on all British military 80s except for the first (1948) batch. On the first 1500 vehicles, there should be a rubber seal attached to the bottom of the frame by drive screws and washers.

The frame pivots at its base so that it can be folded forwards onto the bonnet, and there are three different types of pivot attachment. The original type, found on Land-Rovers built before the middle of the 1950 model year, consists of a pivot bolt with castle nut and split pin. The last vehicle fitted with this arrangement was 0611-0748; all 0630-series Welders built during 1950 also had it. The second type of windscreen pivot arrangement is rather simpler, with the pivot bolt being held in place simply by a split pin. However, this arrangement seems to have been unsatisfactory and did not last very long. With chassis number 0611-5324, a third arrangement was introduced, this time with a special locking nut on the end of the pivot bolt. All types may have washers on the pivot pin to 'fit' the windscreen frame to the bulkhead, as bulkheads vary in width by as much as ⅜ inch.

The windscreen is held securely in the upright position by means of two clamp-type fasteners attached to bosses on its bottom rail that hook over brackets on the bulkhead. On 1948, '49, '50 and the first '51 models, these clamps have straight arms. Late in the 1950 calendar year, clamps with curved arms were introduced. The first vehicles with these have chassis numbers 1610-1420, 1613-2794, 1616-1310, 1630-0004, 1633-0004, 1636-0008, 1663-0043 and 1666-1507.

The windscreen frame has two forward-projecting brackets welded to it about half way up. One function of these is to support the hinges for the optional sidescreens, but they are also used to carry a rear-view mirror on vehicles built before the sidelights moved to the wings in the summer of 1951. The mirror itself is a Lucas 540 (part number 062561), a round item on a cranked stem which is attached to the windscreen bracket by a single-bolt clamp; on later vehicles the mirror is bolted through the front wing. Normally only a driver's side mirror is fitted.

The optional windscreen ventilator panel in the open position; the wing nut secures a crude 'lock' which rotates through 90 degrees to hold the panel shut. The correct type of armoured cable for the semaphore trafficators can be seen.

When the optional semaphore trafficator arms (see *Electrical Components*, pages 35-38) are fitted, they are bolted to the top of the windscreen frame. Their control switch goes on the bracket welded to the inner edge of the windscreen frame bottom rail. Early frames do not have this bracket, and the trafficator kit was supplied with a separate bolt-on bracket.

Wings, Bonnet and Grille Panel

Three different types of front wing are fitted to the 80-inch Land-Rovers, although there is a fourth sub-variant for early North American specification vehicles (see page 60). From the earliest days, a circular rubber door buffer was fitted to each front wing just ahead of and above the wheelarch cut-out; however, it does appear that some early vehicles built before about October 1948 may not have had this from new.

The first 1500 vehicles should have front wings in which the top, front and inner valance are a single assembly, to which an outer side panel is bolted. These go with the fabricated bulkhead and with the first type of pressed bulkhead. The second type of wing has an unchanged side panel but a modified top, front and inner valance pressing. This should be fitted to vehicles up to and including 1610-3898, 1613-6865, 1616-3017, 1663-0078 and 1666-2022; all 1951 Station Wagons and Welders should also have this type of front wing.

The third major type of wing was introduced in production for the final 1.6-litre models and was therefore not associated only with the 2-litre models. Its top, front and inner valance pressing is spot-welded to the outer panel along a line which corresponds to the join between the two pieces of the 1949-51 wing. These wings also have a modified front panel, with a pressed and punched hole for the sidelight, with a small 'eyebrow'; they go with the final type of 80-inch bulkhead, which has no provision for sidelights.

A wing mirror should be fitted to the driver's side wing on vehicles which have this third type of front wing; earlier vehicles have a mirror attached to the windscreen frame. The mirror is the same Lucas 540 as the earlier type, with a circular head and cranked stem. The metal of the head and stem should be painted gloss black. Home market Station Wagons were also fitted with semaphore trafficators let into the trailing edge of the wing panel.

There are also three types of grille panel and grille fitted to 80-inch Land-Rovers. Vehicles built before mid-1950 should have their headlamps concealed behind the grille. On these models, the grille panel is characterised by three large rectangular apertures in the upper part, with a single narrower aperture running across the bottom. The grille itself contains no headlamp cut-outs. An oval Land-Rover badge is bolted through the grille to a strip of metal behind. This badge is approximately 5 inches wide and is made of cast brass on a few very early models; subsequent badges are made of aluminium alloy.

Expert opinion differs on the correct colour for these badges, but it looks as if there were three variations. The very earliest had a red rim and red letters on a black background, the two colours corresponding to the major colours in the Viking ship badge on Rover saloons. Probably all the brass badges were painted this way. Later vehicles with Light Green paint on their bodies had badges with red letters on a Light Green background. When the change to dark green paint was made in 1949, the background colour changed with it; the rim and letters were painted yellow because red would not have showed up very well.

From May 1950, a second type of grille and grille panel were fitted. The first basic model to be fitted with the new type was 0611-1547, and the first Station Wagon 0620-0311; none of the 1950-model Welders on 0630-prefix chassis had it. This second type of grille contains circular cut-outs for the headlamps, and is fitted to a redesigned grille panel. This panel has two circular headlamp apertures flanking a large central rectangular aperture, with three smaller apertures below. A few early examples have the 5-inch Land-Rover badge, bolted through to a strip of metal as before, but most have a larger oval badge $7\frac{3}{16}$ inches across. This is stamped from aluminium alloy and has the words 'Birmingham, England' underneath the Land-Rover name. It is bolted through the grille to a metal strip in the same way as the earlier type.

The third type of grille and grille panel were fitted to 1952 and '53 models. The grille panel is generally similar to the 1950-51 type, but the grille is shaped like an inverted T and leaves the grille panel around the headlamps exposed. The bottom edge of the grille is clipped to the lower edge of the grille panel, and two bolts then hold it in place at the top. These two bolts also hold the $7\frac{3}{16}$-inch oval Land-Rover badge in place.

To prevent the bonnet from chafing on the top edge of the grille panel, all 80-inch Land-Rovers have a strip of khaki-coloured webbing fastened to that panel with split rivets. This rubbing strip and its fastenings are exactly the same on all three types of grille panel.

The bonnet panel is a single piece of curved Birmabright, with two galvanised steel hinges at the bulkhead end. It slides sideways off its hinges to improve access to the engine. On either side towards the front is a galvanised bracket on which the windscreen frame rests when folded forwards; each bracket has a webbing buffer strip riveted to its top face. Alongside each bracket is a clamp to hold the windscreen frame in position; these brackets face

The first two types of front wing are indistinguishable externally (above) and have the outer panel bolted to the top along flanges on the inside, while the third type has this line of spot-welds (left) and should have the sidelight in a pressing in the front panel. The round rubber buffer is designed to prevent the unrestrained door from damaging the wing when opened.

forwards on 80s up to and including 1610-1482; thereafter they 'trail' on the bonnet. Also screwed to the bonnet on each side is a small 'sheradised' staple, which engages with the bonnet catch on the wing. These bonnet catches and their fittings should also have a 'sheradised' finish.

With the optional bonnet-top spare wheel stowage position, a strengthening dome and four rubber support blocks (fitted at 12, 3, 6 and 9 o'clock) are fitted on the outside of the panel. The bonnet prop rod is a simple metal pole which can be swung up from the left-hand inner wing and engaged on the underside of the panel. It should have a dull grey galvanised finish.

SEAT BOX AND CAB FLOOR

The first 1500 Land-Rovers have unique features in this area, but its construction on all subsequent 80-inch Land-Rovers is the same. The largest section is the seat box, which incorporates lockers and has sill panels which extend forwards to meet the bulkhead. There are then two floor sections, which flank a gearbox cover or transmission tunnel. On later 80s,

Khaki webbing should be riveted to the top edge of the grille panel to prevent chafing. Also visible in this picture is the yellow-on-green badge used from June 1949 approximately.

The original 'lamps-behind' grille and front panel are seen in this picture (above) of Brian Carvey's 1950 model. The fan visible is an aftermarket addition to improve cooling, and the brass plate at the bottom of the grille carries the vehicle's name – 'Bessie'.

The later 'lights-through' front end has a completely different grille panel, as seen here on a 1951 model with the grille itself removed – and then in place.

these floor sections are separate panels; on the first 1500 vehicles, the floor is integral with the seat box and there are other detail differences.

The seat box itself incorporates a locker on either side, the one on the right giving access to the fuel tank and the one on the left being for storage. There are two hinges riveted to each locker lid, their other ends being bolted to the angle plate that runs along the back of the seat base. Each lid has a single 'sheradised' hasp screwed and bolted to its forward edge. These hasps mate up with turn-buckles held by screws and nuts to the front of the seat box, which Rover literature calls the heelboard.

The petrol locker lid has a retaining strap to hold it in the open position for refuelling. This strap is made of webbing and has a hook at its free end. At the other end it is fixed to the capping on the rear body by a self-tapping screw. Both locker lids may have rubber protectors riveted to their front outer corners; these were optional fittings.

Between the two lockers is a centre panel which incorporates a hinged cover plate giving access to the centre power take-off control knob when one is fitted. On 1948-49 and early '50 models, this cover plate is rectangular and has a piano-type hinge at its rear edge. Later vehicles have a shield-shaped cover plate. The first chassis to have the later type are 0610-3885, 0620-0094 and 0630-0022. Both types of cover plate have a spring clip at their front edge.

There is an inspection cover for the gearbox in the centre of the heelboard. The original type is fitted on chassis numbered up to and including 86-1500; the cover is hinged on 1.6-litre models built before the summer of 1951, and the very last 1.6-litre Land-Rovers have the 2-litre type of cover with fixing prongs instead of a hinge.

Three different types of gearbox cover are fitted, and three different floor panels mate up with them. It is not possible to mix and match with these components. On all three types of floor panel, the redundant pedal holes in the passenger footwell are covered with a blanking plate.

The earliest gearbox cover and floor panel are fitted to the first 1500 models only (86-0001 to 86-1500). The bellhousing cover on these early models is much squarer and more nearly symmetrical than the later type. All examples have two drive screws to attach the cover plate for the reverse stop to the right-hand side of the gearbox cover. According to Rover parts catalogues, only the first 180 examples (86-0001 to 86-0180) have a cover plate in the driver's side floor for the pedal adjuster, but in fact some later examples also have it while some examples within this number range do not. The floor panels on the first 1500 vehicles extend only to the rearmost edge of the bulkhead, and the gap in each footwell is bridged by a separate toeplate.

The second type of gearbox cover has a much wider bellhousing cover and is not symmetrical, extending much further on the left of the vehicle's centre-line. This and its matching floor panels are fitted to all vehicles from 86-1501 up to and including 0610-3884, 0620-0093 and 0630-0021. The third type of bellhousing cover is generally similar but has a larger cover plate for the gearbox reverse stop, and is fitted with its matching floor panels to all subsequent 80-inch Land-Rovers.

Rover improved the dust-sealing arrangements

after the first 1500 vehicles had been built, but these earliest Land-Rovers have no rubber weathershields for the controls in this area. Subsequently, rubber seals were fitted, all of them too simple to deserve the title of gaiter.

The handbrake lever aperture in the heelboard is protected by a simple flat rubber weathershield. This is riveted to the heelboard and the rivets are capped. Similar fixings are used for the rubber weathershield across the transfer gear lever aperture in the right-hand side floor panel. As for the gear lever aperture, there are two types of protective rubber seal. The first, held to the gearbox cover by capped rivets, is found on vehicles from 86-1501 to 0610-1032. Subsequent vehicles have a seal with a shaped lip which holds it in place without the need for rivets.

Doors and Sidescreens

The doors on all basic models of the 80-inch Land-Rover come up to waist height only; above that are sidescreens with sliding windows. These were optional on very early 80s and standard thereafter. The doors on the 80-inch Station Wagon are completely different (see pages 53-58).

Two different types of door were used during 80-inch production. The first type, used on 1.6-litre models, has no outside handle, while the second type, used on 2-litre models, does have one. The two different types of sidescreen are each appropriate to only one style of door.

Neither type of door has a separate frame; instead, the alloy 'skin' is folded back to create top and side sections that are then reinforced with alloy stiffeners. Except on the earliest vehicles, both types have at their upper rear edges the same steel gusset plate, which is held in place by a combination of pop rivets, screws and nuts. Both types also have the same galvanised steel top capping plate (fixed by rivets and pop rivets), and the same two galvanised steel hinges (held by nuts and bolts).

The earliest 80s have no weather seals on their doors, and front and rear rubber seals were not introduced, according to parts catalogues, until chassis number 0610-1747 in approximately August 1950. However, it seems clear enough that some earlier vehicles did have them – possibly mainly those intended for export – and that others had them fitted as a service modification. The seals are held in place by retainer strips riveted to the doors.

The latch fitted to the inside of the door is simply that; there is no means of locking the doors. The same type of latch was used throughout Series I Land-Rover production. On 1952 and '53 models, however, the door panel is drilled to allow a simple 'sheradised' steel handle to pass through into the back of the latch so that the door can be opened from the outside. During the 1953 model year, the rubber grommet which prevented the spindle of the outside handle chafing on the door panel was changed; the later type came in with chassis numbers 3610-1070, 3613-0779, 3616-0652, 3630-0004, 3633-0005, 3636-0003, 3663-1331 and 3666-0289.

The seat box covers the fuel tank, always fitted under the right-hand 'locker' lid (above); this one is on a 1953 model. The locker lid is held open by a webbing strap attached to the rear body capping (left); a hook passes through the hole in the lid.

The main distinguishing feature between early and late sidescreens is the presence on early models of a canvas flap at the rear lower edge, allowing the inside door latch to be reached from outside when the sidescreens are fitted. Sidescreens are fitted to the doors by passing the two long threaded rods at their lower edges through the door tops and bolting these up inside the doors; these fixings are the same for both types. Both sidescreen types also have the same weather sealing arrangements: these consist of a large canvas flap at the rear, crudely riveted to the outside of the sidescreen frame; a rubber draught strip at the front held in place by upper and lower retaining strips; and a rubber draught strip on the lower edge to seal the gap between door and sidescreen. On earlier vehicles (up to 86-2500) these lower draught strips are laboriously fixed to the sidescreens by drive screws and washers; on later examples they are attached by spring clips.

The windows in both types of sidescreen are made of Perspex. The fixed front pane is the same on

The first or '1.6-litre' type of door has no outside handle but has a simple latch on the inside. The access flap in the sidescreen is clearly visible here.

The 2-litre models have external door handles with a bare metal finish; this one has become rusty. The sidescreen has no canvas flap.

This 1.6-litre sidescreen has the canvas flap and a finger-hole in the sliding Perspex section.

On this later 2-litre sidescreen, the sliding section has a clear knob bonded to it. The later, flat, type of sidescreen hinge can just be seen.

all 80s, but there are two patterns for the sliding rear portion. On all 1.6-litre models and on the first 2-litres, it has a finger cut-out in its leading edge. On later 2-litres, from chassis number 2610-3085 in early 1952, a Perspex knob is bonded to the inside of the window and there is no cut-out; this window also has an aluminium frame. During production of the 1949 models, the window channels were simplified, the original type with separate retainers being replaced by self-retaining channels at chassis number 866-6250.

The sidescreens are hinged to the windscreen, and three different types of hinge are found. The first type, found on all but the very last 1.6-litre models, is essentially thick wire bent into a Y-shape. The second type is a flat plate, and found from chassis numbers 1610-3311, 1613-5971, 1616-2551, 1630-0004, 1633-0007, 1636-0009, 1663-0078 and 1666-1974. The 2-litre models built in the first year or so of production have this type, and then a third and broadly similar type is fitted from 2610-5443, 2613-5779, 2616-3456, 2630-0014, 2636-0005, 2663-1953 and 2666-1021, all built towards the end of 1952-model production.

On all sidescreens, the window frames are of galvanised steel. Only the large rectangular Birmabright plate which forms the lower half of the sidescreen is finished in body colour.

Back Body and Tailboard

The back body of the basic 80-inch Land-Rover always consists of three main elements. These are the two main body halves and the floor panel, all of them made of Birmabright alloy. The whole back body assembly is bolted to the chassis.

The back body on vehicles up to and including 0611-0304 has a straight front panel; subsequent back bodies have a 'kinked' panel, with the top slightly behind the bottom. This allows room for the fatter 'shovel' type of seats with their hinged backrests which were introduced at the same time in the 1950 model year (see *Seats*, pages 51-52).

All the upper edges of the body are protected by galvanised steel cappings, the front one being narrower on the later type of body with 'kinked' front panel. The four corner cappings also incorporate sockets for the hood sticks, and the two extra corner cappings on either side of the tailboard opening have dowels to secure the tailboard in the closed position. In addition, there is a galvanised protective strip at the rear of the floor across the tailboard opening.

The spare wheel is stowed inside the body at the front (the optional bonnet mounting is described in *Wings, Bonnet and Grille Panel*, pages 39-40), and held in place by a special clamp with a spring clip. From early 1950, the fixing of this spring clip changed; the earlier type is often referred to as the 'big clamp' and the later one as the 'small clamp'. The earliest vehicle with the new arrangement is 0611-0305; all 0630-series Welders have the earlier style of fixing.

There are also stowage clips inside the body for the jack handle and starting handle. Each tool is always stored in two clips, the jack handle on the left-hand body panel and the starting handle on the front panel. The floor panel is always finished in body colour paint and the factory did not supply any floor covering. Towards the summer of 1952, the floor panel was modified with stiffeners welded underneath; the first vehicles with it have chassis numbers 2610-5377, 2613-5479, 2616-3400, 2630-0014, 2633-0014, 2636-0005, 2663-1986 and 2666-1015.

There are several fittings on the outside of the body. The rear lights (see *Electrical Components*, pages 35-38) are fitted to the two rearward-facing body panels, which were pre-drilled for the purpose. There are also ten hood lacing brackets, two on each side just behind the cab for the optional three-seater hood, two more on each body side and one on each of the rearward-facing panels. On early vehicles these brackets are all of the same 'staple' type, fitted to the body panels with screws and nuts. However, beginning with chassis number 866-6001 in June 1949, the brackets on the body sides were changed for welded cleats, although the staple brackets remained at the rear. These cleats were positioned closer together than the staple brackets had been.

The left-hand rear panel also bears an oval Land-Rover badge, attached by two screws and nuts, and always the same type and size as the grille badge. The right-hand rear panel is provided with a square black number plate, which has rounded corners and is normally secured with four screws.

There are also two important tailboard fittings on each side of the rear body. The first of these is the galvanised support chain, which is sleeved in Vynide to match the seats and is attached to each wheelarch box by a bolt, spring washer and nut. The second is the locking wedge or key, also attached to a chain from the rear-facing body panel, again by a bolt, spring washer and nut.

The tailboard itself remained the same throughout 80-inch production. It is fabricated from Birmabright, with galvanised steel cappings to reinforce the top and sides. These incorporate eyes which fit over the dowels on the body cappings when the tailboard is closed. On vehicles between 866-6001 (June 1949) and 0610-5462 and 0630-0027 (late 1949), the tailboard eyes have rope cleats designed for use with the fixing rope of the contemporary 'zig-zag lacing' hood (see *Canvas, Cab and Hard Top*, pages 45-48). In the middle of the tailboard is a reinforcing alloy rib, which has a simple L-section on early vehicles and a stronger top-hat section on later examples.

Two large galvanised hinges are bolted to the tailboard's outer side. Slightly smaller hinges were fitted from chassis number 866-6001 in June 1949. On the inside of the tailboard is a hook for the support chain at each top corner. The first 1500 vehicles have no weather seals, but from 86-1501 there are rubber weather strips on each side and at the bottom, in each case located by retaining strips held to the tailboard by rivets and pop rivets. The side seals and their retaining plates are in two sections, the upper one being the shorter.

The front or transom panel of the back body has a straight face and wide galvanised capping on early vehicles like this 1950 model (far left), but is 'kinked' and has a narrower capping on later ones like this 1951 example (near left).

The back body is generally similar on all 80-inch Land-Rovers. This picture of a 1953 model also shows the rope cleats welded to each side outer panel.

The tailgate chains should have a green Vynide covering.

The hood sticks form a self-supporting framework. These are on a 1950 model, and are the later type with pronounced curvature in the horizontal pieces running across the body.

The galvanised capping at the front of the back body also carries various fittings for the seats in the driving compartment (see *Seats*, pages 51-52).

PAINT COLOURS (BODIES)

The utility versions of the 80-inch Land-Rover came with just one standard colour: green. However, two greens were used.

The precise change-over point has not been established beyond doubt, but it appears that all vehicles up to 866-6000 (and contemporary 867-series Station Wagons and 868-series Welders) were painted in Light Green, which bears ICI code PO30-2602. This is also known as 'No.2 Green', a name probably derived from the list of 1948 Rover saloon car paints on which the colour was listed as no.2 between no.1 Sundown and no.3 Grey. It can be matched by a Mercedes-Benz paint sold under code LR-L5, 21 line. On all subsequent vehicles the colour was generally known as Bronze Green, which has ICI code PO30-2651. Hard tops were finished in Ivory, which has ICI code PO30-2155.

The finish of all these colours should be semi-matt; no standard 80-inch Land-Rover ever left the factory with gloss paint.

CANVAS, CAB AND HARD TOP

When the Land-Rover was announced in 1948, Rover planned to sell it in very basic form without any body superstructure at all; in fact, even the doors were intended to be optional. However, a full-length canvas tilt (or 'seven-seater hood') very quickly became standard equipment, and a short canvas cab cover (or 'three-seater hood') became optional. Metal cabs and metal rear bodies also became available at extra cost.

HOOD AND HOOD SUPPORTS

The three-seater hood is supported by a detachable tubular steel framework consisting of three parts. The main one is a hooped hood stick which fits into the sockets in the cappings at the front corners of the body. This is then braced to the windscreen frame by two tie rods which attach to the hood sticks by bolts with wing nuts.

When a full-length hood is fitted, a second hood stick fits into the sockets in the cappings at the rear corners of the body. This rear hood stick is braced to the front one by a tubular tie rod on each side, fitted to each hood stick by more bolts and wing nuts, and located just below the radius of the hood stick on each side.

There are two different types of hood stick. All 1948-49 models, and '50 models with chassis numbers up to and including 0610-5463 and 0630-0027, have sticks with a flat horizontal section. All later 80s have the second type of stick, with a pronounced curvature in the horizontal section which encourages water to drain off the roof of the hood. Front and rear hood sticks are identical in each case, but each type of hood stick is suitable for use only with the correct type of canvas hood.

Both the three-seater and full-length hoods are made of the same heavy-duty khaki canvas. The three-seater type consists of two sections, one being the roof and rear quarter-sections, the other being the rear curtain. The rear curtain contains two rectangular 'windows' made of gauze, and has five reinforced slots for its fixing straps at the top. Down each side are three loops, through which are threaded the two long webbing straps attached to the rear of the canvas cab roof section.

The three-seater hood is held in place by metal loops and webbing straps with dull-finish buckles. Nine metal loops hold the front of the hood to the windscreen frame, one strap on each side holds the hood to the tie-rods, and two long straps hold the rear hood valance to the body. In addition, each of the rear quarter panels is secured by three quick-release fasteners along the leading edge.

There are three different types of full-length hood. The first one, fitted to all vehicles up to and including chassis number 866-6000 in June 1949, is distinguished by having webbing straps to attach it to the sides and rear of the body. Both the later types have rope fixings in place of these straps. The second type, fitted to subsequent vehicles up to chassis numbers 0610-5462 and 0630-0027, is distinguished by a zig-zag pattern of lacing at the rear. Both these types go with the flat type of hood sticks. The third type was fitted to all subsequent 80-inch models and goes with the curved hood sticks.

All three types of full-length hood have webbing straps and buckles inside to hold them to the hood sticks, but the earliest type also has two short webbing straps on each side and two long webbing straps attached to the rear roof valance. These additional straps are threaded through staples on the side and rear body panels to hold the hood in place.

On the second and third types of hood, the fixing rope is threaded through the lower edge of the canvas; it emerges in two places on each side to go over the cleats on the body sides, and in the rear curtain is laced through eight reinforced eyelet holes. There are two different lengths of rope for the rear curtain, one 56 inches long and the other 90 inches long (or 99 inches, according to some Rover parts catalogues); the longer type is necessary with the second type of hood, where the zig-zag lacing pattern uses up the extra length.

The rear curtain is detachable on the first type of hood but is stitched to the hood valance on the second and third types. It has extension 'wings' which wrap around the sides of the main hood; each one then attaches to the hood sides by a single webbing strap which passes through a buckle on the main hood. All original rear curtains have two rectangular windows, which are made of greenish khaki gauze on the first examples and of heavy celluloid on hoods made after late 1949. Replacement hoods supplied by Rover after about 1954 have a single Perspex rear window, which was introduced in anticipation of new UK traffic regulations that came into force on 1 January 1956.

The third type of seven-seater hood could be fit-

The three-seater canvas cab on a 1949 model in position (top) and with the rear curtain rolled up to give better ventilation (above). Also visible are the staples on the body sides and the spare wheel fixing bracket. The grab-handles on the rear body cappings were an optional extra.

The rear sections of the three-seater hood fit over the hood sticks (near right), which in turn fit into sockets in the galvanised body cappings. Webbing straps and buckles hold the three-seater hood to the hood sticks (far right) and also tension the fabric. This view shows the rear curtain, looking towards the rear of the vehicle.

Webbing straps are also used to hold the canvas to the staples on the body sides.

The full-length hood on the 1949 AA Land-Rover has the original type of gauze window coverings. Note how the removable rear curtain is held in place by webbing straps laced neatly through loops.

The third type of full-length hood could be fitted optionally with a fume curtain behind the driver. This is it in place, showing how its webbing straps loop around the front hood stick. This vehicle has the optional inward-facing rear seats.

ted optionally with a canvas partition or 'fume screen' behind the driver. This is a separate panel containing two rectangular windows, in gauze on early examples and celluloid on later ones. The partition is held to the front hood stick by webbing straps and buckles – three at the top and two down each side. Two further straps on the bottom edge attach the panel to the body.

An optional extra for all seven-seater hoods was an additional pair of webbing straps and buckles fitted to each side near the top. These allowed the sides of the hood to be rolled up and fixed in the open position. Many export models built after March 1952 had two windows in the sides of the hood; these were identical in size and type to the windows used in the rear curtain. Rover also offered a kit for installing windows in earlier hoods. However, neither the hood nor the conversion kit was available on Land-Rovers sold in Britain.

TRUCK CAB

The truck cab was introduced as an optional extra in June 1952, but was available on export models some time earlier. It could be, and commonly was, retro-fitted to earlier 2-litre and 1.6-litre models. It consists of two major elements, both made of Birmabright alloy.

The first of these elements is the roof. This slopes upwards from front to rear and is braced with three stiffening ribs on the outside. The second element is the rear panel, which contains an aperture for the rear window. This window may be a single fixed pane of glass or two sliding panes with metal finger-plates and a simple hook-type catch to keep it closed. The bottom of each side extension of the rear panel and its two rear corners are reinforced with galvanised steel cappings.

Rubber seals are attached to the front, sides and rear of the roof, and additional rubber blocks in each corner. The roof is attached to the windscreen frame by a bolt and an adjustable link in each corner, and to the rear panel by bolts. The rear panel is attached to the rear body by long studs which go into the hood stick supports at the front of the body, and

The metal truck cab was painted in Ivory, unless to special order. It is seen here on Dave Davies' 1949 model, 866-7732. Note the stiffening ribs on the roof.

additional support is provided by an angled piece of metal running across the top of the rear panel. There is also an extra packing piece for the spare wheel, to prevent it fouling the rear panel of the cab.

A tropical roof could also be bought, although in theory it was for export only. This is simply a second alloy roof panel which bolts to the main cab roof and is held slightly above it by the stiffening ribs and by six distance pieces along the sides. The theory is that cool air is able to circulate in the gap between the two panels, thus reducing the effect of the sun's heat on the cab itself. The design was successful enough to remain in production for Land-Rovers until the early 1980s.

Hard Top

The hard top became optional from February 1950. It consists of four major elements – a roof panel, two side sections and an upper tailgate.

The roof panel has the same profile as the truck cab roof at the front, and this joins to a flat rear section. Three stiffening ribs run from front to rear; very early examples are narrower than later types and have slots which may have been intended as lashing points. Early canopy sections are also fabricated from four pieces of metal, and early roofs have no spot-welded join between the canopy and the main roof. A tropical roof was an additional option – again, in theory for export only – and has five distance pieces on each side as compared to the three found on the truck cab.

The two side sections are L-shaped when viewed from above and have reinforcing plates at each lower corner. These plates are normally galvanised but may have been painted to match the rest of the hard top on very early hard tops with the narrow stiffening ribs. The side sections may either be plain (to give a van body) or have a single fixed window in each side. These windows are of glass and are rubber-glazed; they became an option on export models during 1950. At the rear, each side section carries a rubber side seal for the upper tailgate and a simple loop-type catch for the upper tailgate lock.

The side sections are held to the rear body cappings by long studs and brackets, and there are rubber seals and filler pieces between upper and lower body panels. The roof section is fitted to the windscreen frame in the same way as the truck cab roof, and there are rubber seals above the cab doors, between side panels and roof, and above the upper tailgate. The roof is bolted to the side panels.

The upper tailgate has a fixed rear window made of glass and rubber-glazed. It also has a T-shaped handle on the outside and a locking lever on the inside; both should have a chromed finish. Two large hinges hold the upper tailgate to the roof panel, and a spring quadrant on each side holds it open when required; these hinges and quadrants should have a 'sheradised' finish. On very early tailgates, the hinges were external rather than concealed.

Interior

Dashboard

Two types of steering wheel are used on the 80-inch models. Both have three sprung spokes and a diameter of 17 inches. The wheel fitted to Land-Rovers built in 1948 and early '49 is actually the 1946-47 Rover car type, with each sprung 'spoke' consisting of two wire spokes. This wheel is also found on some Land-Rovers built around the middle of 1949, although these later ones do not have the groove for the car's trafficator switch.

The second type of wheel is the one used on the P3 saloon cars of 1948-49, and each of its sprung spokes consists of four wires, arranged in pairs. Land-Rover enthusiasts refer to this one rather confusingly as the 'four-spoke' wheel, even though it still has

An interesting collection of features on Brian Carvey's 1950 80-inch model. The steering wheel is the 'four-spoke' type. An optional combined water temperature and oil temperature gauge is fitted on the lower left of the facia, replacing the blanking plate which normally covers the redundant hole for the LHD steering column. The optional passenger's side wiper motor is fitted, and the heater is a later Smith's type, complete with demisting assembly. The additional mirror stuck to the windscreen is not an original feature.

three primary spokes. It was probably first used on Land-Rovers early in 1949 and then took over completely later in the year.

The rim of both steering wheels is made of black plastic and the metal spokes have a chrome finish. The black Bakelite centre boss has a switch of the same material to control the headlamp main beam. Stamped into the plastic alongside it is the word 'DIP' with an arrow pointing left. Both letters and arrow should be painted white. The steering column should be painted black along its whole length. It is supported by a bracket bolted to the driver's side of the bulkhead. This bracket, and the clamp that holds the column to it, should be galvanised.

The 80-inch Land-Rover has a small instrument panel in the centre of the dashboard, shaped like a narrow elongated oval and fixed by four set screws and washers to a pod welded to the bulkhead behind. The front surface of the instrument panel is painted the same colour as the body. Both right-hand and left-hand drive panels are the same, but some 1949 models have an extra warning light for the headlamp main beam set into the centre of the panel above the oil warning light. This is actually a US-market fitting that was probably used because of overstocking of US-specification parts at the factory.

There are four main circular apertures in the instrument panel. Reading from the left, these contain the Lucas PLC6 L133 ignition and lights switch (which incorporates the ignition key lock in its centre), an ammeter with upward-pointing needle, a petrol gauge with downward-pointing needle, and a speedometer with distance recorder (but no trip counter). The latter may read in either miles or kilometres, depending on the market the vehicle was built for.

Instrument panel on a 2-litre model shows the later '30-30' type of ammeter. The black knob of the panel light switch to the left of the combined ignition and lighting switch is rarely found in good condition, as the Bakelite tends to crack. Just visible at the bottom of the picture is the curved metal handle of the hand throttle.

The only one of these instruments to change during 80-inch production was the ammeter. Initially a Lucas type with a scale reading from −20 to +20 and a red-tipped pointer, this was later changed for a Lucas CZU 26 (part number 36047) with a scale reading from −30 to +30. It is not clear when the change took place.

There were also two types of speedometer drive cable. The earlier type has a ribbed outer casing and is found on all 1948 and '49 vehicles, on 1950 models up to and including chassis numbers 0610-5830 (basic) and 0620-0140 (Station Wagons), and on all 1950 Welders in the 0630-series. The later type has a plain outer casing.

Outboard of the combined ignition and lights switch is a Lucas PS15/1 L4 pull switch above two electrical sockets for an inspection lamp. The pull switch operates the instrument panel lights, and should have a black Bakelite knob; these knobs tended to crack at their threaded ends, and later replacement types have clear plastic bodies with a black top. The sockets have coloured plastic rims, the upper one being black and the lower red.

The instrument panel normally has three warning lights (there are four on those 1949 models with the US-specification main beam warning lamp). Two of these are between the combined ignition and lights switch and the ammeter: the upper one has an amber lens and is for the choke (which Rover called the mixture control), while the lower one with a red lens is for the ignition. The third warning light is in the lower centre of the panel, between the ammeter and the fuel gauge, and has a green lens with a disc behind it out of which the letters 'OIL' are punched. Some of the earliest vehicles may have had red oil warning lights.

The early warning lights have metal bodies with plastic lenses, and are found on all 80-inch models built up to the middle of the 1951 model year. The final vehicles fitted with this type have chassis numbers 1610-1655, 1613-3213, 1616-1501, 1623-0080, 1626-0020, 1630-0003, 1633-0003, 1636-0007, 1663-0042 and 1666-1476. Some of these early warning lights fit flush with the instrument panel, and some stand slightly proud of it; both types were supplied by Lucas under the same part number, and they appear to have been fitted interchangeably on the assembly lines.

A second type of warning light is fitted to subsequent 1951 models and to most '52 models. These later Lucas WL3/1 lights have the lens and bezel moulded as a single plastic part. The instrument panel wiring harness which goes with them incorporates different bulb-holders. They have Lucas part numbers 38084A (red, ignition), 38085A (green, oil, but without the word 'oil' on the lens) and 38086A (amber, choke).

The last 1952 models and all '53 models once again have warning lights with separate lenses, but these now have plastic rather than metal bodies; the first chassis to have them are 2610-5067, 2613-3551, 2616-2760, 2630-0007, 2633-0012, 2636-0005, 2663-0632 and 2666-0967. However, the bulbs in these warning lights are all 12-volt types this time, whereas the earlier ignition light only had a 2.5-volt bulb.

Additional instrument dials were available as optional extras. The very earliest may have been marked only with the name of their manufacturer (Jaeger), but the majority came with the Land-Rover logo on their faces. An oil temperature gauge came with the optional oil cooler (see *Options and Accessories*, pages 62-64), and a combined water temperature and oil pressure gauge may be fitted. In both cases, these are usually located in the flat part of the bulkhead alongside the main instrument panel on the left-hand side of the vehicle. The same position is used for both right-hand drive and left-hand drive vehicles, as it affords the simplest runs for the associated cabling and tubing.

Underneath the instrument panel are three bulkhead controls. On the left is the starter button, which should have a black alloy knob and is the same on all 80-inch models. Next comes the curved metal handle of the hand throttle, 'sheradised' and again the same on all 80s. Finally, on the right is the choke or mixture control, which has a black plastic knob with white letters reading 'Cold Start', and is mounted on a bracket bolted through the bulkhead to a bracket on the engine side. Bolted to the bracket on the cab side is a metal box containing a Lucas S4C switch, which is activated by the choke cable and operates the choke warning lamp.

There are two types of choke control cable and three types of support bracket. The early support bracket consists of two pieces of steel screwed together, and is fitted to all 1948 and '49 vehicles, and to '50 models up to and including chassis numbers 0610-4682, 0620-0106 and 0630-0021. The second type of support bracket consists of two pieces of steel welded together, and is fitted to subsequent models built in the 1950 model year, up to and including chassis numbers 0611-1527, 0620-0311 and 0630-0030. The third type of bracket, fitted to all subsequent 80s, is a single piece of steel.

The early type of choke cable is fitted with the first two types of support bracket, and the later type only with the third. The earlier choke cable has a single fixing nut on the bulkhead side of the support bracket; the later type has a second nut on the switch side of the bracket, together with a shake-proof washer.

When the optional semaphore trafficators are fitted (see *Electrical Components*, pages 35-38), a Lucas TS82 control switch (part number 310392) is fitted to the windscreen frame.

The clutch and brake pedals pass through the floor panel and act on cross-shafts which pass through the chassis frame itself. These are on a 1950 model.

HANDBRAKE

Two different types of handbrake lever are found on the 80-inch Land-Rovers. The earlier type is 'waisted', while the later type has a shaft of constant diameter. The change took place in 1950, the first vehicles with the new type being 0610-5379 (basic), 0620-0121 (Station Wagon) and 0630-0029 (Welder). Both types of lever should have a black-painted shaft. Left-hand drive handbrakes are attached to a cross-shaft and are not interchangeable with right-hand drive types. The first LHD 80s with the 'straight' rather than 'waisted' lever were 1950 models, 0611-1807 for the basic models and 0620-0326 for the Station Wagons. However, LHD Welders did not change until the first 1951 example, chassis number 1633-0001, was built.

The rubber dust-seals around the base of the clutch and brake pedals are original equipment, but the rubber matting in the footwell is a non-standard if practical addition.

PEDALS

The clutch and brake pedals are mounted on rods which pass through the toe-board, the holes having rubber grommets, to cross-shafts below the floor. The accelerator is a pendant type, with a distinctively shaped pedal which pivots from the toe-board. Early accelerator pedals have a full-width cross-shaft, but a short cross-shaft is fitted from 1610-2848.

Both clutch and brake pedals have large, flat toe-pads with raised 'pips' to give grip. One side of each pedal is turned up, again to improve grip; this is the right-hand side on the clutch pedal and the left-hand side on the brake (ie, adjoining sides when installed). The pedal rods are fitted into eyes on the ends of rod-type levers which run to the cross-shafts.

The pedals should all be finished in black. The brake and clutch pedals may be fitted with rubber pads, which were an extra-cost option. These are fitted with their ribs running from side to side.

SEATS

Unless to special order, all 80-inch Land-Rovers have three separate seats in the front compartment. These seats come in four different types for the basic vehicles, and a fifth type that is unique to the Station Wagons and described separately (see page 54).

The first type of seat is fitted only to the first 150 vehicles, chassis numbers 86-0001 to 86-0150. Its backrest is little more than a padded and curved horizontal bar, and is identical to the type fitted on pilot-production vehicles during early 1948. The second style of seat is generally known as the 'spade' type because of the shape of its backrest, which tapers towards the top, and this should be fitted to all remaining 1948 and '49 vehicles, and to 1950 models up to and including 0611-0304 (basic models) and 0630-0030 (Welders).

The third pattern of seat has a squarer backrest and is known as the 'shovel' type, again on account of its shape. This was introduced probably in March 1950, and is found on all subsequent 1950 models, on all 1951 models, and on 1952 models up to and including chassis numbers 2610-2280, 2613-1713, 2616-1499, 2630-0002, 2633-0008, 2636-0001, 2663-0150 and 2666-0354. The fourth and final seat, fitted to the remaining 1952 models and all 1953 models, is distinguished by its padded backrest.

The first or pilot-production type of backrest is supported on two short brackets bolted to the rear body capping. It is, quite literally, a backrest rather than a seatback. It consists of a curved and padded strip, about 5 inches deep, which is located just above the rear body capping. The original upholstery was probably black.

The second or 'spade' type of seatback has an aluminium alloy inner panel, with green Vynide upholstery. Two sprung loops are attached to the rear of each seatback by four set bolts, each with one spring

The 'spade' type of seat back on a 1949 model (top left); note how each seat back is sprung against the rear body capping. The wedge-shaped cushions are correct for the model. 'Shovel' seat backs on a 1951 model (top right). The cushions have slightly more shape than the earlier type. The last type of seat back fitted on 80-inch models was the 'padded' variety (above left), seen here on a 1953 2-litre. The undersides of the cushions (above) have two locating rubbers, and the centre is covered in brown hessian.

and one plain washer. The free ends of these curved brackets are bolted to small reinforcing brackets, which in turn are bolted to the top surface of the galvanised capping on the driving compartment's back panel. Each backrest also has a rubber buffer held to it by a screw and a nut.

The third or 'shovel' type of seatback has a steel inner panel and green Vynide upholstery. Each seatback is arranged to tip forwards on two long 'sheradised' hinges bolted to the seatback. The lower ends of these hinges are bolted through the back panel. Each hinge bears a hollow extruded rubber buffer block, held in place with securing blocks and rivets. In addition, to each hinge is riveted a retaining strap made of canvas webbing. Eyelets in the free ends of these straps fit over studs (in some cases with distance tubes as well) held to the back panel by screws and nuts, thus holding the seatback upright.

The last type of seatback is also upholstered in green Vynide. It hinges at its bottom corners on brackets held to the seat base by screws and nuts. To the rear of each seatback are attached a leather retaining strap (on the left) and a leather buffer pad (on the right). The retaining straps have eyelets which fix over studs held to the rear body capping by drive screws. The rear capping also bears a pair of rubber buffers for each seat, again secured by drive screws.

The seat cushions are always wedge-shaped and covered in green Vynide. There is a four-piece wooden seat frame, and the exposed underside of this has a natural brown hessian covering. Screws with cup washers hold the Vynide to the wooden underside, and two black rubber dowels are also screwed to this. These dowels locate in the seat box to hold each cushion securely in place.

Some 80-inch Land-Rovers may also be fitted with inward-facing seats in the load-bed. These seats have hinged bases and can be folded upwards to leave the floor of the load area clear, a webbing strap holding them in place. In theory, they were available for export only. They are upholstered in green Vynide, their metal frames are galvanised, and they are usually accompanied by galvanised guard rails bolted to the capping on each side of the tailgate.

The original Clayton heater (right) had a slightly more greenish paint finish than the reproduction item pictured here. Note the blower fan control knob on the bulkhead above the heater, and the quadrant for the engine speed governor control below the instruments. The heater tap (far right) is screwed into the thermostat housing. This example is seen on a pre-production model.

HEATER

The 80-inch Land-Rover was never fitted with a cab heater as standard, but a heater was made available as an optional extra by 1949. This heater is made by Clayton Dewandre and its maker's plate reads 'Clayton Type CB'. A round box bolted to the bulkhead on the passenger side of the cab, it has an attractive grey-green metallic stove-enamelled finish; modern reproduction heaters have gunmetal paint with a silvery finish.

A water pipe tapped into the engine thermostat housing brings hot water into the heater box, and the heat is then distributed to the cab through a series of vanes and flaps. Different versions of this basic heater were fitted to commercial vehicles of all types in the late 1940s and 1950s, and it is not uncommon to find a Land-Rover which has been fitted with one of these, probably taken from a scrapped vehicle.

Early in the 1953 model year, the Clayton heater was replaced by a black Smith's unit of similar general appearance, and soon afterwards a demister assembly, consisting of crude hoses and outlets bolted to the windscreen frame, was introduced. The Smith's heater was made available from chassis numbers 3610-0134, 3613-0225 and 3616-0090, but could also be retro-fitted to earlier vehicles.

STATION WAGONS AND WELDERS

Right from the beginning, Rover recognised that the Land-Rover would be an extremely versatile vehicle. As a result, several special variants became available during the production life of the 80-inch model – most notably the Station Wagon, the Welder, the Fire Engine and the Military types. Production of these was overseen by the factory and they were all built in quantity. The Fire Engines and Military models are covered in separate sections (see pages 108-115 and 116-125 respectively). There were, of course, also 'aftermarket' conversions, often one-offs, about which almost no information is available. Restorers of any such unique vehicles are therefore on their own...

THE 80-INCH STATION WAGON

The 80-inch Station Wagon was not a very successful model, mainly because its coachbuilt body inflated its purchase price and its status as a passenger-carrying vehicle – on the home market – incurred Purchase Tax, from which the basic Land-Rover was exempt. Just 651 were built between October 1948 and the summer of 1951, and no 2-litre edition was ever catalogued.

The chassis of the Station Wagon is essentially the same as that of the basic Land-Rover, but is fitted with the optional heavy-duty rear springs and has small 'box' extensions on the rear cross-member to support the overhang of the rear body. At least one vehicle also appears to have been fitted with a chromed bumper, but the normal production bumper was shared with the basic 80-inch Land-Rover of the time.

The electrical components are the same as on basic Land-Rovers for the most part, although all Station Wagons seem to have had export specification flashing trafficators. These operate through the tail lamps, circular Lucas 488s (each with a twin-filament bulb) fitted to the thin strip of panelling below the tailboard aperture. At the front, the side-lamps are designed to take twin-filament bulbs, one of the filaments operating as the flashing indicator.

The Station Wagon's front wings, bonnet and grille panel are shared with other 80s, except that all Station Wagons have their spare wheels mounted on the bonnet and therefore have the optional mounting kit on that panel. They should also have a unique Birmabright alloy spare wheel cover, held in place by a large winged nut in the centre and painted to match the bonnet panel. In theory, two types were available, one to suit 6-inch tyres and the other to suit the optional 7-inch size.

The bulkhead on Station Wagons is a modified version of the standard one, with an extension added to the top. On the passenger compartment side it also incorporates two oddments trays or shelves above the instrument panel. To the outer edges of the steel panel are bolted the wooden uprights of the front frame, and as a result the body aft of the front wings is slightly wider than the body of a basic 80.

KYM 725, chassis number R0620-0035, is an early 1950-model Station Wagon finished in two-tone green. It has been restored by Ken Wheelwright. The spun aluminium alloy spare wheel shroud was unique to the Station Wagons and is a rare find today.

Above these, further wooden pieces form the windscreen frame and header panel, and the whole assembly is finished off with Birmabright skin panels. It is notable that the panel below the windscreen does not contain any fresh-air ventilators; the opening quarter-lights in the doors were presumably intended to fulfil that function.

The windscreen is also completely different from the standard type, being a single pane of glass rather than a two-piece divided 'screen. It is also fixed in position rather than hinged, and is rubber-glazed with a single-piece seal incorporating a wedge strip. Two windscreen wipers are fitted as standard, both driven by a single motor concealed behind the oddments trays at the top of the bulkhead panel.

The cab area is unique to the Station Wagons, having a seat box which covers only the fuel tank and transmission tunnel, leaving the left-hand side of the vehicle clear for a special tipping seat. The arrangement is identical on both LHD and RHD models. The cab floor which matches up with this seat box is therefore also unlike the type on basic Land-Rovers.

There is light green carpet on the gearbox cover, and a separate piece of carpet is held by press studs to the inspection cover in the transmission tunnel. The floor panels are covered with ribbed black rubber sheeting (made by the now-defunct North British Rubber Company), which covers all the horizontal surfaces but stops short at the vertical surfaces of the gearbox cover and bulkhead. There are two pieces on the left-hand side, the second one running under the seat, which is mounted directly to the floor.

There should also be fibreboard linings to the footwells and fibreboard facing panels on the lower bulkhead below the bottom of the instrument panel. This fibreboard is light green and is held to the bulkhead by self-tapping screws with cup washers. Two spring clips on the fibreboard hold the starting handle across the lower half of the bulkhead. Fibreboard is also used for the rather crude door trim panels. There are chromed door release handles inside, and sill locking levers with a chromed finish are set into the ledges beneath the door windows.

The three forward-facing front seats are again unique to the vehicle. The centre and right-hand seats are modified versions of those found in contemporary basic models, but the left-hand seat has a tubular frame finished in the body colour, and tips forward to allow access to the rear. The direction indicator switch – whether for semaphores or flashers – is mounted on an extension bracket on the steering column, as on 1946-47 Rover saloons.

The Station Wagon back body shares no common components with the back body of the basic 80-inch Land-Rover. Whereas bodies for basic models were built up at Rover's Solihull factory, Station Wagon

The Tickford-built body looks very square from behind, and overhangs the rear chassis cross-member by some distance. The draw bar and the visible part of the rear cross-member are painted to match the adjacent body colour, while the rest of the chassis is black. Note the yellow-on-green badges at front and rear.

bodies were assembled by Salmons-Tickford at Newport Pagnell. They were built by traditional coachbuilding methods, with aluminium alloy panelling over a wooden framework bolted together and reinforced with metal flitch plates.

The alloy used is the standard Land-Rover's Birmabright, and the wood is mahogany – used in preference to the coachbuilder's favourite seasoned ash because it was more likely to stand up to tropical conditions. Each element of the wooden structure would have been shaped by hand, so reconstruction of these bodies is a skilled and time-consuming business, and very much more expensive than the reconstruction of a basic Land-Rover's body.

In essence, the back body consists of two wooden side frames with extensions at roof level that meet up with the front frame. These side frames incorporate the rear side window surrounds and the bracing for the lower side body panels. They are held together by a straight wooden beam across the rear at roof level, and by three curved roof bearers. The back body of the Station Wagon overhangs the rear chassis cross-member by several inches.

The Birmabright skin panels are held to this

Details of a Station Wagon under restoration by Andrew Ings show the bulkhead side extensions (near right) and top extension (far right) unique to the model. Note how the alloy outer skin panels are wrapped around the bulkhead sides.

The Tickford-built body has an ash frame (above); these rear side members are normally invisible. The roof (above left) is supported by wooden spars like this one.

The upper and lower tailgates of the Station Wagon body (left) open independently. The lower tailgate support chains (far left) should be sleeved like this. Note the locker under the rear seats, already occupied by wiring and perhaps not best suited to the stowage of any items needed in a hurry or often!

wooden framework by coachbuilder's nails. The rear side panels incorporate swage lines which avoid a slab-sided appearance, and the roof is a single sheet of Birmabright alloy.

The rear side windows are made of glass and are divided into two sections, the forward one fixed and rubber-glazed, while the rear section slides in an unpainted aluminium channel. The sliding glass section has a round glass knob bonded to its leading edge and there is a hinged metal stop on the frame.

At floor level, there are wooden battens to form a support frame for the flat metal floor panel. Then at each side are metal wheel boxes, which extend from the backs of the front seats to the rear of the vehicle. These are painted in the main body colour and carry the inward-facing rear seats, which are described below. In the rearmost end of each one is a flap which gives access to an unlined locker; these flaps have piano-type hinges at their top edges and are held closed by spring clips. The exposed portion of the rear floor is covered with the same ribbed black rubber used for the front footwells.

Like the rest of the Station Wagon body, the doors are built on wooden frames and are completely different from their counterparts on the basic Land-Rover. The doors are full-height, so the wooden frame runs around the door windows as well as around the main lower panels. The wooden frames are, of course, panelled in Birmabright, and their outer panels have swage-line features which blend into similar styling lines in the rear side panels of the body. Station Wagon doors also have concealed hinges, fitted to the leading edge of the door frame and to the wooden pillars of the front body frame.

The Station Wagon dashboard has the standard instrument panel, but also two large shelves at the top. The doors each have a single check-strap.

The varnished wooden garnish rails and upholstered door trim panel are further unique features on what was still essentially a utility vehicle. The small mirror on the door has been added to improve safety and is not an original feature.

The doors also contain separate metal window frames, with downward extensions which allow the windows to wind down into the doors. There are cable-operated winding mechanisms mounted to these and to the insides of the wooden door frames; the cables are made of Teleflex. At the forward end of the metal frames are opening quarter-lights in chromed metal frames, which pivot centrally on pins concealed in the upper and lower elements of the main window frame. There is also a simple catch – an unpainted bronze casting – on the lower frame of the opening quarter-light. The window panes themselves are all made of glass rather than the Perspex used for the sidescreen windows on basic models.

The tailboard is divided into upper and lower halves. The lower half hinges downwards like the tailboard on other 80-inch models, but it has a wooden frame and Birmabright outer and inner skins. Retaining chains hold it in the open position, and near the top a chrome-plated T-handle with a key lock in the centre operates rods that engage in catches on the body sides to keep it closed. An oval 'Land-Rover' badge is mounted at the upper left, and the number plate hangs centrally, beneath a single D-lamp that acts as the stop-light.

The upper half of the tailboard is essentially an aluminium frame for the single-pane rear window, which again is glass rather than Perspex. Three hinges hold this to the wooden upper body cross-member, and on each side a spring-assisted quadrant bolts to the wooden body side frame. Locking screws with knurled nuts on these quadrants fix the upper tailgate in either the open or the closed position. There are also nickel-plated lifting handles in the centre of the lower window frame member, one each on the inside and outside.

The whole of the back body is lined with fibreboard, and a large ivory-coloured interior lamp sits in the centre of the rear roof. Spring clips on the back of the seat box, just above floor level, hold the wheelbrace and jack handle. There are also four individual inward-facing seats mounted above the wheel boxes in the rear, and the cushion of each one can be raised out of the way and secured with a strap.

Paint colours for the Station Wagons had a little more variety than for the utility versions of the 80-

inch Land-Rover. Early Station Wagons, built when the basic models were still Light Green, had Light Green as the main colour and either Light Grey or Ivory panels inside the body side strakes. When the basic vehicles switched to Bronze Green, some vehicles were built with this paint up to waist level and with Light Green tops. Eventually, Bronze Green took over completely and the vehicles were no longer painted in two colours.

WELDER

The Land-Rover Welder was designed by Rover jointly with the Lincoln Electric Company Ltd of Welwyn Garden City and became available from October 1948. Rover gave these vehicles their own chassis numbering sequence during 80-inch production, but only penny numbers were built – just 91 before the 80 gave way to the 86 in 1953. As a result, the Land-Rover Welder is a very rare model today. Welders were available on later Series I Land-Rovers, but they were always viewed as a special conversion and not as a factory-produced model.

The Welders on the 80-inch chassis should be fitted with an engine speed governor, an oil cooler and a radiator with a larger header tank than standard. They have a centre power take-off and a special cranked control lever which differs from the straight control lever normally used with the centre power take-off. No centre seat is fitted, and in its place is a

The three-abreast front seats of the Station Wagon are rather more elaborate than those in the standard Land-Rover. The left-hand seat tips forward (left) to give access to the rear. Note that even the seat box is different from standard, covering only two-thirds of the vehicle's width. The retaining straps on the rear seat cushions (below left) can be used to hold the cushions upright and make more room to carry loads in the rear. The ribbed black rubber flooring is correct for these vehicles. The headlining (below) is made of coloured millboard. Note the large central roof light, another unique feature.

This view of Richard Lines' 1952 80-inch Welder shows how the Lincoln SA150 arc welding generator was mounted in the middle of the vehicle. The support cradles for the gas cylinders rest on a bar which runs across the tailgate opening. The indicator lights bolted to the rear capping are not original equipment. The Welders had several items of special equipment as standard, including this 10-blade engine fan (right). The brass tap, of course, is for the heater. This bellows arrangement on the throttle (far right) acted as a damper to prevent the engine revs rising suddenly when the load was taken off the welding generator.

housing to protect the belt-drive from the power take-off pulley to a Lincoln SA 150 Arc Welding Generator, fitted in the body with its controls and dials facing towards the rear. To the body of the generator is fitted an M-shaped support frame with twin hooks on either side to take the lengths of electric cable supplied with the vehicle.

According to sales literature for the Welder, a lidded locker was fitted to the centre of the load floor behind the generator for equipment stowage. However, no surviving Welders appear to have had this fitted, and it may have been on prototypes only. Both in the sales literature and in reality, the area around each wheel arch is boxed in and given a lid that hinges from the rear body side capping in order to create additional stowage lockers.

In the rear of the load bed are two support cradles for gas cylinders; these cradles rest on the floor and are angled backwards to rest on a support bar across the top of the tailgate aperture. The intention was that oxy-acetylene welding equipment and the attendant cylinders of oxygen and acetylene could be carried in the vehicle in addition to the arc-welding equipment.

Certain items of welding equipment were supplied with the vehicle and complete its specification.

The Lincoln SA150 arc welding generator was driven by three rubber belts from a triple pulley on the gearbox power take-off, whose control lever was cranked forwards to reduce the risk of an operator catching fingers in the revolving belts.

An oil temperature gauge, standard on the Welder, was fitted to the bulkhead alongside the blanking plate for the LHD steering column (or RHD on LHD models). Note the stop bolted to the quadrant control for the engine speed governor. The Clayton heater differs slightly from the standard Land-Rover accessory and may not be correct for the vehicle.

There are two 30-feet cables, the first a ground cable fitted with lugs and a ground clamp, and the second an electrode cable fitted with a lug and an electrode holder. Both cables are of Lincoln's own manufacture, the electrode cable being a Stable Arc type. In addition, each Welder should come with a face shield, a wire scratch brush and a chipping hammer.

Welders were normally finished in the same paint colour as the contemporary basic Land-Rover.

EXPORT VARIATIONS

The 80-inch Land-Rover was not produced with the same variety of detail specifications to suit overseas markets as became necessary with later types. The only significant variations, apart from left-hand steering, were those on Land-Rovers built for export to the USA.

The export of CKD (Completely Knocked Down) vehicles for overseas assembly started in 1950, when vehicles were numbered in the standard sequences; 1951 and later CKD vehicles had their own chassis number sequences. As some elements of these CKD vehicles would have been sourced locally in the country of assembly, and as no records have come to light, it is not possible to list all the detail variations with any degree of accuracy.

Some vehicles were also built or bodied overseas, the former being the case with the Belgian Minerva Land-Rovers and the latter the case with the German-built Tempo vehicles.

LAND-ROVERS FOR THE USA

Exports of Land-Rovers to the USA began in late 1949, and these vehicles differed in two principal respects from those for other territories. They had special (probably laminated) glass in their windscreens to meet local regulations, and they had special lighting arrangements which demanded a unique wiring harness.

The US authorities refused to allow the then standard bulkhead-mounted sidelamps, so the apertures for these were blanked off with a metal plate and the sidelights – Lucas 488 with white lenses – were mounted in the wing fronts. Each wing front was punched to receive the sidelight, and provided with three fixing holes for it.

Different rear lighting arrangements were also needed, so round stop-and-tail lamps – Lucas 488 with red lenses – replaced the D-shaped ones always found on other 80-inch models. They were let into the rear panels, one on either side, and a cover plate was riveted over the fixing holes for the D-lamps.

The US authorities demanded that the rear number plate should be mounted centrally, so Rover attached a special mounting bracket to the centre of the tailboard with rivets and pop rivets, and added a Lucas lamp (part number 53093E on 1951 models, 53101E/J on later models) above it to illuminate the number plate when the sidelights were on.

Lastly, US regulations also demanded a main beam warning lamp on the dashboard. Rover therefore fitted a small telltale with a blue lens into the centre of the panel above the oil warning light.

MINERVA LAND-ROVERS

The Belgian Minerva company, based at Mortsel near Antwerp, constructed a number of Land-Rovers to meet a Belgian military contract. Although these are described in Rover records as CKD vehicles, Solihull probably shipped out very little more than the drivetrain, leaving Minerva to build the chassis and bodies and to trim the vehicles. As such a large proportion of each vehicle was built in Belgium, and the Minerva Land-Rovers differ considerably from the Rover-built product.

Probably unique to the Australian-assembled 80-inch Land-Rovers were the large logos on the right-hand front wing and the tailgate. These have faded since this 1951 model was built, but it looks as if the lettering was originally painted in yellow at both ends of the vehicle.

This restored ex-military Minerva Land-Rover is now in the hands of Dutch enthusiast Huub Houben. The characteristic sloping wings are in evidence, as are the side exhaust with its unique ribbed heat-shield and the single 'pigtail' towing-eye on the front dumb-iron. The second rear-view mirror would probably not have been fitted when the vehicle was new, and the yellow placard on the radiator grille is of course the rally plaque from an enthusiasts' gathering.

Minerva rear view shows cross-member without power take-off hole, characteristic shape of the tilt rear panel, jerrycan holder and spare wheel mounting. The low height of the centre rear body panel can just be seen. Interior differences (below right) include windscreen clamp brackets and central tool locker in place of a third seat – carpet on the floor is not original! Restored grille badges in early (bottom) and later (top) forms show their original attractive black and red enamel finish.

Between September 1951 and October 1956, a total of 9905 vehicle 'sets' were shipped from Solihull to Minerva. The majority were built up with 80-inch wheelbase chassis even though the 1954-56 deliveries were numbered in the sequences reserved for 86-inch models. Those which entered military service were used by the Belgian Army, Air Force, Navy and Gendarmerie, although some were stockpiled in Belgium and did not enter service until very late. Some remained in service into the 1990s.

Minerva also built small numbers of vehicles for civilian owners, and among these were a handful of 86-inch models, which are confusingly numbered within the same sequence as the 80s.

The chassis of the 80-inch Minerva Land-Rover is broadly similar to the standard left-hand drive Solihull-built type. The rare civilian versions have a power take-off aperture in their rear cross-members, but the military models do not. Military models also carry a towing hook at the centre of this cross-member and a five-pin trailer lighting socket on the right-hand side. The tyres are 6.00 × 16 type on standard well-base rims, although 6.25 × 16 tyres (probably of Belgian manufacture) were also fitted when the vehicles were in service. The engine is the standard 2-litre siamese-bore type, but the exhaust is unique to the vehicles. The front downpipe runs to a silencer box carried outside the left-hand chassis rail between the second and third cross-members, and the tailpipe emerges from the left-hand side ahead of the third cross-member.

The electrical system is unique to these vehicles, having twin 6-volt 120 amp/hour batteries instead of the single 12-volt type. One battery is in the standard position under the bonnet, and the second is underneath the driver's seat. The system has a positive earth up to chassis number 3663-1532, and a negative earth thereafter. Flashing front and rear indicators are standard equipment.

The whole body is made of steel rather than the Birmabright alloy of the standard Land-Rover. Front wings and grille are unique, the former being noticeably angular with a sloping front face instead of the curved front of the Rover product. A sidelight and amber indicator light are carried at the bottom front edge of the wing, and there is a single mirror on the driver's side wing. The grille is also unique to the model, covering only the central aperture in the grille panel and bearing a Minerva badge at its top. On either side, the smaller apertures in the grille panel are covered by small slatted grilles. There was originally a single 'pigtail' towing eye on the left-hand (driver's side) dumb iron, although most vehicles seem to have been fitted with a matching item on the right-hand dumb-iron during service.

There are in fact two different grille badges, one with the oval Land-Rover logo below the Minerva name and the other bearing the words 'Licence Rover' and 'T.T.' (for 'Tout Terrain' or 'All-Terrain') at the bottom. Both have black and red enamel backgrounds, with lettering and other raised elements unpainted. It is probable that the type with the Land-Rover badge is the earlier, and that the later type was introduced around 1954, after a legal wrangle soured relations between Minerva and Rover.

The windscreen differs in detail from the Rover type, and has different fastening clamps; a full-width ventilator panel is standard. The doors on all military Minervas are similar to the early 80-inch type in overall appearance, and have no handles; in consequence, the sidescreens have flaps. However, civilian versions on both the 80-inch and 86-inch wheelbases have recessed handles similar to those on the Solihull-built 86-inch models. The back body has a fixed rear panel on military versions; this reaches only three-quarters of the way up the two rear-facing side panels. High up on the left-hand side of the rear panel is a jerrycan holder, which is matched on the right-hand side by the spare wheel holder. However, civilian models have a drop-down tailgate and no jerrycan holder, and the spare wheel is mounted conventionally within the back body. The tilt is a seven-seater type, but unique to the Minerva models, and the basic military models have two inward-facing bench seats over the rear wheel boxes.

TEMPO LAND-ROVERS

There were also some unique military Land-Rovers built in Germany from left-hand drive chassis (probably chassis with bulkheads) sent out by Rover. There were probably around 190 of these, all 2-litre 80s built in the first half of 1953. The bodywork and final assembly were by Vidal und Sohn of Hamburg, who traded under the Tempo name, and the vehicles were all used by the West German Border Patrol Guards (*Bundesgrenzschutz* or BGS) for patrolling the border with East Germany.

The Tempo Land-Rovers have standard left-hand drive chassis, but with the fuel tank repositioned at the rear left-hand side and a negative earth electrical system with a heavy-duty Bosch dynamo (type LJ/GKM 300/12/1400 R3). The original tyres would have been 6.50 × 16 size.

Like the Minerva Land-Rovers, the Tempo vehicles have all-steel bodies. Although the frontal styling is similar to the Rover product, the wings actually have hinged lockers in their curved front parts, with hasps and turn-buckle fixings on their lower front panels. There is a sidelight in each locker lid, and a swivelling spotlight on the driver's side wing. The grille carries a Tempo badge above the Land-Rover one. A siren is mounted on each dumb iron just ahead of the grille panel, and some vehicles have capstan winches. The bonnet panel carries a large flat map-locker and there is a full-width ventilator flap at the top of the bulkhead. The windscreen hinges above this flap and is supported on the bonnet by a bracket on either side of the map locker.

The rear body is notable because it is much taller than the Rover type, its waist-line being at the base of the windscreen glass. The doors have recessed handles and detachable top sections with sliding windows, and there are lifting handles under the body sides, behind each rear wheel. The tailgate is a drop-down type, and the spare wheel is carried on the right-hand side of the rear panel. The hood and its frame are carried permanently attached to the rear body sides, rather in the fashion of a car's fold-down convertible top.

Inside, the Tempo vehicles have an additional instrument panel located above the standard Rover item. This carries a direction indicator switch, a control and tuner for the sirens, and a spotlight switch. A heater with demister apparatus is standard, and the two front seats have tubular frames. In the rear are a pair of inward-facing benches, mounted on the wheel boxes.

OPTIONS AND ACCESSORIES

Several optional extras have already been dealt with in the most appropriate sections. However, there are others which deserve some discussion. In addition, all 80-inch models were supplied when new with a comprehensive set of tools – which is a rare find these days.

The tool kit from 'Bessie', Brian Carvey's 1950 model. The tool roll is made of black hessian.

This view of Brian Bashall's 1948 chassis shows clearly the drive shaft running from the gearbox to the rear power take-off, which is fitted with a rare capstan winch.

A six-spline rear power take-off fitted with the correct guard plate. Below it is the correct extension plate for a tow hitch.

Another option for the rear power take-off was this drum, needed to power belt-driven machinery. It is fitted to a pre-production Land-Rover.

A capstan winch could also be fitted at the front, and always came with this sturdy-looking rope guide.

Tools

The 80-inch Land-Rovers were supplied with a small number of major tools and a tool roll containing a selection of hand tools.

The major tools were a wheelbrace of the familiar top-hat shape, a screw-type jack with separate extension bar and wooden handle, a hand-operated tyre pump with connector, a starting handle and a grease gun. Export models also had a tyre lever.

The hand tools came in a black hessian tool roll with two string ties. There were 11 tools: a tyre pressure gauge (with the Rover crest stamped into its body), a tommy bar, a box spanner, a 7-inch spark plug wrench, combination pliers, a screwdriver made out of a single piece of steel rod looped around to form the handle, a small Lucas distributor screwdriver and feeler gauge, a King Dick adjustable spanner, two double-ended spanners (one with 3/16 and 1/4-inch AF sizes, the other with 5/16 and 7/16-inch sizes) and a single-ended 3/8-inch AF spanner. All these tools except the screwdriver are the same as those supplied with Rover saloon cars between 1949-53.

Power Take-Offs

The 80-inch Land-Rovers can be fitted with power take-offs (PTOs) from the gearbox to drive machinery located either in the vehicle body or at the rear. The centre PTO is controlled by an additional lever in the centre of the vehicle, and its three-belt pulley is found underneath the centre section of the seat box. The rear PTO is driven by an additional propshaft and its main housing is bolted to the rear cross-member. The propshaft passes through the circular aperture in the cross-member and drives the output shaft through a gear train. There are two types of output shaft, the earlier having 10 splines (on PTOs numbered up to 86-0400) and the later one having six splines. The rear PTO output may be protected by a galvanised steel guard, or may be connected to a horizontal drum-type pulley for use with belt-driven machinery.

The rear PTO may be used to drive a capstan winch, an extremely rare accessory which is only suitable for use with the six-spline output shaft. A similar capstan winch may also be fitted at the front of the vehicle, driven by a shaft from an adapted vibration damper on the crankshaft nose. This front PTO was introduced in October 1950, but could be retro-fitted to earlier vehicles.

The front winch is mounted on a support plate bolted to the bumper and the front cross-member, which is reinforced by five distance tubes through which the bolts pass. Some may have had riv-nut fixings instead of bolts. Front winches numbered 86-0201 onwards have some differences from the earlier types. In all cases, a rope guide is also bolted to the front bumper. This rope guide and the centre plate around the capstan should be unpainted; the capstan itself and the main support plate should be black; and there is a black knob for the winch control rod which protrudes through the support plate.

An optional extra often fitted with the PTOs is an engine oil cooler, introduced late in 1950. This takes the form of seven wound coils in a frame bolted to the chassis cross-member ahead of the radiator and to the grille panel. Pipes run from this to the sump and to the oil pump. An oil temperature gauge is also installed on the dashboard.

TOWING EQUIPMENT

Several types of towing equipment were available. These were all jaw types, not the modern ball-type of tow hitch. One type had the jaws angled sharply away from one another, while a second had parallel jaws. Yet a third type was available, held to the rear cross-member by four bolts instead of the two of the other types, and with a handle on its pin.

There were also three types of tow plate, all of which bolted to the rear cross-member. The standard type was used unless a rear PTO was fitted, in which case a longer tow-plate cleared the PTO and was accompanied by an angled anchor plate. A rare third type was for use with a combine harvester.

Note that some 80-inch Land-Rovers may be fitted with a 2-inch diameter tow ball on the rear cross-member. Supplied with the Brockhouse trailer (see pages 126-127), this differs from a modern 50mm towball in being slightly larger and lacking a flattened top.

MISCELLANEOUS EXTRAS

The extras not covered elsewhere in this section include a radiator chaff guard (of which there were three types), a radio set (two types, one with short and medium wave reception, the other with medium and long wave), floor mats, a flag staff, radio interference suppressers (for the condenser, coil, dynamo, fuel pump and wiper motor), a 'cool-ride' seat pad (introduced in March 1950), and a speedometer to show tenths of a mile on its rather cluttered dial. Quite rare was a foot support, which was bolted to the side of the driver's footwell on RHD vehicles to prevent a driver's wet boot slipping off the accelerator pedal and becoming wedged against the side panel. Also available was a 15cwt trailer built by Brockhouse, which is described in detail separately (see pages 126-127).

APPENDICES

IDENTIFICATION, DATING AND PRODUCTION FIGURES

Land-Rovers built before October 1950 have their chassis numbers on a plate attached to the engine side of the bulkhead on the left-hand side. This plate is made of brass on models built up to the end of 1949 approximately, and of aluminium alloy on subsequent vehicles (for rather less than 12 months). It seems probable that the brass plates were originally nickel-plated with black lettering, while the alloy plates have black printing on a natural metal-coloured background.

From October 1950, it became necessary to fit a transfer box instruction plate explaining the workings of the selectable four-wheel drive system. This was fitted to the bulkhead on the cab side, just above the gearbox cover, and Rover used it to carry the chassis number as well; the bulkhead plate therefore disappeared. Reproduction transfer box plates are available. All 80-inch models also had the chassis number stamped into the left-hand side engine bearer on the chassis.

Note that what is commonly called the chassis number is actually a vehicle identification number. On 1.6-litre vehicles, it is sometimes possible also to see a three- or four-digit number stamped in smaller figures alongside or underneath the Rover chassis number. This is, strictly, the build number of the chassis, and has no relevance today.

The engine number is stamped on the left-hand side of the cylinder block at the front, on the machined surface just ahead of the exhaust manifold. Before the new chassis numbering system was introduced on 1951 models, it is typically within a few hundreds of the chassis number.

Engines rebuilt by Rover always had the original number ground off and a rebuild plate – usually brass and probably originally nickelled – screwed to the block next to the dipstick. Those rebuilt by the British Army were usually treated in the same way, but the brass military rebuild plates are often found on the rocker cover or elsewhere on the engine.

The gearbox number is on the right-hand side of the gearbox casing top cover. Like the engine number, it is normally within a few hundreds of the chassis number on Land-Rovers built before the middle of 1950. The axle number is on the top of the axle casing, on the left-hand side and usually next to the breather, for both front and rear axles.

Accessories such as the rear power take-off and its housing are also numbered in separate series, beginning in each case at 86-0001. This series retains its 86-prefix throughout, never switching to the 866, 0610 and other prefixes used on the vehicles.

Other serial numbers and manufacturing date codes are stamped on Land-Rover components. Carburettors have a four-figure code on their body castings, such as LB51. In this case, L is the Solex application code, B stands for February (A to M were used, with I excepted), and 51 stands for 1951. Coils are stamped on their ends with the month and year of manufacture. Control boxes are hot-stamped with the month and year of manufacture underneath. Differentials are sometimes stamped with a

The chassis number will be found stamped on the chassis frame, on the left-hand engine bearer.

On vehicles built before October 1950, the chassis number is stamped into a plate screwed to the engine side of the bulkhead. This one is actually on a pre-production model, R.19. Some later plates were alloy; this one is brass.

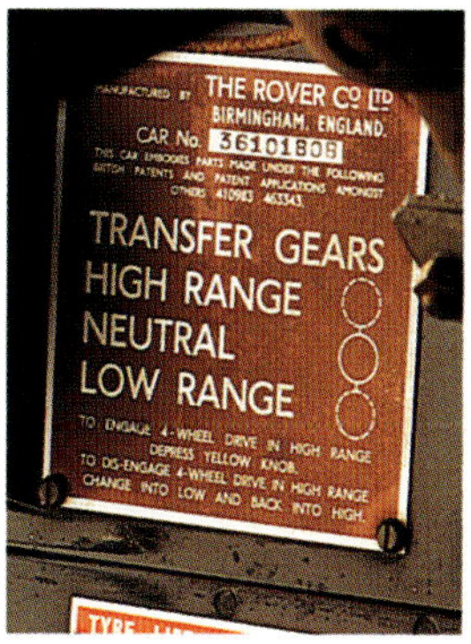

On vehicles with the selectable four-wheel drive transmission (and no freewheel), the chassis number is found on the transfer box instruction plate alongside the instrument panel.

serial number on top of their flanges; this is typically within a few hundreds of the chassis number on vehicles built before mid-1950. Distributors have a date of manufacture expressed in figures (eg, 9.49) on a lozenge-shaped plate (early examples) or stamped directly into the metal casting (later examples). Dynamos are date-stamped on their bodies with the month and year of manufacture. Fuse boxes are hot-stamped with the month and year of manufacture on one side. Radiators have a disc with the month and year of manufacture soldered to their top tanks. Starter motors are date-stamped with the month and year of manufacture on their bodies. Wheels made after early 1949 are date-stamped with the month and year of their manufacture in a circle.

Chassis Numbers

1948 models
R86-0001 to R86-3000 (all models). NB The prefix R is for RHD models only; LHD models have an L prefix.

1949 models
R866-3001 to R866-7920 (basic vehicle), R867-0001 to R867-0070 (Station Wagon), R868-0001 to R868-0010 (Welder). NB The prefix R is for RHD models only; LHD models have an L prefix.

1950 models
R0610-0001 to R0610-9999 (basic vehicle), R0611-0001 to 0611-5440 (basic vehicle), R0620-0001 to 0620-0480 (Station Wagon), 0630-0001 to 0630-0030 (Welder), 0710-0001 to 0710-0050 (2-litre prototypes). NB The prefix R is for RHD models only; LHD models normally but not invariably have an L prefix. The R prefix became omitted from home market vehicles, beginning with 0611-0348, 0620-0265, and 0630-0001. The 2-litre prototypes also had no prefix letter. Vehicles shipped as CKD for overseas assembly were numbered within the main sequences.

1951 models (last 1.6-litre)
1610-0001 to 1610-3971 (basic vehicle, home), 1613-0001 to 1613-6120 (basic vehicle, LHD)*, 1616-0001 to 1616-3268 (basic vehicle, RHD export), 1623-0001 to 1623-0080 (Station Wagon, LHD), 1626-0001 to 1626-0020 (Station Wagon, RHD export), 1630-0001 to 1630-0004 (Welder, home), 1633-0001 to 1633-0007 (Welder, LHD), 1636-0001 to 1636-0009 (Welder, RHD export), 1663-0001 to 1663-0081 (CKD basic vehicle, LHD), 1666-0001 to 1666-2320 (CKD basic vehicle, RHD). NB * The final chassis number in this sequence is suspect: parts catalogues refer to a change made at 1613-6866.

1952 models (first 2-litre)
2610-0001 to 2610-5569 (basic vehicle, home), 2613-0001 to 2613-6424 (basic vehicle, LHD), 2616-0001 to 2616-3614 (basic vehicle, RHD export), 2630-0001 to 2630-0014 (Welder, home), 2633-0001 to 2633-0013 (Welder, LHD), 2636-0001 to 2636-0004 (Welder, RHD export), 2663-0001 to 2663-1985 (CKD basic vehicle, LHD), 2666-0001 to 2666-1092 (CKD basic vehicle, RHD).

1953 models
3610-0001 to 3610-4122 (basic vehicle, home), 3613-0001 to 3613-4613 (basic vehicle, LHD), 3616-0001 to 3616-4007 (basic vehicle, RHD export), 3630-0001 to 3630-0008 (Welder, home), 3633-0001 to 3633-0007 (Welder, LHD), 3636-0001 to 3636-0007 (Welder, RHD export), 3663-0001 to 3663-7268 (CKD basic vehicle, LHD). NB No records exist for 3666-series CKD basic vehicles with RHD.

Note In these lists, the identifying prefix and vehicle serial number are separated by a dash to aid clarity. This dash is not found on the actual vehicles. Final chassis numbers given are based on surviving despatch records held by the British Motor Industry Heritage Trust. It is possible that some despatch records have been lost, and that final chassis numbers were higher in some cases.

Engine Numbers

1948 and 1949 models
86-0001

1950 models
0610-0001 (with L prefix on LHD models), 0710-0001 (prototype 2-litre engine)

1951 models (last 1.6-litre)
1610-0001 (RHD), 1613-0001 (LHD)

1952 models (first 2-litre)
2610-0001 (RHD), 2613-0001 (LHD)

1953 models
3610-0001 (RHD), 3613-0001 (LHD). NB B40 Rolls-Royce engines: just 50 Mk.IIB B40 engines were built, 33 for the evaluation vehicles and 17 spares. Their numbers were B40-518, B40-53, B40-556 to B40-605, and B40-609 to B40-610.

Note In these lists, the identifying prefix and engine serial number are separated by a dash to aid clarity. This dash is not found on the actual engines. Only commencing numbers can be given.

Factory reconditioned engines Engines reconditioned by Rover were renumbered. The reconditioning plate has the part number, which may be identified as follows:

245579 (1948-50, engines originally numbered up to 0610-00200)
245581 (1950-51, engines numbered from 0610-00201)
245583 (1952-53, see supplementary information below)

The 245583 part number is followed by a serial number and identifying codes. A typical number would be S0015/20/10, which breaks down as follows:

S Engine reconditioned at Solihull; L indicates an engine reconditioned at the London service depot in Seagrave Road; K is also found and is not yet explained.
0015 Serial number, in this case the 15th of its type.
20 The increase in bore size in thousandths of an inch (90 indicates liners fitted with standard bore; 91 with 0.010in bore increase; 92 with 0.020in increase).
10 The under-size of the reground crankshaft in thousandths of an inch.

Gearbox Numbers

1948 and 1949 models
86-0001 (with L prefix on LHD models)

1950 models
0610-0001 (with L prefix on LHD models)

1951 models
1610-0001 (RHD), 1613-0001 (LHD)

1952 models
2610-0001 (RHD), 2613-0001 (LHD)

1953 models
3610-0001 (RHD), 3613-0001 (LHD)

Note In these lists, the identifying prefix and gearbox serial number are separated by a dash to aid clarity. This dash is not found on the actual gearboxes.

Axle Numbers

1948 and 1949 models
Front axle 86-0001 (with L prefix on LHD models); rear axle 86-0001

1950 models
Front axle 0610-0001 (with L prefix on LHD models); rear axle 0610-0001

1951 models
Front axle 1610-0001 (RHD), 1613-0001 (LHD); rear axle 1610-0001

1952 models
Front axle 2610-0001 (RHD), 2613-0001 (LHD); rear axle 2610-0001

1953 models
Front axle 3610-0001 (RHD), 3613-0001 (LHD); rear axle 3610-0001

Note In these lists, the identifying prefix and axle serial number are separated by a dash to aid clarity. This dash is not found on the actual axles.

86-INCH & 107-INCH MODELS

The 86-inch and 107-inch Land-Rovers were announced in September 1953. Both represented Rover's response to customer requests for more carrying capacity. The 86-inch replaced the original 80-inch model and offered 25% more load capacity (although its 1000lb payload was not increased). The 107-inch, with its six-foot load bed, was aimed at the pick-up market, and was in fact initially known as the Land-Rover 4-Wheel-Drive Pick-Up.

The 1954 models were in some respects transitional types, with the same 2-litre engine as the superseded 80-inch models. For 1955, both the 86 and the 107 were fitted with a revised version of the 2-litre engine and a number of detail changes were made. However, relatively few specification changes were made after that; Rover had now fine-tuned the design enough.

A seven-seater Station Wagon model on the 86-inch chassis was made available from the beginning, but its 107-inch equivalent with 10 seats did not appear until June 1956. All the 86-inch models went out of production just under a year later, when the new 88-inch Land-Rovers arrived, and the utility versions of the 107-inch gave way to the new 109-inch models at the same time.

Rob Ivins' 107 pick-up shows the blue-painted chassis used on 1954 models. The spare wheel was normally mounted on the bonnet on the 107 pick-up.

Ray Adams' 1955 86-inch was one of many originally delivered for military service through the Ministry of Supply. The amber indicator lamps and the rear mud-flaps are not original features.

However, the 107-inch Station Wagon remained in production and was never replaced by a 109-inch equivalent. In fact a 107 Station Wagon was the very last Series I Land-Rover to be made, since the new Series II 109-inch Station Wagon lagged some months behind the other Series II models announced in April 1958, the 107-inch Station Wagon remaining in production until the new vehicle was ready in the summer of 1958.

CHASSIS

CHASSIS FRAME AND BUMPER

The chassis frames of the 86 and 107 Land-Rovers are ladder-frame types made of 14swg steel, with box-section side members. The 86-inch model's side rails are formed from four strips of steel welded together along their edges to form the box-section. On the 107-inch model, each face of the box-section consists of three strips of steel welded end to end; the side-rails are also some 1½ inches deeper in the middle of the chassis than those of the 86.

The 86-inch chassis has five cross-members; the 107-inch chassis has six, the additional one being located just behind the rear axle. All cross-members except the second (below the engine) and third (supporting the gearbox) have large circular apertures for additional driveshafts used with the power take-offs. The 107 Station Wagon has a special chassis frame which is described in the section devoted to this vehicle (see pages 88-92).

The rear cross-member extends beyond the chassis side rails to provide support for the rear of the body, and carries five vertical body mounting brackets. There is also an outrigger on each chassis rail, alongside the gearbox cross-member. These outriggers curve forwards on both 86 and 107 models and support the bulkhead; the 107's are deeper to match the deeper chassis side rails. Just behind the third cross-member is an additional outrigger on each side. Viewed from above, these have an almost triangular shape on the 86-inch models, but are rectangular on the 107s.

Chassis frames on 1954-model 86s and 107s are painted to match the bodies – green on the 86s and blue on the 107s. The same applies to all Station Wagons, but 1955 and later basic vehicles, of both wheelbase lengths, have their chassis finished more conventionally in black.

The front spring-hanger brackets welded to the chassis side rails are the same on both 86s and 107s. However, the rear spring hanger brackets differ. On 86s, the front pair are welded to the side rail where it curves upwards, and therefore point backwards.

On 107s, they are welded to a straight section of the side rail, and therefore point downwards. There is also more chassis overhang behind the rear pair of hangers on a 107 than there is on an 86. Other brackets welded to the chassis are generally similar to those on the 80s.

The front bumper has integral support brackets, and is bolted to the chassis frame. Both bumper and brackets should be galvanised. The battery casing and air cleaner support are bolted to the frame at the front, and are always finished in black, regardless of the chassis colour. The rear cross-member carries two lifting handles with a galvanised finish. On early models it also carries a draw bar, which should be painted to match the chassis. This draw bar became an optional extra towards the end of 1954, however, and was only fitted to special order on 86-inch chassis from 5710-2760, 5713-1995 and 5716-1177, and on 107-inch chassis from 5720-0394, 5723-0935 and 5726-1114.

The U-shaped axle check-straps are attached to the chassis by plates and set bolts, as on the 80s. These plates and the bolt-heads should be painted black, while the straps are made of webbing. All 86-inch models have the same type of check-straps, and all 107-inch utilities have a second, longer type.

Springs and Dampers

The front road springs on both 86 and 107 Land-Rovers are 'handed' and must not be changed from side to side; the stiffer one of the two is designed to compensate for the extra weight of the driver. Front springs on 86-inch models have ten leaves, while those on 107-inch models have only nine on vehicles built before approximately the end of the 1954 calendar year, and 11 on those built subsequently. The changeover point is at chassis number 572-00469, which was the last one to be fitted with nine-leaf springs.

The rear road springs on 86-inch and 107-inch models are also 'handed', those on 86s having 11 leaves and those on the 107s having ten. The 107 springs have a greater camber to suit the vehicle's greater payload, and as a result the body sits quite high off the ground at the back when unladen. All road springs, both front and rear, should have a black painted finish.

Front dampers on 86s differ from those on the rear axle, and those fitted to 107s are both different from the 86 types and different between front and rear axles. When heavy-duty springs are fitted on an 86-inch model, the 107 type dampers are used. On 1954 models, the lower ends of the dampers are retained by a washer and self-locking nut; on 1955 and later models the bottom of the damper is retained by a split pin and washer. Washers and self-locking nuts are used on the top damper mountings of all 86s and 107s.

The chassis of the 1955 86-inch model is painted in the conventional black. The rear shackle for the front spring and the heat shield on the exhaust pipe can be seen.

The leading spring hanger bracket on the 86-inch chassis points backwards, as on this 1955 example.

When the springs are correctly set, the rear spring shackle should sit at about 45 degrees to the vertical, as on this 86-inch model.

Axles

Both front and rear axle casings on the 86-inch and 107-inch Land-Rovers are finished in black; crown-wheel and pinion sets always give 4.7:1 reduction gearing. Like the axles fitted to 1951 and later 80-inch models, those on 86s and 107s all have spring washers on the studs which hold the differential housing to the axle casing.

All 86-inch and 107-inch Land-Rovers have the same front axle casing as the 80-inch models fitted with 2½-inch wide road springs. The swivel pin arrangements on the 86s and 107s are identical in principle to those of the 80-inch types. The only important difference is an invisible one, as the two sections of the axle drive-shafts are connected by universal joints rather than Tracta joints.

Most of the visible elements in this area are the same as those of the 80-inch models. However, 86s and 107s have different swivel pin bearing housings and different top swivel pins, the latter being splined like those on the later 80s. In the 1960s, Rover made available a kit for owners to convert the original swivel pins with their cone and spring steering dampers to a type which used a pin and thrust washer steering damper.

There are three different types of steering lock stop bolt, one fixed and two adjustable. These were always fitted in matching pairs, the longer bolts being used on 107s to suit that model's larger wheel and tyre combinations.

The rear axle casing is different from its equivalent on the 80-inch models, being stronger in order to cope with the greater payload of the 86 and 107 models and also having mountings to suit 2½-inch wide road springs.

Wheels and Tyres

The standard wheels on the 86-inch and 107-inch models are the same 16-inch well-base pressed steel discs found on the 80-inch types. As on the 80s, they are stamped with a date of manufacture (eg, 10.55 for October 1955) on their outer faces. Split-rim

The wheels on 1954 107-inch models were painted Blue or Grey, to contrast with the bodywork. The freewheeling hub fitted is a period accessory.

types also exist, and are once again found mainly on vehicles originally delivered for military use.

On the 86-inch models, the wheel discs are painted in the body colour. However, on 107-inch types built in the 1954 and 1955 model years, the wheels are painted in a contrasting colour – Blue wheels with a Grey body and Grey wheels with a Blue body. Later 107s normally have wheels painted Green or Beige to match the body colour, or Blue with a Blue or Grey body.

Tyres fitted as original equipment to the 86-inch models were 6.00 × 16 size. A 6.50 × 16 size was optional and was common on military 86s; there was also a 7.00 × 16 option, which was fitted as standard to the 86-inch fire engines. This 7.00 × 16 size was also standard on all 107s.

The standard tyres on both 86 and 107 models were either Dunlop RK3s or Avon TMs. Alternative 6.00 × 16s were the Dunlop T28, and the 6.50 × 16 type was the Dunlop T29A. In the 7.00 × 16 size, the three options were the road-biased Dunlop Forts, a Dunlop tyre with a curved-bar tractor tread, and a sand tyre of unspecified make.

Brakes

As on the 80-inch models, the braking system of the 86s and 107s uses Girling components. Once again, there are hydraulically operated drum brakes on all four wheels and the parking brake is a mechanically operated drum on the transfer box output shaft. All 86-inch models have 10-inch wheel brakes.

The 10-inch wheel brakes are fitted only to 107s built before April 1954 approximately (the chassis number at changeover is not known). Later 107s have 11-inch drums with wider linings (a change which allowed Rover to increase the vehicle's payload from 1170lb to 1500lb); twin leading-shoe brakes are fitted on the front axle while the rear axle has the leading-and-trailing-shoe type.

The brake fluid reservoir tank is not the same component as on the 80s, although it is visually similar. Its Girling part number is 3000522W. As on the 80s, both the tank and its screw top should be black, and there should be a blue and orange Girling decal on the tank. The clip-type bracket which holds the tank to the chassis is the same as on the 80s.

There are two types of master cylinder, neither of them the same as the type fitted to the 80s. Both should have a plated metal finish. Girling part number 3102348 is used on all vehicles with 10-inch wheel brakes, while those with 11-inch brakes have part number 3102541 W, which has a longer body and is also larger in diameter. The rear of the larger master cylinder protrudes into a hole cut into the chassis outrigger which supports the petrol tank.

The visible parts of the wheel brakes on both 10-inch and 11-inch systems should be painted black. The brake pipes should be left unpainted, but their clips are black. The flexible hoses would originally have been black rubber. The transmission brake is a 10-inch diameter drum, identical to that on the 2-litre 80s. Its visible parts should also be painted black.

Steering

Like the 80-inch models, the 86 and 107 Land-Rovers have a Burman Douglas worm-and-nut steering gear. However, there are several differences. In addition, the recirculating ball system of the later 88s and 109s was used as a service replacement, and as a result some 86s and 107s have this type of steering. The original worm-and-nut type brings with it a dipswitch and central horn button on the steering wheel. The recirculating ball type has the horn push relocated on a bracket mounted to the steering column, and the dipswitch is relocated in the driver's footwell. This later type of steering is described in

more detail in the section dealing with the 88 and 109 models (see page 98).

The steering box on the 80-inch models often put too much strain on the bulkhead and caused it to crack or split. As a result, Rover relocated the steering box of the 86 and 107 models on a black-painted bracket on the chassis rail. The steering tube, of course, is longer than on the 80s to suit the relocated steering box, which is not the same as the 80-inch type. There is also a flat rubber seal where the steering column passes through the bulkhead, instead of the large shroud fitted to 80s.

ENGINE

All the 86s and 107s were fitted with 2-litre petrol engines. However, there were two distinct types. On 1954 models the engine remained the same as on the 2-litre 80s, but for the 1955 season a new version was fitted.

The reasons for this are quite complicated, and go back to the introduction of Rover's inlet-over-exhaust engines in the P3 60 (1595cc four-cylinder) and 75 (2103cc six-cylinder) saloons in 1948. It was, of course, a version of the 60's engine which went into the Land-Rover, fitted with a cast iron rather than aluminium alloy cylinder head.

Rover then decided to enlarge the swept volume of these engines by increasing the bore of the cylinders. The larger bores left no room for water passages between them, which presented no problems in the four-cylinder Land-Rover engine. However, there were doubts whether this 'siamese-bore' design would provide adequate cooling for the six-cylinder engine, which would be subjected to the greater stresses of prolonged high-speed motoring in the latest P4 saloon car range.

The 2-litre siamese-bore engine did go into production for the 80-inch Land-Rover in 1951. For the six-cylinder, however, Rover repositioned the cylinder bores further apart within the block to leave room for water passages between them; within the company, the redesigned engine was always known as the 'spread-bore' type. This spread-bore six-cylinder engine went into production in 1953 for the Rover 90 saloon, and with it came a spread-bore four-cylinder for the Rover 60, with the same 1997cc capacity as the existing Land-Rover engine.

The engine bay of Rob Ivins' 107-inch pick-up shows the original 'siamese-bore' 2-litre engine used in 1954 models. The radiator header tank would originally have been finished in the matt black of which traces are still visible, the original battery would have been black, and the original coil would have had a black top rather than a red one. Interesting period accessories are the gold-coloured Lucas container for spare bulbs on the bulkhead and the large orange Fram by-pass oil filter towards the front of the engine bay. The washer bottle has of course been added to meet road traffic regulations. Note how the bulkhead has a single bracing strut – always on the opposite side to the steering column.

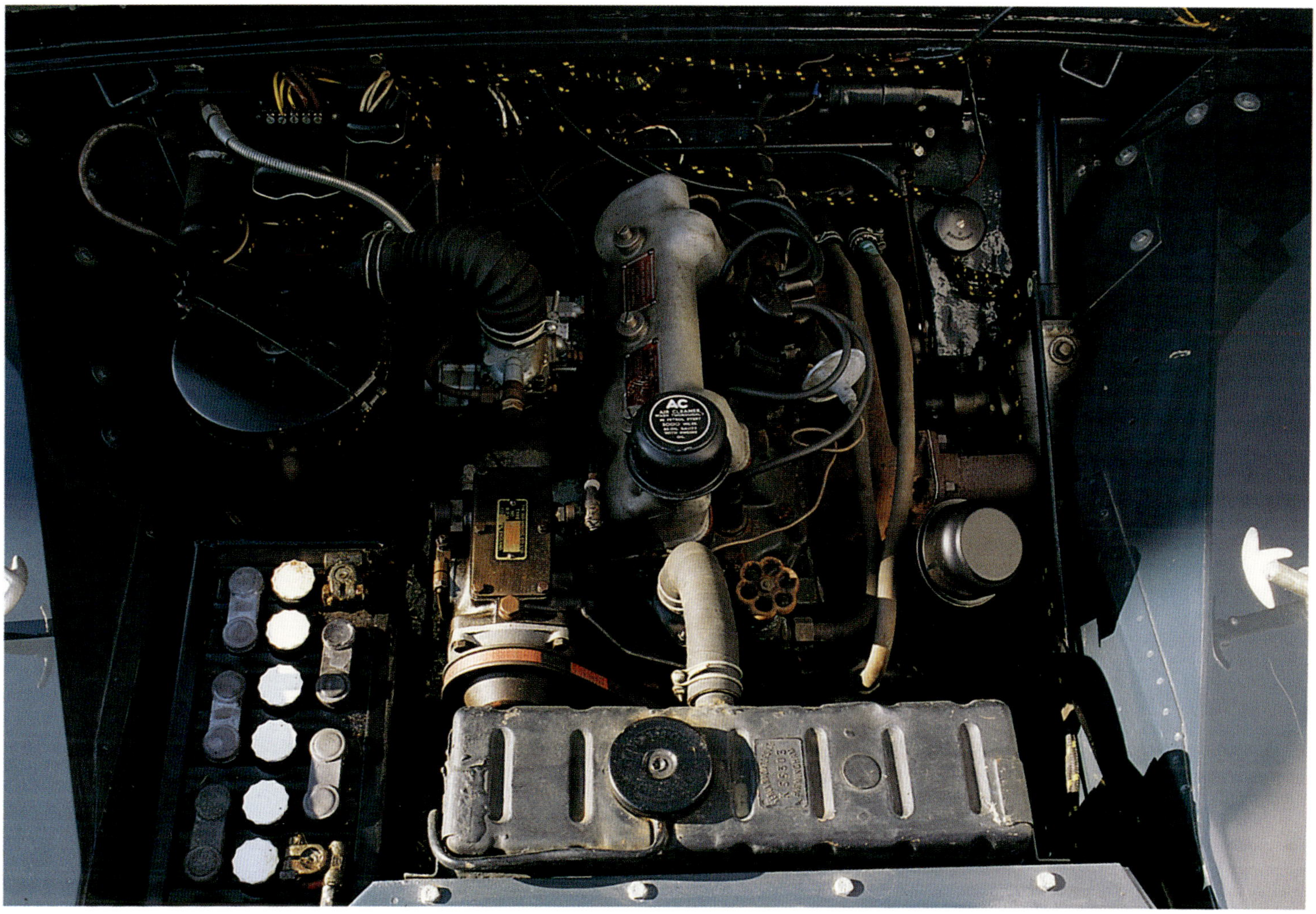

The later 'spread-bore' engine in John Taylor's 1955 86-inch Station Wagon has a different air filter, without the pre-cleaner. All details, black battery included, appear to be correct. This engine is also fitted with the optional engine speed governor.

The cylinder blocks of these two engines had to be machined on a different line from the original 2103cc six-cylinder and 1997cc siamese-bore engines.

During the 1954 model year, Rover was therefore building two different 2-litre engines: the siamese-bore type for the Land-Rover and the spread-bore type for the Rover 60. For 1955, the anomaly was resolved, and Rover switched entirely to spread-bore engines. The 2103cc six-cylinder of the Rover 75 was redeveloped as a spread-bore engine of 2230cc, and the spread-bore 2-litre 60 block was used for the Land-Rover, albeit with a cast iron cylinder head instead of the alloy head used on the saloon engine.

Block, Head and Sump

The 1954 siamese-bore engines are identical in most respects to the 2-litre engines fitted to the final 80s. The later spread-bore engines are visually similar but have some important differences. The cylinder heads of both engines are nevertheless identical. The cylinder block of the spread-bore 2-litre should be painted grey.

The most obvious identifying feature of the later engines is that they have a disposable-element oil filter on the right-hand side of the cylinder block. This filter should incorporate a black-painted metal canister which screws on over the paper element. The exhaust manifold is different from the earlier type, with its four inlet pipes more widely spaced. It should be finished in the same matt silver as the earlier type. The later oil pump has minor differences from the type on siamese-bore engines, and the sump is also different, having a similar curved profile at the front but a pronounced step at the rear.

The fan on the siamese-bore engines is the same as that on the 2-litre 80's engine, with a welded construction. However, the spread-bore 2-litre engine has a different fan, riveted together and having a reinforcing plate. Both types of fan should be painted black.

Fuel System

The fuel system of the 86-inch and 107-inch Land-Rovers is similar in principle to that of the 80-inch models. Fuel is drawn by an electric pump on the bulkhead from a chassis-mounted tank, through a sediment filter, to the carburettor. An oil-bath air cleaner is again fitted. However, there are important differences, both between these models and the 80s, and between the 1954 and 1955-56 models.

The fuel tank is once again a 10-gallon type, still painted black. However, it is not the same as the 80-inch type (the most obvious difference is a 'square' lower trailing edge instead of a shaped type) and has a double-skinned bottom instead of an undershield. It is bolted directly to the chassis outriggers. Only two types of sediment filter are fitted, both seen earlier on the 2-litre 80s. One has a rectangular tap, the other a 'hooked' type, and they appear to have been fitted as alternatives throughout the period of 86 and 107 production.

The carburettor is once again a Solex 32 PBI-2. Jetting on 1954 models is the same as on the 2-litre 80s; later 86s and 107s have different jetting, but the overall appearance of the carburettor is unchanged. The fuel pump on all models is the same SU AUA 58 L type as on the 2-litre 80s.

All 1954 models have the same AC air cleaner as the 80s, and this should be finished in black. However, on the 86s and 107s it has a short straight pipe running to a metal elbow on the carburettor. A different air cleaner is fitted for the later spread-bore engine: this has no centrifugal pre-cleaner on its side and has slotted intakes around its top rim. It is linked directly to the carburettor by a ribbed flexible hose.

Cooling System

The cooling system on the 86 and 107 models is the same as on 80-inch types, but a 10lb radiator filler cap was optionally available instead of the standard 4lb type. The 10lb cap appears to have been specified mainly with power take-off installations and in some overseas territories where higher running temperatures are desirable. In addition, the oil recommendation plate on the front panel above the radiator has a different list of oils from the one on the 80s.

Exhaust System

The three-piece exhaust system of the 86-inch and 107-inch Land Rovers shares no components with the two-piece type fitted to the 80-inch models. The 86s and 107s have a common front pipe with two heat shields and a common rear silencer; as on the later 80s, the silencer is 'handed' to suit left- or right-hand drive vehicles. Between front pipe and rear silencer is an intermediate pipe, longer on the 107s than on the 86s to allow for the difference in the wheelbase length.

The front pipe is not mounted to the chassis frame at all, but is held in place by a flange which fits over the four studs of the exhaust manifold on the engine, and by a sliding flange which is held to a fixed flange on the intermediate pipe by three bolts.

The intermediate pipe is clamped to a flexible mounting which itself bolts to the chassis frame; it is then held to the silencer box by a flange with four bolts. On right-hand drive models, the rear silencer is supported by a clamp bracket around the tailpipe. This bracket is bolted to a flexible mounting, itself bolted to the chassis frame. On left-hand drive 86s and 107s, the rear silencer is mounted to the chassis in two places. There is a bracket welded to the silencer box itself, and this bracket is bolted to a flexible mounting, in turn bolted to the chassis frame. The tailpipe is then supported by a clamp bracket (again not the same as the right-hand drive type) and flexible mounting bolted to the chassis.

TRANSMISSION

Like the 80s, the 86s and 107s have a four-speed primary gearbox with synchromesh on third and fourth gears only. There is a two-speed transfer box, which carries the drum-type parking brake on its output shaft. All vehicles have selectable four-wheel drive.

Clutch and Bellhousing

The flywheel and flywheel housing on 1954 model 86s and 107s are the same as those on the final 80s. There is an alloy mounting for the starter motor, which is held by three bolts to the front of the flywheel housing. On 1955 and later models, the flywheel housing has two studs and the starter motor bolts directly to these. The clutch is again a Borg and Beck type, and is the same as that fitted to the last 80-inch models.

There are also two types of bellhousing. The first type, fitted only to 1954 models with the siamese-bore engine, is the same as that on the final 80s, and has a dowel on its left-hand side to help in locating the gearbox. It is held to the gearbox by three bolts. The second type, associated with the later spread-bore engine, has no locating dowel and is bolted to the gearbox by four bolts. It also differs from the earlier type at the rear of the starter motor. Both types should be unpainted.

Primary Gearbox and Controls

The casing of the primary gearbox on 1954 models is the same as that of the last 80s; there are minor differences on subsequent models. The casing should always be unpainted, and should have a brass drain plug in its underside. The dipstick on all 86 and 107 gearboxes differs from the 80-inch type, having a longer and less hooked handle.

The gearchange lever is not 'handed' as on the 80s. Its rod should be painted black. The same black plastic knob is used, however, with white painted lettering.

Transfer Box and Controls

The transfer box casing differs from its 80-inch equivalent, with a different speedometer drive hous-

Sidelights are mounted in the front wings; those on Station Wagons are twin-filament Lucas 488 types which double as flashing indicators.

ing bolted to its rear end. The transfer box casing, speedometer drive housing and front output housing should all be unpainted.

As on the later 80s, the transfer box ratio selector lever has a red plastic knob and its rod is painted black. A second control lever, with a yellow plastic knob and black-painted rod encased in a coil spring, engages drive to the front axle when the transfer box is in high ratio.

Propeller Shafts

Both front and rear propeller shafts have splined sliding joints and are finished in black. The 86-inch and 107-inch models use the same front propshaft as the later 80-inch models. On 86s, the rear propshaft is the same as the front one; 107s of course have a longer rear propshaft.

Electrical Components

The 86-inch and 107-inch models continued to use a positive earth 12-volt electrical system, consisting largely of Lucas components. The battery supplied with new vehicles would have had a black rubber casing. As on the 80s, the original terminal connections on the battery leads would have been the clamp type, and the earthing strap would have been a braided wire type with no outer sheath.

The 1955 and later 86s and 107s have rear lamps like this one – a Lucas model 518, familiarly known as the 'pork pie' lamp.

Semaphore trafficators were normally fitted to the windscreen frame in the same way as on 80s, but on this 107 a neat installation was made on the rear pillar of the cab.

The wiring harness should have an outer casing of black cotton braid with an interwoven yellow stripe, while the cables inside are braided and lacquered. Front harnesses are the same on 86s as on 107s, but the long-wheelbase model has a longer rear harness.

The voltage control box is a Lucas model RB106, part number 37138A, and the same as fitted to the final 2-litre 80s. The separate fuse box is another Lucas item, part number 37131A, and carries a single 25-amp fuse. The two are bolted to a plate which also carries the fuel pump and is held to the bulkhead by three bolts.

The dynamo is not the same as that fitted to the 2-litre 80s, but is another Lucas item, model C39 PV/2 (part number 22258D). Some versions have a separate cover band, while others do not. The 1954 siamese-bore engines have a Lucas M418G type G76 starter motor (Lucas part number 25514) with three-bolt fixing, but the later spread-bore engines have an M418G type FA 64 (Lucas part number 255330) with two-bolt fixing.

The ignition system incorporates a Lucas distributor. On 1954 siamese-bore engines, this is a 'fat' DM2 type, similar to the one on 80-inch models and having Lucas part number 40330A. The later spread-bore engines have a different distributor, with Lucas part number 40504A. Both types have unpainted bodies, and brown or black Bakelite caps with the ignition leads in their sides. From engines 5711-9698 and 5713-8230, spread-bore types built in 1955, a different vacuum unit is fitted.

The coil on 1954 and '55 models is the same B12 type as is fitted to 80s, with Lucas part number 45012B. From 1956, however, the coil is an HA12 with Lucas part number 45054E. Both types should be mounted with their top pointing towards the centre of the vehicle. The spark plugs were originally the same Lodge CLN type as fitted to 80-inch Land-Rovers, and their suppressers are once again the same as the 80-inch type.

The horn is bolted to the front chassis cross-member, and the two different types that exist appear to have been alternatives. The Lucas type – not the same as that fitted to 80s – has an offset adjuster and is a model HF 1235 with Lucas part number 069399F. The alternative Clearhooter type has a central adjuster.

As on the 80s, only the driver's side of the vehicle had a windscreen wiper on the 86s and 107s unless a second one was specified as an extra. The motor in all cases is bolted to the inside of the windscreen frame. All 1954 and '55 86s and 107s, together with the first of the 1956 models, have the same Lucas motor as on the 80s. This has a black crackle-finish body with squarish contours and has Lucas part number 75197A. From early in 1956, Lucas part number 75113E was fitted, which has a more rounded body with a plated silver finish.

LIGHTING

The 86-inch and 107-inch Land Rovers have two different types of headlamp. Sidelamps remained the same throughout production for the basic models, although a special variety was fitted to Station Wagons and to North American vehicles. Rear lamps are more complicated, as there are three main types plus a fourth for North America and Australia. In addition, there are two types of red reflector fitted at the rear of these models.

On all 86s and on 107 models built before the introduction of the 88s and 109s in spring 1956, the headlamps are the same type as fitted to the final 80-inch Land Rovers. These are Lucas F700s (with Lucas part number 553935), and they are screwed to the grille panel through their rims. The outer rims are painted to match the vehicle's body colour. RHD and LHD types differ; there are other variations from country to country; and the French export type appear to have been fitted with yellow bulbs. The second type of headlamp, fitted to 1958-model and later 1957-model 107 Station Wagons only, is the same as found on 88s and 109s and has Lucas part number 553921.

The sidelights of the 86 and 107 Land Rovers are mounted in the wing fronts, and have Lucas part number 052558, as on the final 80s. North American vehicles and Station Wagons, however, have a different lamp (Lucas type 488) with a twin filament bulb, which doubles as a flashing turn indicator.

At the rear, the D-lamps seen on the 80s are found only on 1954-model 86s and 107s. All later examples have a round lamp which is familiarly known as the 'pork-pie' type because of its shape. This is a Lucas model 518, part number 53393A. Rear lighting arrangements on all models exported to the USA and Australia have differences from standard (see page 93).

Some 1955 86s and 107s have 'pork-pie' lamps with reflectors in their lenses, but these appear to have been discontinued because their reflective surfaces were too small to meet lighting regulations. Later vehicles have stand-alone circular reflector plates fitted to the lower body corners. The first type of reflector plate, used only during the 1955 model year, has a diameter of 1$\frac{29}{32}$ inches; later 1955 and all subsequent models have a larger type, 2¼ inches in diameter.

TRAFFICATORS

Semaphore trafficators were an optional extra for the 86s and 107s. The Lucas type SE 100 trafficator units should be mounted on brackets at the top of the windscreen frame. The cables then run down the outside of the frame uprights, to which they are each held by a single clip. A Lucas control switch (part number 310392) is fitted to a black-painted metal bracket clamped to the steering column.

The windscreen frame carries 'shark's teeth', over which the soft top is fitted.

The windscreen frame of Station Wagons does not normally have the 'shark's teeth' found on soft-top models.

Pivoting arms on the frame support the windscreen when it is folded forwards over the bonnet.

BODY

BULKHEAD AND WINDSCREEN

A single design of bulkhead is used for all the 86 and 107 Land-Rovers. This is quite different from the bulkheads used on 80-inch models, mainly because it incorporates a much-enlarged instrument panel and provides shelves for oddments stowage. It is also considerably taller than the 80-inch type, standing several inches above the bonnet edge and incorporating ventilator panels.

This bulkhead has a prominent 'shelf' running across its upper section. The shelf is divided into three sections, the centre one being for the instru-

A scissors-type bonnet prop (above) was used on all 86s and 107s. The front panel of 86s and 107s (right) has three rectangular cut-outs at the bottom, and one larger one between the headlamps.

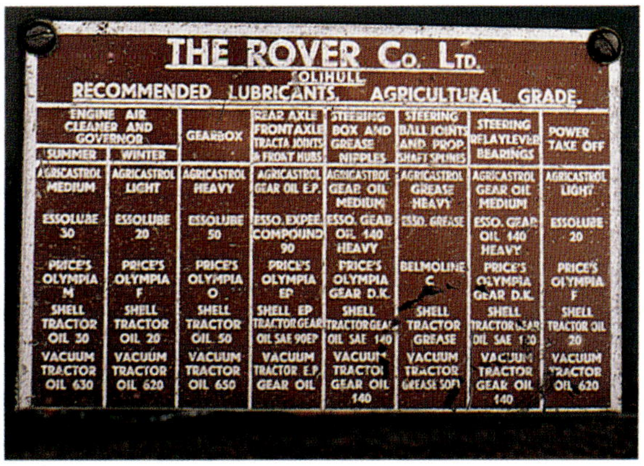

The rearward extension of the grille panel has a plate badge screwed to its centre. On early models the list of recommended lubricants is brief (right), but later models have a plate with a much more comprehensive set of recommendations (below right). It is not clear when the change took place, but it probably occurred during the 1955 model year.

ment panel. There are also rectangular cut-outs below the top rail to accommodate the ventilator flaps, which are a standard fitting. Wire mesh fly screens, an optional extra, can be fitted behind these. A large, shaped sealing rubber is fitted to the top edge of the panel to seal the gap between windscreen frame and bulkhead.

Further down, the 86 and 107 bulkheads have welded tube housings for the door hinges (80-inch bulkheads have open flange-type mountings). In addition, there is a tie bar on the opposite side to the steering column, bracing the bulkhead to the chassis frame alongside the engine; this tie bar should be painted black, whereas the rest of the bulkhead is in the body colour. The floor sections of the bulkhead's toe boxes extend as far as the rearward extensions of the main panel and leave no gap to be filled by the front floor panels.

The windscreen frame of the 86 and 107 models is completely different from that fitted to the 80s. It is shallower, finishing immediately below the glass area and not incorporating a lower panel. As on the 80s, it is made of galvanised steel and has two panes of glass. Vehicles shipped to France and Algeria had the special glass – presumably laminated – also fitted to US export examples.

The frame still pivots at its base so that it can be folded forwards onto the bonnet, and the pivot is effected by a bolt and special locking nut, similar (but not identical) to the arrangement on the final 80-inch models.

Two small angle brackets are bolted to the inside top corners of the windscreen frame, and act as anchor points for a hood, truck cab or hard top. The inside bottom corners incorporate slotted platforms which accommodate long bolts that pivot in the windscreen clamp brackets on the bulkhead; by tightening a wing nut on each of these, the windscreen can be held firmly upright.

On soft-top 86-inch models only, there is also a pivot arm attached to a bracket on the top rail of the windscreen on both sides; this acts as a support for the windscreen when it is folded down over the bonnet, and is held in place by the bonnet clamps. The windscreen top rail of soft-top models also has fixing lugs (familiarly known as 'shark's teeth') for the canvas roof. These lugs are unnecessary, of course, on vehicles fitted with metal tops, but it appears that Rover was not always consistent and used supplies of whichever windscreen was available – some Station Wagons have windscreens with these fixing lugs.

A rare optional extra is a sun visor which bolts to the windscreen. This was probably sold mainly for export models.

Wings, Bonnet and Grille Panel

The front wings are different from those fitted to the final 80-inch models. They consist of three separate pressings: a single pressing forms the inner wing and top panel, a second pressing forms the side panel, and the third is the front closing panel. This front panel has a scalloped indentation for the sidelight. Both wings were sometimes drilled to take wing mirrors, but normally only one mirror was fitted and the redundant hole would then be filled with a bolt. This has a plain washer visible on the top surface of the wing, and the nut on the underside is kept tight by a spring washer.

The grille panel, however, is the same as that fitted to the last 80-inch Land-Rovers, and is made of aluminium alloy. It has two circular apertures for the headlamps flanking a large central rectangular aperture, and there are three smaller apertures below. On the top edge of the grille panel, a strip of sand-coloured webbing held in place by 12 bifurcated rivets serves as a bonnet rest.

The wire mesh grille has the same inverted T-shape as on the final 80s, and is once again clipped to the grille panel at the bottom and bolted to it at the top. The two bolts which hold the grille in place also pass through a 7$\frac{3}{16}$-inch wide oval Land-Rover badge. On Station Wagon models, these bolts also hold a second plate badge, which hangs below the oval and reads '4-Wheel Drive Station Wagon'.

As on 80-inch models, the bonnet panel is a single piece of curved Birmabright, with two hinges at the bulkhead end. However, both panel and hinges are different from their 80-inch counterparts. All Station Wagons have their spare wheels stowed on the bonnet, and 107 pick-ups normally do as well. The bonnet-top spare wheel stowage kit was optionally available for other models and consists of a strengthening dome fitted on the outside of the panel. The bonnet prop rod on all models is a scissors type, consisting of two flat metal arms. One end is attached to the underside of the bonnet, the other to the left-hand inner wing.

Seat Box and Cab Floor

There are no differences here between the 86 and the 107 models. As on the 80-inch Land-Rovers, the largest section is the seat base, which once again incorporates lockers. The sill panels which run forwards to join the bulkhead, however, are separate panels, and the floor section is in one piece with a separate bellhousing cover which mates up with the front bulkhead. The seat base is braced at the rear by corner brackets, which bolt to the rear of the sills; these brackets are different from those on 80-inch models.

The lockers in the seat base give access to the fuel tank (on the right) and provide storage (on the left). Each locker lid has two hinges which are attached by pop rivets to the lid and by set screws and nuts to the angle plate at the back of the seat base. There is a single hasp at the front edge of each locker, each attached by rivets and each mating up with a turnbuckle held to the heelboard by 'sheradised', countersunk bolts and nuts.

Between the two lockers is a plain centre panel; on models equipped with a centre power take-off, there is a different panel which incorporates a hinged cover plate to allow access to the power take-off controls. On all models, there are three studs on the front of the heelboard, to which the seat cushion retaining straps attach.

The floor panel runs the full width of the vehicle and incorporates the gearbox cover. On top of the gearbox cover is an inspection plate, which swivels on a nut in one corner and is held closed by a wing nut at the opposite corner. On the right at the top of the gearbox cover panel is also a cover for the four-wheel drive control rod, attached by bolts and nuts.

The 86 and 107 models have shaped rubber gaiters for the controls which emerge through the floor panel and heelboard. In all cases, these are held in place by retainers. The redundant handbrake slot in the heelboard (on the left for RHD vehicles and on the right for LHD examples) is covered with an alloy blanking plate.

Doors and Sidescreens

The front doors of all 86-inch and 107-inch Land-Rovers have the same metalwork. Only the 107-inch Station Wagons have rear side doors, and these are covered in the section on those vehicles.

The doors of the 86 and 107 Land-Rovers are very different from those of the final 80-inch models. Instead of a sloping rear face, they have a straight one, and instead of the protruding door handle, which is vulnerable in dense vegetation, the 86s and 107s have large recesses in the door panels, and a strong handle shielded within them.

As on the 80-inch models, the doors come in two sections, the main door reaching up to waist height only and the sidescreen (now a standard fitting) being bolted in place to form the upper part of the door. Land-Rovers exported to Canada have unique features in this area, as described in *Export Variations* (see page 93).

Door cappings and hinges are once again galvanised, but the hinges are not of the same type as on 80-inch models. As on earlier Land-Rovers, the doors have front and rear sealing rubbers, but these are fitted to the windscreen, body sill, bulkhead and the front of the rear body rather than to the doors themselves as on 80-inch models.

Despite superficial similarities, the sidescreens are different from those fitted to the final 80-inch models. On 1954 and early 1955 models, both fixed and sliding windows are made of Perspex. By about February 1955, the Perspex had been replaced by glass, although there were some transitional sidescreens with Perspex sliding sections and glass fixed panes.

The load-bed of the 107-inch pick-up is protected by rubbing strips.

As on the 80-inch models, the window frames are made of galvanised steel but the rectangular alloy panel which forms the bottom half of the sidescreen should be painted in body colour. On very early sidescreens, this panel has 90-degree corners, but on later examples it has neatly radiused corners; it is not clear when the change took place.

The sidescreens once again bolt through the door tops in two places, and at their bottom edges a sealing strip retained by spring clips prevents water ingress. Unlike earlier models, the sidescreens are also hinged to the bulkhead; they therefore have different hinges from those found on the final 80-inch models.

Back Body and Tailboard

The back body on the 86-inch and 107-inch Land-Rovers is similar in design to that of the 80-inch models, consisting of two side 'halves' and a separate floor panel, all made of Birmabright alloy. However, the join between the two body halves at the front is concealed by a prominent galvanised cover plate which was never fitted to the 80s, and the 86s and 107s have very few back body components in common with the earlier models. The 86-inch back body also shares relatively few components with the much longer and deeper 107-inch type. The 86-inch body is held to the chassis by 12 bolts, but there are 18 bolts to do the job on the 107-inch models.

On both 86-inch and 107-inch Land-Rovers, the body sides all have galvanised cappings. These are supplemented on 86s by vertical protection strips of galvanised steel on the two rear body corners and on 107s by similar strips at all four corners of the body. As on the 80s, there are galvanised corner plates incorporating the hood-stick sockets, but these are not the same as the 80-inch variety; their downward extensions are truncated whereas the 80-inch type form complete triangles.

The hood-lacing cleats on the body sides are the same welded type as on the final 80s, the 86-inch body having three cleats on each side and the 107-inch body five. The rearward-facing body panels are once again drilled for lights, and on the left-hand rear panel is the same oval Land-Rover badge, while the right-hand rear panel supports the registration plate. Vehicles exported to North America or Australia once again have special features in this area. Each rear panel again has a single staple-type hood-lacing bracket, and the tailboard key and its chain are the same as on the 80s.

However, the tailboard support chains on the 86 are longer than the 80-inch type, and the 107's chains are even longer. Both varieties are sleeved with canvas or Vynide, and both are attached by means of a pin and split-pin to a mounting plate bolted to the wheelarch panel. This plate is much larger than the 80-inch type.

The jack handle and starting handle on both 86s and 107s are not carried within the back body load area but are held in clips to the front of the body and are accessible when the driving compartment seats are tipped forwards. The 107 body also has lidded stowage lockers in the wheelboxes, just behind the wheels themselves. These lockers have two hinges and are held shut at the front (or inboard) end by a single hinged hasp that slots over a turnbuckle screwed to the wheelbox. Hinges, hasps and turnbuckles are all galvanised.

Spare wheel stowage arrangements also differ from the 80-inch type, and once again the 86 and 107 differ from one another. The 86s have a fixed clamp bolted through the galvanised capping at the front of the body. To keep the wheel firmly in place, this clamp is supplemented by a rest on either side, each one again bolted through the body capping and standing above it. On the 107, the clamp is fitted to the vertical cover plate which conceals the join between the two body halves at the front, and additional supports for the spare wheel are welded to the body capping.

Both 86 and 107 models have the same galvanised protecting strip at the rear of the floor across the tailboard aperture, although this is not the same as its 80-inch counterpart. There is no floor covering on either the 86 or the 107, but the floor of the 107 models should have four galvanised steel tread plates which run the full length from front to rear; these were designed to protect the rear body of the 107 from the damage likely to be caused by the heavier and bulkier loads the vehicle could carry. There should be similar tread plates on the wheelbox sides (one on each), and two shorter ones on each wheelbox top, running between the front panel and the locker lids. Two more short strips should run vertically on each side of the front body join cover plate, and yet another should run horizontally on the front panel above each wheelbox.

The tailboards on the 86 and 107 models are not the same as those on the 80s, and the 107 tailboard is taller than the 86 type to match the deeper body sides. Both North America and Australia were demanding centre-mounted number plates by the time the 86s and 107s entered production, so models exported to those countries have a number plate mounting bracket secured to the tailboard with rivets and pop rivets.

Both 86 and 107 tailboards have galvanised top cappings, but there are no side cappings. Instead, there is a simplified design of side reinforcement strip, incorporating the eyes for tailboard locking and doubling as sealing rubber retainers; the side rubbers are actually riveted to these angle strips. The sealing rubbers extend upwards only as far as the eyes; above them is a thick rubber buffer block, attached to the body sides by drive screws with washers. The bottom seal is also riveted to an angle strip, itself riveted to the tailboard.

Hinges are different from those on the 80s, but common between 86s and 107s. The same is true of the hooks which hold the tailboard chains. Lastly, the 107 tailboard should have four tread plates mounted to its inside surface, matching the tread plates on the floor of the load bed.

Paint Colours (Bodies)

The basic 86-inch models were available in Green, Blue, Grey or Beige. Green is also sometimes known as Deep Bronze Green and Blue as RAF Blue. Beige appears to have been for export only. Hard tops and Tropical roofs were normally finished in Ivory.

The 107-inch models were initially available in only two colours – Blue and Grey. For the 1956 model year, these colours were supplemented by Green and Beige (for the wheel colours associated with these body colours, see page 69). As on the 86, Beige was primarily intended for export, although it may have been used on a few home-market 107 models.

The Land-Rover Series I Club has done considerable research into the original paint colours and has come up with the following reference codes for Herberts paints:

Blue	37262
Bronze Green	0428
Grey	37263
Ivory	0416

The Beige used on export models is more problematical. It appears to be the colour also known as Sand which is available from ICI under line reference number PO30-3182. However, this match has not been confirmed.

The correct Grey has a pinkish tinge and appears to have been the same as the Dove Grey used on Rover cars. Its ICI line reference number is PO30-3270. It is not the same as the later blackish grey, known as Mid Grey or Light Welsh Grey, which was used on Series II and later models.

Canvas, Cab and Hard Top

Hood and Hood Supports

The 86-inch Land-Rover was never supplied with a 'three-seater' hood like that available for the 80-inch models. All 86-inch hoods were full-length types, similar in concept to their 80-inch equivalents. As on the 80-inch, the 86-inch hood covered both load area and cab. However, the hood of the long-wheelbase 107-inch models was more strictly a tilt cover for the load bed, and was supplied only with a metal truck cab.

The supporting structure of the hoods on these vehicles once again depends on tubular hood-sticks braced together by tie-rods, but the hood-sticks themselves are different from those on earlier models. There are two hood-sticks on 86-inch models, and these are supplemented by a third one of a different type on 107-inch models.

The front and rear hood-sticks of both 86-inch and 107-inch models fit into sockets in the cappings at each corner of the body. To each capping is then bolted a simple clamp, which holds the hood-stick firmly in place. A tie-rod runs between front and rear hood-sticks just below the curved section on each side, and is attached to them with screws and nuts. The tie-rod on 107-inch models, of course, is considerably longer than the one on 86-inch types. An intermediate roof support rod is bolted between these tie-bars mid-way between the two hood-sticks, and on 107-inch Land-Rovers this is supported by a vertical rod on each side which is fixed to the body side cappings by screws and nuts. Hood-sticks, clamps and central roof support are the same on 86s and 107s, but the central vertical supports are unique to the long-wheelbase models.

The supporting structure for the cab area of the hood is far more rigid on 86-inch models than on the earlier 80s. It consists of a vertical channel bolted to each side of the front hood-stick, together with a

The hood sticks are held in their sockets by bolts and clamps on 86s and 107s. This is an ex-military 86, and one of the rear grab rails normally fitted to such vehicles is visible behind the hood stick.

horizontal support and drain channel at the top. This horizontal section is bolted at the front to the windscreen frame. Each section also has its own rubber weatherseal.

The actual canvas hood of the 86-inch models is made of the same khaki material as earlier types but is easy to distinguish from them because it has a prominent seam running right across the roof section. As on the 80s, however, the rear curtain is stitched to the hood and has side 'wings' which can be held in the closed position by means of a strap and buckle on each side. Once again, there are two rectangular rigid Perspex windows in the rear curtain.

The 86-inch hood is held to the body by a rope threaded through its lower edges. This rope provides three loops which fit over the three cleats on each side of the rear body. The rope is also laced through eight reinforced eyelets in the bottom of the rear curtain, and a single rope hook on each curtain 'wing' allows the rope to be tied off after it has been pulled tight.

A canvas fume curtain behind the driving compartment was an optional extra on 86-inch models. It attaches to the front hood-stick by six webbing straps with buckles, and has a single rectangular celluloid window. Also optional on the 86-inch – and fairly rare – is an additional pair of webbing straps and buckles on each side of the hood near the top. These allow the sides of the hood to be rolled up and fixed in the open position. Many export models also have two Perspex windows in the sides of the hood; as on the 80-inch, these are identical in size and type to the windows used in the rear curtain. This type of hood, however, was not available on 86-inch models sold in Britain.

Unlike the 86-inch hood, the 107-inch tilt came in two colours – blue and green. Only blue was available initially, but green was introduced shortly after the 1955 season started, at chassis numbers 5720-0151, 5723-0307 and 5726-0321. At the same time the front fixing straps were altered and the blue tilts were modified in line with the new green type. Webbing straps should always be blue or green to match the hood fabric. It would be logical to suppose that the blue tilt was always supplied with a blue or grey body, while the green one was always supplied with green or beige vehicles.

As the 107-inch canvas is a proper tilt cover, it has curtains both front and rear. The rear curtain has 'wings' with fixing straps like those on the 86-inch models; the front curtain, however, has smaller 'wrapovers', held in place by two straps on each side. Both front and rear curtains contain two rectangular Perspex windows, and some export models have two identical windows in each side of the tilt cover.

Like the 86-inch hood, the 107-inch tilt is held in place with straps inside and rope outside. On early models, there are just two straps for the centre stick and front curtain, but in models built from late 1955 there are six. The fixing ropes come in three pieces: a 100-inch length for each side of the tilt, a 99-inch length for the rear curtain, and a 168-inch length for the tilt top and sides.

It was also possible to order a tonneau cover for the 107-inch pick-up bed. This is made of the same canvas material as the hood and comes in blue or green only.

TRUCK CAB

The truck cab optionally available on 86-inch models and standard on 107-inch pick-ups is broadly similar to its equivalent on the 80-inch Land-Rovers. However, none of the major parts are in fact the same.

The roof panel slopes upwards towards the rear of the cab and has three longitudinal stiffening ribs on the outside. It is held to the windscreen frame by adjustable brackets. Under the edges of the roof are rubber seals in retainers, those at the side being divided into two so that one covers the door aperture and the other is sandwiched between the roof and the side section of the rear cab panel. Only the rear seal is the same as the 80-inch type.

The rear panel has a two-piece sliding window, which uses the same Perspex, finger pulls and locking catch as the 80-inch truck cab. The side sections of the rear panel have alloy reinforcing plates at their vertical leading edges only (on the 80-inch these plates are rectangular and cover the full length of the side section). There are also cappings at the leading edges of these side sections, and these carry rubber door seals. The cappings are galvanised and unpainted, but the reinforcing plates should be painted to match the cab.

A truck cab came as standard on 107-inch pick-ups, and was optional for 86-inch models. The cappings on the truck cab and back body (left) are galvanised.

The roof panel is bolted to the rear panel of the cab, and this in turn is secured to the rear body capping by long bolts. There is a simple rubber seal between the rear panel and the rear body capping; 86s have a different seal from 107s. Finally, the tropical roof panel is the same as the 80-inch type. As on earlier truck cabs, it is held to the main roof stiffeners by screws and nuts, and supported by three distance pieces on each side. Most examples were fitted to vehicles for export, but it appears that some found their way onto home market models.

Hard Top

Like the hard top available for the 80-inch Land-Rovers, the optional hard top for the 86-inch models comes in four sections – roof, two sides, and upper tailgate. No hard top was ever catalogued for the 107-inch Land-Rovers, although some examples were certainly built; the Rover Mobile Service School, for example, used a 107-inch hard top, and other examples were built to special order for expedition work. These vehicles all seem to have had a truck cab and a separate enclosed rear body.

The roof panel has a sloping canopy section joined to a flat rear section, with three stiffening ribs running from front to rear. The optional tropical roof – mainly found on export models – is attached to these stiffeners and is also held to the main roof panel by five alloy distance pieces on each side.

The two side sections incorporate rear panels which stand on either side of the tailgate aperture. All three lower corners on each panel have galvanised steel reinforcing plates. The side sections may either be plain or have a single fixed window in each side, this latter being an export-only option in theory, although most Land-Rovers supplied to the Civil Defence in Britain (which had RGC and SXF registrations) also had them. When fitted, these side windows are made of toughened glass and are rubber-glazed.

Like the side pieces of the truck cab, the fronts of the hard top side sections carry cappings and door seals. Each vertical surface alongside the tailgate aperture has a rubber seal for the upper tailgate, a simple loop-type catch for its lock, and a spring quadrant to hold it open. On earlier examples, these spring quadrants have a turn-wheel to lock their support arms; later ones have a notch at the top to support the sliding arm and hold the tailgate in the open position.

The dashboard of this 107 Station Wagon typifies the layout on 86s and 107s of all types. Note the horn push on a steering column extension. The heater and mesh flyscreens were optional extras, as was the fabric spare wheel cover just visible through the windscreen. The rubber pedal pads were standard on Station Wagons but optional on other models, and the floor covering was standard on Station Wagons. Note also the flasher unit, in the bulkhead cubby behind the steering wheel; even though flashers were standard on Station Wagons, Rover made no attempt to conceal the additional electrical components!

The side sections are fitted to the rear body in the same way as on the 80, with rubber seals between upper and lower body panels. There are further rubber seals between side sections and roof, between roof canopy and windscreen frame, and above the cab doors. The roof bolts to the body sides in the same way as on the 80s. The upper tailgate is identical to the 80-inch type, but on 1956 and later models it could be optionally fitted with a keylock; this lock came as part of a set of three, the other two being on the cab doors.

INTERIOR

DASHBOARD

The steering wheel of the 86 and 107 models is the same as the final 80-inch type, but its support bracket is different. This bracket is supplemented by a galvanised reinforcing plate on the bulkhead.

The instrument panel is also completely different to that fitted to 80-inch models. It is larger and incorporates two round dials which are much clearer than the earlier small gauges. The panel itself is held to the bulkhead by five set screws, which should be 'sheradised'. The instrument panel is painted the same colour as the vehicle's bodywork.

The large dial nearer the driver is the speedometer and the one further away is divided into three segments. The upper left segment contains the ammeter, the fuel gauge is at upper right, and the bottom segment contains a red warning light for main beam. The speedometer contains a mileage recorder (but no trip counter) and is calibrated in miles or kilometres, depending on the market for which it was intended. The speedometer cable has a smooth outer casing and is fitted with ferrules made of brass or nylon, the latter probably being later service replacement items.

In the centre of the instrument panel is a black plastic rotary switch (Lucas part number 031415) for the lights; US models have a different switch (Lucas number 031412). In the centre of this switch is the barrel lock for the ignition. At the top left of the panel are the two plastic sockets for an inspection lamp, the upper one being black and the lower red. At top right is a black plastic pull switch for the instrument panel lights, similar to but not the same as the switch used for this purpose on 80s.

There are three warning lights on the panel, all Lucas type WL3/1 with separate glass and bezel, as used on the later 80-inch models. At bottom left is the green oil warning light (Lucas part number 38085A), matching it at bottom right is the amber mixture warning light (Lucas 38086A), and in the centre above the rotary light switch is the red ignition light (Lucas 38084A).

Below the instrument panel are two bulkhead controls; 86s and 107s did not have a hand throttle as standard like that on the 80s. On the left is the starter button, a Lucas model ST 18 and not the same as that on 80s despite visual similarities. On the right is the choke or mixture control, with a black plastic knob labelled 'Cold Start' in white. Once again, this cable is visually similar to the item fitted to later 80s but is not the same. The choke cable support bracket is nevertheless the same as that on later 80s, and the choke warning light switch is the same Lucas part number 31109A.

HANDBRAKE

The handbrake lever is visually similar to the lever on the final 80s, with a straight black-painted shaft and a push button in the end. As before, the LHD and RHD types differ, the LHD type being attached to a cross-shaft.

PEDALS

As on the 80s, the clutch and brake pedals are mounted on rods which pass through the toe-board to a cross-shaft under the floor, while the accelerator is a pendant type. The pedals are all visually similar to their 80-inch counterparts, but not one of them is actually the same. Also worth noting is that the clutch and brake pedal levers (between the pedal rod and the cross-shaft) are pressed rather than forged items as on the 80s. Where the pedals pass through the floor panel, they should be sealed against water ingress by rubber and felt seals.

The pedals should all be finished in black, and those for the brake and the clutch may be fitted with optional rubber pads, identical to those available on the 80s.

SEATS

The seats on 86-inch and 107-inch models are completely different from those on earlier Land-Rovers. They are upholstered in leathercloth, which may be green, embossed green, blue or grey. As on the 80-inch models, there are three abreast as standard in the driving compartment, and the backrests of all of them hinge forwards like those on the later 80s.

Each backrest is bolted to a pair of long galvanised brackets which pivot on curved support brackets; the pivot is effected by long split pins with spring washers at each end to prevent rattles. The support brackets are themselves bolted to the body. Riveted to the top of the left-hand bracket on each backrest is a retaining strap made of leather, which holds the backrest upright when attached to a stud screwed to the galvanised capping of the back panel. On this back panel are also mounted two rubber buffers for each seat, held in place by drive screws.

The seat cushions are flat rather than wedge-shaped as on the 80s; a rearward slope is achieved on the 86s and 107s by a sloping top to the seat box. The wooden base of each cushion has two rearward projections which locate in slots in the upturned rear edge of the seat box. In addition, two rubber buffers are screwed to the wooden base of each cushion. Each cushion also has a single leather retaining strap, held to its base by a wooden block and designed to clip over a stud on the seat box.

THE DE LUXE CAB

The 107 models were available from the beginning with a De Luxe specification, which consisted of full trim for the cab and a number of other convenience features for its occupants. The idea behind this appears to have been to offer a vehicle which could compete effectively in the pick-up market, where customers were used to rather less utilitarian specifications than came as standard on Land-Rovers. Some elements of this De Luxe trim were also used in Station Wagon models on both wheelbases, but the basic 86 was never available with De Luxe trim.

The De Luxe cab has trim of one sort or another covering the roof, lower doors and floor; the only metal visible is around the windows and windscreen, on the dashboard, on the steering wheel support and on the seat base. Starting at the top, the roof is lined with Ivory-coloured Hardura (plastic-covered felt), held in place by a pair of ivory-painted metal hoops screwed to the roof panel. There are also two panels of similar material above the windscreen, with a retaining moulding in the centre.

The seats and trim in the De Luxe cab are invariably blue on 1954-55 models; grey and green were made available for later 107s. The De Luxe seats use standard cushions with a padded single-piece backrest, upholstered to match the rest of the interior. The rear of the cab, the footwells and the centre of the bulkhead are lined with matching leathercloth material, and the metal retainers holding the bulkhead trim in place are painted to match. Meanwhile, the whole of the floor, transmission tunnel and bellhousing cover is carpeted with a single piece of black plastic-covered felt. This floor covering has matching plastic edging pieces to protect the vulnerable corners around the bellhousing cover.

There are door trims as well, which include map pockets and padded rolls, and the lower part of the sidescreen has a separate trim casing. On 1954-55 models this is accompanied by a spring catch for the sliding window; later trim casings differ slightly to suit a screw-type window catch.

The De Luxe specification also includes a number of convenience items. An interior lamp is mounted at the top of the rear cab wall; early types have a plain lens and later ones have a moulded type. This lamp has an integral switch, and is equipped with its own fuse box mounted on the right of the dashboard. The sliding section of the rear cab window has a simple locking catch, and in some cases the metal finger-pull on standard types appears to have been replaced by a knob bonded to the glass.

The door handles are also lockable, although only the right-hand one has a keylock; this appears to have been the case on both RHD and LHD vehicles! The left-hand door handle can be locked only from the inside. Both cab doors are also fitted with bright metal pull handles on the inside.

Inside the cab of a 1954 107 pick-up. The cushion of the centre seat has obviously been replaced at some time, and the darker grey of the bellhousing cover suggests some repainting. The link mats on the floor were a period option.

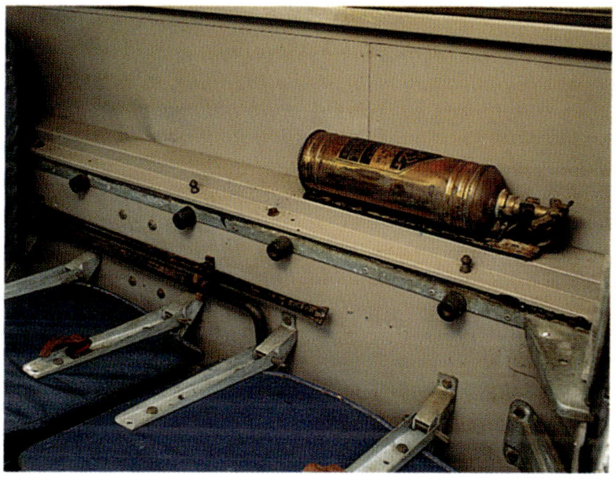

Large tools were stored inside the cab of the 107 pick-up, in clips behind the seats. The brass fire extinguisher is a period accessory.

HEATER

A recirculating heater was available as an optional extra for the 86-inch and 107-inch models. This is Smith's type 620, similar to but not the same as the optional heater on the 80s. It is fitted by three studs with spacers to the left-hand side of the bulkhead centre panel, below the instrument panel. The heater unit comes with twin demisters, which consist of flexible pipes leading upwards to nozzles screwed to the windscreen bottom rail.

Two pipes run from the heater through the bulkhead, one running to the water pump inlet pipe (when the standard item is replaced by a tapped pipe) and the other to a tap valve screwed into the thermostat housing. The blower fan is operated by a rotary rheostatic switch (Lucas part number 076613) mounted on the dashboard, to the left of the starter switch.

The heater itself is relatively common, especially on home-market models, but the matching unit for the right-hand side of the vehicle is very much rarer. This is the same Smith's 620 type, with a blanking plate over the outlet for the demister pipes. The two heaters are connected by a pair of water pipes, and the second heater has its own blower control switch, again located on the dashboard.

A further optional extra – also rare – is a heater for the rear compartment. This has a different heater unit, which is fixed to the front panel of the rear body by three brackets in the place normally occupied by the spare wheel. The wheel, of course, is relocated on the bonnet. This rear heater has its own blower control switch (the same type as for the front heaters) and is connected to the front heater by two long water pipes.

STATION WAGONS

With the arrival of the 86s and 107s, the Welder disappeared from Land-Rover catalogues as a separate model, although it was still possible to buy a basic 86 and then have it kitted out with welding equipment by Lincoln. The Fire Engine remained available, now on the 86-inch chassis, and the Station Wagon was reintroduced on the short-wheelbase chassis – this time with a Rover built metal body which kept costs down.

A long-wheelbase Station Wagon followed very much later in June 1956, almost three years after the 107-inch chassis had been introduced in pick-up form. The Station Wagon had a very different chassis from the 107 utility models, and its late introduction meant that Rover was unwilling to modify it further to the 109-inch wheelbase that became the long-wheelbase standard a few months later in the autumn of 1956. As a result, the 107 Station Wagon remained available right through the production

period of the 109 Series I chassis, and was not replaced until the Series II 109 Station Wagon was ready in mid-1958, after all the other Series I models had gone out of production.

THE 86-INCH STATION WAGON

The chassis of the 86-inch Station Wagon has no differences from the chassis of the basic 86-inch Land Rover. However, the rear cross-member carries a step on two coil-sprung hinges. This step has a black rubber mat, retained by four edging strips which are riveted to the step itself. There is also a rubber buffer attached to the cross-member to prevent the step chafing against it. The wheels of these vehicles should normally be painted to match the body.

The front bulkhead, windscreen assembly, wings, grille panel and grille are all standard items. However, the Station Wagon comes with an additional badge on the grille which reads 'Four Wheel Drive Station Wagon'. This badge hangs below the standard Land Rover oval with its black-painted background and is finished to match it; there is a special backing plate for the badge assembly and the whole is held to the grille by two screws and nuts with washers. In addition, the bonnet panel comes with a spare wheel carrier as standard.

The 1954- and 1955-model 86-inch Station Wagons have standard lighting arrangements with semaphore trafficators, but 1956 models have flashing direction indicators as standard. These are the same as the optional items fitted to basic 86-inch

The dashboard of a left-hand drive 86-inch Station Wagon, formerly operated by the NAAFI in Germany. The heater is correct for the vehicle. The safari roof (left) of the Station Wagons was always painted Ivory.

The grille and back body of both 86 and 107 Station Wagons carry this special badge.

Trimmed doors and black floor coverings characterise the 86 Station Wagon's driving compartment. The front of the roof (right, above) is held to the windscreen frame by brackets. The roof-mounted courtesy light (right, below) located between the roof ventilators is unique to the Station Wagons.

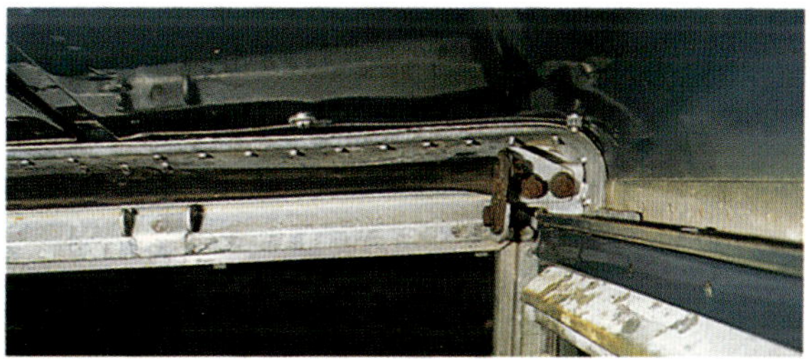

This view shows how the upper body sections bolt to the lower ones on the 86-inch Station Wagon, and also illustrates the rear door lock and release lever.

vehicles, and operate through the standard sidelights and tail-lamps. Although many vehicles were modified in service, the factory specification never included additional amber lamps.

The lower rear body of the 86-inch Station Wagon is the same as that of the basic 86-inch, complete with cappings and (redundant) rope cleats on the body sides. The left-hand rear panel carries a second 'Four Wheel Drive Station Wagon' badge underneath the standard Land-Rover oval. This additional badge is held to the body panel by two pop rivets.

The tailgate aperture also carries unpainted, galvanised cappings which bear the rubber lower door seals. The right-hand capping also has the pivot brackets for the hinges, and the left-hand capping and a support bracket fixed to the body also hold the striker plate for the door lock. There is a rubber seal for the lower edge of the door across the bottom of the tailgate aperture, and its metal retainer is held to the body floor by drive screws. Also bolted to the floor on the right of the tailgate aperture is a sliding check strap assembly for the door.

The upper side panels of the 86-inch Station Wagon are L-shaped Birmabright pressings which incorporate the rearward-facing sections of the upper body on either side of the rear door. They contain fixed windows in both side and rear sections. These windows are made of toughened glass and are glazed to the body sides by rubber sealing strips with narrow rubber strip inserts which expand them and keep them in place.

The three lower corners of each panel are reinforced with triangular galvanised cappings, the one at the right-angle between side and rear faces of the panel consisting of two triangular pieces making a right-angle. There are further vertical cappings on each side of the rear door aperture, and to these are fixed the rubber upper door seals and their retainers. The right-hand capping also bears the pivot bracket for the top door hinge, and this is held in place by two bolts. The panels themselves should be finished in the main body colour, but the capping pieces should have an unpainted, galvanised finish.

These upper panels are attached to the lower body sides by L-shaped brackets, a large one at the front and a smaller one at the rear on each side. A long stud passes through each bracket, through the capping of the lower body, and is then secured by a nut with a plain washer and a spring washer. There is a rubber sealing strip on every surface where upper and lower body panels make contact, and an additional small draught excluder rubber and filler piece at the front lower corner of each upper body side panel.

At the front of each upper body side panel is a vertical capping, again with a galvanised finish, which is attached to the panel by three bolts. These cappings serve both as reinforcement for the panel and as retainers for the rubber upper door seals, which are held to them by seven rivets on each side. It is worth noting that the upper and lower rear body panels do not fit together neatly; the upper section always overhangs the lower.

John Taylor's left-hand drive 86-inch Station Wagon typifies the breed. This model has two inward-facing seats on each side in the rear (left). Note the tubular metal supports and the webbing strap which is used to retain the seat cushions when they are folded up against the seat backs. The black rubber floor covering is correct for this vehicle.

The rear door is made in two pieces, a lower section and a window section. The lower section (which is identical to the right-hand front door panel) has a galvanised top capping which is riveted in place, together with two hinges on its right-hand outer side. The angled edge of the upper hinge should face downwards, while the angled edge of the lower hinge should face upwards. There is a door handle on the left-hand side, and this is fitted with a keylock (the assembly is not the same as the door handles fitted to the side doors, although it is visually similar). There are no rubber seals on the lower part of the door, all seals being attached to the lower body panels. The main door panel should be finished in body colour, the cappings and hinges should all have a galvanised finish, and the door handle should be finished in black.

The upper section of the rear door is essentially a steel frame with a rectangular Birmabright filler

This 107 Station Wagon is also owned by John Taylor. The galvanised capping on the rear body and the profusion of rivets make the rear doors look rather fussy. This is a 1958 model and therefore has some features from the contemporary 88 and 109 models, such as the later type of steel grille panel (right).

panel riveted in place. It has a fixed glass window, with rubber glazing and filler strips to expand the rubber and hold it in place. Pop-riveted to the lower edge of the panel is a rubber strip, which seals the join between upper and lower door sections. At the top right of the frame, a hinge is bolted to the door. The upper door frame and the hinge should have a galvanised finish, while the Birmabright filler panel should be painted in the body colour.

The Station Wagon body is topped off by a roof panel. On 1954 models this has just two ventilators which are held to the main panel by drive screws; on 1955 and later models there are four ventilators of the same design. The main roof panel has three longitudinal ribs on its upper surface, and is riveted to the sloping canopy section above the cab, which is a separate pressing and is essentially the same as the roof of the truck cab. There is a single 'Alpine light' in each side of the main roof panel.

The main roof panel should be painted in the body colour; when a tropical roof is fitted, both this and the ten alloy distance pieces which separate it from the main roof should be finished in Ivory. The Alpine lights are Perspex on 1954 models and glass on 1955 and later vehicles. In either case, they are rubber-glazed to the roof, and the main glazing rubbers have slim rubber filler strips to expand them and hold them in place. The differing thicknesses of the Perspex and glass Alpine lights mean that their glazing rubbers are not interchangeable.

The roof panel is held to the body sides and rear by 14 bolts, the four in the rear corners being longer than the others. There are rubber seals sandwiched between roof and upper body panels, and a further rubber seal above the windscreen frame, in the latter case stiffened by a metal strip and held to the canopy by four drive screws. There is an adjustment bracket in each front corner of the roof canopy, to enable the roof assembly to be fitted tightly to the windscreen frame. In addition, the roof canopy carries the top rubber seals for the doors, in each case riveted to a retainer strip which is in turn screwed to the underside of the canopy.

Paint options were limited to Blue and Grey, and there appear to have been no Green 86-inch Station Wagons. Wheels were painted to match the bodies; details of chassis colours are given in the section on the 86-inch chassis (see page 67).

The 86-inch Station Wagon has a special interior trim which mixes certain elements of the 107 De Luxe cab trim with parts unique to the Station

Wagon. On 1954 and 1955 models the basic trim colour is either blue or grey; on 1956 models green trim is (in theory) a further choice. There is no roof lining in the rear of the vehicle, although the cab area uses the headlining of the De Luxe trim.

The front floor covering and the trim in the footwells and on the bulkhead above the transmission tunnel are like those in the De Luxe cab. However, all trim panels are in the same colour, either blue or black. Additional loose floor mats are fitted in the footwells. Door trims are the same as those of the De Luxe cab, and the doors also have bright metal pull handles, window catches (two types, changing for 1956 models as with the De Luxe cab), a keylock on the right-hand side and an internally lockable handle on the left-hand door. As on other models with door locks, the lockable door is the right-hand one, irrespective of whether the vehicle has left-hand or right-hand drive.

In the rear of the Station Wagons, the floor is covered by a black rubber mat, held by a galvanised retainer strip across the door sill. There are four inward-facing rear seats, trimmed to match the rest of the interior. On 1956 and later models, these seats have finishers on their sides and front.

The backrests are fixed, hooking under the galvanised body side capping and then bolting through the wheelarch. The seat cushions pivot around bolts holding their support brackets to the backrest brackets. The seat cushions can be folded up against the squab when not in use, and in this position each cushion is retained by a strap attached to the upper bodywork. These straps are made of webbing and are coloured to match the interior. When in use, the seats rest on black rubber buffers – one for each seat – screwed to the wheelarch, and on tubular steel U-shaped leg supports that are painted black.

There is no trim on the rear body sides, on the back panel, or on the rear door. All these areas are untrimmed metal, finished in the main body colour.

The 107-inch Station Wagon

The 107-inch Station Wagon is very much rarer than the 86-inch model, the production total of 7001 vehicles including just 239 for the home market. Chassis production figures are also inflated slightly above the actual total of Station Wagons built because they include a few dozen military ambulances built on Station Wagon chassis.

The long-wheelbase Station Wagon differs much more from its basic 107-inch counterpart than the 86-inch Station Wagon differs from the basic short-wheelbase Land-Rover. It has a number of unique parts and also incorporates several items from among the optional extras listed for the basic models. After the 88 and 109 models replaced the 86s and utility 107s, the 107 Station Wagon took on a number of parts from these newer vehicles.

The 107 Station Wagon had a unique rear cross-member (above). Note also the rubber tread on the rear step, the rubber buffer mounted to the rear cross-member to prevent the step from chafing, the correct 'pork pie' tail lamps with high-mounted red reflectors, and the configuration of the door hinges. The rear spring hangers (left) on the 107 Station Wagon chassis are mounted further outboard than on other 107s.

The chassis frame of the 107-inch model is one of its unique components, differing greatly from the basic 107 type from the bulkhead rearwards. The side rails sweep down earlier to allow for the flat floor of the Station Wagon body and make space for footwells for the rear seat passengers. There are outriggers for the rear springs, which are mounted outboard of the chassis rather than directly underneath it in order to give greater roll resistance and a smoother ride. The rear cross-member is also unique to the Station Wagon chassis, being rectangular when viewed from behind and lacking an upward taper at its outer bottom edges. This special cross-member means that when optional towing equipment is fitted, both the tow jaw and its supporting bracket differ from the standard 107 type.

The front road springs differ from those fitted to other 107s; although their leaves are the same, there are unique bottom plates. There is also a unique upper steering relay lever. Rear road springs are generally the same as their basic 107 equivalents, although they have longer U-bolts (with a threaded portion 1¾ inches long) and a unique centre locating dowel. As with the basic 107s, the Station Wagons have three types of spring. The first type has ten leaves like the basic 107 spring. The second type,

Station Wagons came with door locks as standard. This one is fitted in the correct position, but has a later replacement barrel.

The driver's footwell (above) of the 107 Station Wagon shows the black floor covering, rubber pedal pads, and special tubular door restrainers. The silver-bodied wiper motor and black demister (right) are correct for the 107 Station Wagon. Note that the standard windscreen clamp is present, even though the windscreen itelf is fixed in position.

Detail of the 107 Station Wagon's body construction: this is the left-hand B/C pillar, just behind the front door.

which was introduced towards the end of the 1956 model year, has 11 leaves; it is found on 1956 models from 8706-00062, 8736-00554, and 8766-00471, and on 1957 models up to and including 1317-00041, 1327-00682 and 1347-00805. The third type has eight leaves and is fitted to all subsequent vehicles. Later 107 Station Wagons with the fully-floating rear axle have the standard 107 check strap on the right-hand side only, and a longer one on the left-hand side.

Dampers, both front and rear, are unique to the 107 Station Wagon, and the rear axle assembly is also not found elsewhere, having a different casing from the standard type with the spring mounting pads further outboard. Either semi-floating or (from April 1957) fully-floating types may be fitted, the latter being easily recognisable because it protrudes through the wheel centre, while the semi-floating type ends in a recess. Wheels are normally finished in the same colour as the body.

The exhaust system is another item which is special to the 107-inch Station Wagon, all three sections being unique. The intermediate pipe is held to the chassis by a saddle clamp at its front end, and there is a pipe clamp for the tailpipe and silencer assembly. This is 'handed' as on other models, emerging on the driver's side. The tailpipe is fitted slightly further forward than on basic 107-inch models, terminating just ahead of the rear spring mounting rather than just behind it.

Like the 86-inch Station Wagons, the 107-inch types have a sprung step bolted to the rear cross-member. All components are the same as their 86-inch equivalents. In addition, all the 107-inch models have flashing direction indicators, which operate through the standard sidelights at the front and through the tail-lamps at the rear, exactly as on contemporary 86-inch models.

There are several subtle differences at the front of the vehicle. The bonnet panel comes as standard with the spare wheel carrier optional on other models and, according to parts catalogues at least, the front wings also differ from the standard type. The radiator grille carries the same 'Four Wheel Drive Station Wagon' badge found on the 86-inch Station Wagons. After the arrival of the 88 and 109 models in autumn 1956, most 107 Station Wagons were fitted with the steel grille panel and chrome-rimmed headlamps associated with these vehicles; in addition, they had the 88 and 109 type of bulkhead rather than the 86 and 107 type.

Other items below roof level are the standard types, as far back as the rear of the front seats. From there on, almost everything about the 107-inch Station Wagon is unique to the model.

Behind the front seats is a half-height bulkhead, which has cappings along its top faces, in the corners, and vertically along its outer trailing edges. These vertical cappings also have the pivots for the lower hinges of the rear door. All the cappings have a galvanised finish, while the bulkhead itself is painted in the main body colour. The bulkhead is mounted to the chassis by one bracket on each side, and these are concealed by cover plates, held to the bulkhead by drive screws and bolts. To the front capping are mounted three rubber buffer pads which support the seat backs, and in the centre of the capping is a stud for the front squab retaining strap.

Above this bulkhead are mounted upper B-post panels. On 1956 models, they are secured to the bulkhead by two right-angled brackets each; on 1957/58 models there is a single bracket on each side. All models have galvanised cappings on the leading and trailing edges of this upper B-post panel, and to these are secured the rubber upper door seals. On 1956 models these cappings are held to the panel by five bolts on each side, the lower two of which also hold a large galvanised capping plate at the bottom. On later models, this additional plate is not fitted and just three bolts hold the vertical cappings in place. The actual panel of the upper B-post should be finished in body colour; all the galvanised cappings have the usual unpainted finish and the bolt heads are 'sheradised'.

Despite the presence of three separate cushions, the back of the front seat in the 107 Station Wagon is a bench type.

The lower rear body is quite different from its equivalent on the basic 107-inch Land-Rover. It is shorter front to rear, it has shaped cut-outs for the rear doors, and it has no rope cleats on its outer side panels. It comes as left-hand and right-hand sections, each one including both the side panel and the panel outboard of the rear-facing door. Behind the wheelarch on each side is a single lidded locker; the lockers themselves are unique to the 107 Station Wagon, but their lids, hinges and hasps are the same as on the basic 107s. On each side panel are also two galvanised steel locating brackets for the rear seats.

Each lower rear body section has the usual galvanised capping. The right-angled rear corner capping (triangular when viewed from the side or rear) is integral with the side capping, and there is a further capping alongside the door aperture. This has a plain face, without the prong for the tailgate fixings seen on basic 107s. There are also galvanised protectors running the full height of each rear body corner, identical to their equivalents on the 107 pick-up. The whole of the rear body is held to the chassis by 10 bolts, of which the four at the front are longer than the rest.

There are further galvanised cappings on either side of the aperture for the rearward-facing door, and these bear the rubber lower door seals. The right-hand capping also carries the pivot brackets for the hinges, and the striker plate for the door lock and its support plate are fitted to the left-hand capping and to the body panel itself.

The left-hand rear panel carries a 'Four Wheel Drive Station Wagon' badge underneath the standard Land-Rover oval, and this is held to the body panel by two pop rivets, exactly as on the 86-inch Station Wagon. The number plate panel is normally screwed or pop-riveted to the rearward-facing right-hand panel, where it is illuminated through a clear lens underneath the tail lamp.

The rear seat in the 107 Station Wagon is a proper bench seat. Note the reinforcing bulkhead which runs across behind the front seats.

There are also two floor sections, again unique to the 107 Station Wagon. The front section runs between the intermediate bulkhead and the front of the rear body, and the rear section covers the remaining section to the back of the vehicle. At the front of each side of this floor section, just behind the B-post, is a check strap for the rear side door. There are four rubber buffers between this floor section and the chassis cross-member which runs below it.

To the rear floor section are riveted four tread strips, running from front to rear and each held in place by 11 drive screws. There is also a sliding check strap for the rearward-facing door at the trailing edge of the floor. This trailing edge also carries a rubber seal for the lower edge of the door, held in a metal retainer which is fixed to the floor by drive screws,

These front door trims (near right) were used on the 86 and 107 Station Wagons, and on the De Luxe cab. The rear doors (far right) of the 107 Station Wagon were also fully trimmed.

The inward-facing seats in the rear of the 107 Station Wagon are both benches.

exactly as on the 86-inch models. There are 10 rubber buffers between the floor and the chassis; pick-up models have 12.

The inside and outside of the lower body sections, and the whole of the two floor panels, should be finished in the main body colour; cappings, as usual, are galvanised, and the tread strips are also unpainted.

The rear side doors normally have sliding windows, although a small number of vehicles were built with fixed glazing; some of these vehicles were delivered to the Royal Family and to the British Army, but there may have been others. The fixed glazing was not a regular optional alternative, but rather a special-order item.

These doors have the usual Land-Rover two-part construction. They have a unique lower panel made of Birmabright alloy with a sloping rear edge. Behind this is a steel framework, bolted together. The lower edge and trailing edges have rubber seals in metal retainers, and there is a galvanised capping at the top. The whole lower panel is held to the B-post by two hinges, both the same, and both fitted with their sloping edges uppermost. There is also a handle in this lower panel, which is several inches higher than the handle in the front door, a quirk which helps to give these early Station Wagons their unique appearance. The main door panel should be painted in the body colour, the cappings should all have an unpainted galvanised finish, and the door handle should be black.

The upper or window section of the rear side door is essentially a steel framework. At its lower edge is riveted a filler panel of Birmabright which should be painted in the body colour; the rest of the upper panel is galvanised and should be unpainted, and the rivet heads should also be unpainted. The single hinge bolted at the top of the upper door section should have the same galvanised finish.

The actual window has a fixed forward section and a sliding rear section. This rear section has a knob half way up its leading edge, and both sections of the window are made of glass.

The window section of the door is held to the lower door by two long threaded studs on the top frame, which pass through the capping at the top of the lower door in the familiar Land-Rover fashion and are bolted to it. There is also a sealing rubber riveted to the underside of the upper section.

The upper rear body sides include the rearward-facing side panel, and they contain a fixed and rubber-glazed side window and a similarly glazed rearward-facing window. This rearward-facing window is one of the few items on the 107 Station Wagon which is interchangeable with its counterpart on the 86-inch model.

Each side panel has a galvanised capping at its vertical leading edge, which also holds a rubber seal for the door in a metal retaining strip. At each lower rear corner are further galvanised reinforcing plates of the usual right-angled triangulated type, and there is an additional triangular galvanised capping at the lower edge beside the aperture for the rearward-facing door. Alongside the aperture is yet another galvanised capping, again holding rubber seals for the door. The one on the right also carries a pivot bracket for the upper door hinge.

These upper rear body panels are held to the lower body sections by brackets and long studs. There is a rubber sealing strip between upper and lower panels, and an additional draught filler piece between the leading edges of the side panels. As on the 86 Station Wagon, the upper body panels are not a good fit and overhang the lower panels noticeably. All the panelwork of these upper sections should be finished in the body colour, while all the galvanised cappings should, as usual, remain unpainted.

The roof panel invariably consists of a main panel with four ventilators and a tropical roof panel mounted above it on 14 distance pieces. As on the 86-inch models, the main roof panel has three longitudinal ribs on its upper surface, and the ventilators are attached by drive screws. Once again, there is a sloping canopy section above the cab, and this is riveted to the main roof panel. A single Alpine light is fitted in each side of the main roof panel. The main roof panel should be painted in the body colour; the Tropical roof and its distance pieces should be finished in Ivory.

The Alpine lights are always made of glass and are rubber-glazed to the roof in the usual Land-Rover fashion, with filler strips to expand the main rubber glazing and hold it in place. Despite appearances, these Alpine lights and their glazing strips are not the same as their equivalents on the 86-inch models.

The roof panel is held to the body sides and rear by 18 bolts, the four in the rear corners being longer than the others. Rubber seals are sandwiched between roof and upper body panels, and there is a further rubber seal above the windscreen frame. As on the 86s, this is stiffened by a metal strip and held to the canopy by four drive screws. Unlike the 86s, however, the 107 Station Wagons also have a small rubber draught seal at each front corner of the canopy. Adjustment brackets in each front corner of the roof canopy allow the roof assembly to be fitted tightly to the windscreen frame.

The roof canopy also carries the top rubber seals for the doors, in each case riveted to a retainer strip which is in turn bolted to the underside of the canopy. There are two of these on each side, one for the front door and the second for the rear.

Like the 86-inch Station Wagon, the 107 model has special interior trim. Once again, this includes elements of the 107 De Luxe cab trim. Colours are blue, grey or green, the latter featuring an embossed leathercloth. The three-piece headlining is made of white plastic-covered felt and is secured by formers and Ivory-coloured retaining hoops. The central roof light, unique to the model, is accompanied by a dash-mounted switch and its own fuse box.

The headlining of the 107 Station Wagon is made of Ivory-coloured fabric, and the centrally-mounted courtesy light is unique to the model.

The front floor covering and the trim in the footwells and on the bulkhead above the transmission tunnel are always black, and there are additional loose floor mats in the footwells. The front door trims are the same as those of the 86 Station Wagon, and the doors are both lockable, the driver's side having an external keylock. The doors also have bright metal pull handles and window catches.

The front seat consists of three separate cushions with a one-piece backrest. This is not the same as the De Luxe backrest, however, and its rear is trimmed with a metal panel painted to match the upholstery. There is also a kick-panel of black plastic-coloured felt attached to the low bulkhead behind the seats by a retaining strip, and black rubber flooring covers the area ahead of the rear seat. The ribbing on this flooring runs from side to side of the vehicle.

The rear side doors are trimmed to match the rest of the interior, and have the same pull handles as the front doors. Towards the end of the 1956 model year, an additional retainer was fitted to each door trim; this modification was introduced with chassis numbers 8706-00062, 8736-00545 and 8766-00491.

The rear seat is a bench type, with a folding backrest. It is retained in the upright position by wing nuts. Its rear panel is made of board, and the metal hinges between cushion and backrest are painted grey. The 107 Station Wagon's seats can in fact be rearranged to make a bed: with the rear seat backrest folded flat, the cushions are then removed from the front seats and slotted in between the rear seat cushion and a ledge on the intermediate bulkhead.

The inward-facing bench seats at the back of the 107 Station Wagon are simply the optional folding seats available on other 107 models. Once again, they are trimmed to match the rest of the interior. There is no floor covering in this area of the body (instead, there are longitudinal tread plates, described above), and there is no trim on the rear body sides, on the back panel, or on the rear door. As on the 86-inch Station Wagons, these areas are painted in the main body colour.

Front seat box area of 107 Station Wagon shows locker cover hasps and their turnbuckles, the leather seat cushion retaining straps, and the handbrake with its dust seal and retainer.

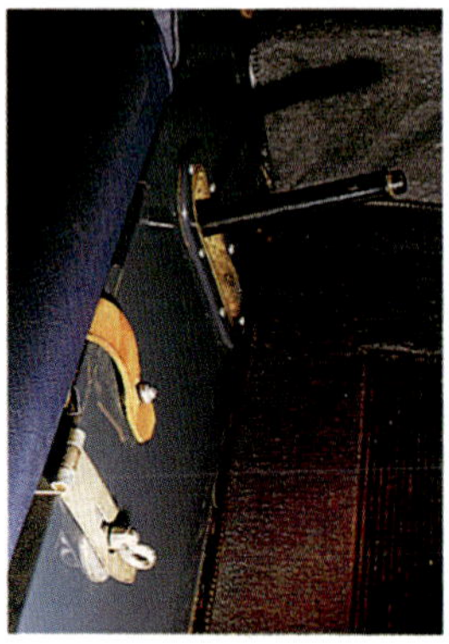

EXPORT VARIATIONS

The Land-Rover was always primarily intended for export markets, and for that reason LHD and RHD variants are given equal prominence in this book. In most cases, Rover was able to export vehicles with a 'standard' specification, although vehicles exported in CKD (Completely Knocked Down) kit form for overseas assembly were often fitted with a variety of locally-manufactured items which differed from those on vehicles assembled by Rover at Solihull. It is simply not possible to list all the variations which were produced under the CKD system, and anyone restoring a CKD vehicle would be well advised to research its original specification carefully.

Vehicles built at Solihull for certain overseas markets also had some deviations from standard. The major ones are summarised below.

LAND-ROVERS FOR THE USA

Very few 107-inch models were exported to the USA, where their distribution and sales were handled by Rootes. The 86-inch model was also not exported in large numbers, but those that did cross the Atlantic had certain special features.

North American vehicles have some differences from standard in their cooling systems, with a special thermostat housing and water pump inlet pipe. It seems probable that most were also fitted with the optional 10lb radiator cap to allow for higher running temperatures.

On the body, there is special windscreen glass (probably laminated), and the rear number plate is fitted to a bracket in the centre of the tailboard. This number plate has its own illumination, exactly as on 80s shipped to the USA. The very few 107 Station Wagons sold in the USA have a special reinforcing bracket for the rear number plate on the rear-facing panel alongside the door. On 1954 basic models, the drilled holes for the standard lights in the rear of the body are covered with riveted plates, again exactly as on US-model 80s.

All US 86s and 107s have flashing turn indicators as standard. The front sidelamp is a Lucas type 488 with twin-filament bulb and clear lens. The rear lamp on 1954 models is a Lucas type 488 with twin-filament bulb and red lens; on subsequent vehicles the twin-filament lamp fitted to contemporary Station Wagons for other markets is fitted. An over-ride in the wiring harness from the indicator switch on the steering column allows the stop lamp to double as a turn indicator in all cases.

LAND-ROVERS FOR CANADA

The primary consideration on vehicles for the Canadian market seems to have been keeping out the cold. Most vehicles, therefore, were probably supplied with a heater. In addition, the driver and passenger doors had special one-piece door seals, although the doors themselves were constructed from separate upper and lower sections in the same way as on Land-Rovers for other markets.

These special door seals are matched by special interior trim for the driving compartment. This appears to be generally similar to the De Luxe trim available in other markets, but has black covering on the dashboard, while all the rest of the cab trim except for the roof sections is in embossed green leathercloth. There are also unique door trims, similar to but simpler than the De Luxe type. In addition, the seat base, locker lids and the front of the rear body are all covered with black felted vinyl, and there are sealing rubbers around the rim of the petrol tank locker.

LAND-ROVERS FOR AUSTRALIA

The 86s and 107s shipped to Australia have a centrally-mounted number plate, like that on their equivalents for the USA.

THE 86-INCH TEMPO MODELS

Following on from the 80-inch Land-Rovers it received in the early part of 1953 (see page 62), the West German *Bundesgrenzschutz* took a further batch of 86-inch models with a modified design. Numbers are unclear, but records suggest that there were no more than 58. These were once again assembled by Vidal und Sohn in Hamburg, probably on the basis of LHD rolling chassis with bulkheads shipped out by Rover, and, like the 80s, they wore Tempo badges. They appear to have been built between 1953-55. The majority are said to have been passed on to the West German Army (the *Bundeswehr*) for further service in the 1960s.

The general configuration of the 86-inch Tempo models is similar to that of the 80s. The electrical system again has a negative earth, and the fuel tank is again relocated at the rear of the chassis. Once again, the bodywork is all-steel, with tall sides and a windscreen which hinges below the glass rather than lower down. The sloping rear door edge is another notable feature.

There are lockers in the front wings as before, but this time the sidelight and an indicator light are more sensibly positioned in the fixed lower panel. There are indicator repeater lamps protruding from the sides of the front wings, and additional convoy lights on stalks mounted on top of the wings. There is a loud-hailer on top of the right-hand wing, and the bonnet carries the spare wheel instead of a map locker. As before, there are sirens ahead of the grille panel. Most vehicles appear to have had capstan winches.

At the rear, some models appear to have had a jerrycan holder in the centre, although others most probably did have a drop-down tailgate. The hood and frame are attached to the body sides as on the 80-inch models.

Inside, the additional instrument panel is now located between the main panel and the steering column. In addition to various switches, it carries a dial gauge – probably a Bosch ammeter. The heater and demister are standard. As on the 80s, there are just two front seats, each with a tubular frame, and there is a pair of inward-facing benches mounted on the rear wheelboxes.

OPTIONS AND ACCESSORIES

TOOLS

Rover provided both major tools and a set of small hand tools with the 86-inch and 107-inch models.

The wheelbrace and starting handle, and the tyre lever on export vehicles, are the same as those supplied with the 80-inch models. However, the grease gun, the tyre pump and its connector are all different. The jack on 1954 models appears to have been the same screw-type as the 80s had, but on later vehicles it is a ratchet type made either by Shelley or Metallifacture; in either of the latter cases, the handle and extension are all of a piece.

The hand tools should be in the same type of black hessian tool roll as those on the 80s. This should contain the same 11 tools, although it appears that on later vehicles two of the spanners were replaced by different double-ended spanners, the first with $\frac{7}{16}$ and ½-inch AF sizes and the second with $\frac{9}{16}$ and $\frac{5}{8}$-inch sizes.

POWER TAKE-OFFS

Both 86 and 107 Land-Rovers can be fitted with a centre power take-off; all 86s can also be fitted with a rear power take-off, as can all 107s except the first 1144 chassis and the Station Wagons. To fit a rear power take-off to those early 107 chassis, it was necessary to change the chassis frame – so probably very few owners did! The vehicles which cannot have the rear power take-off without this modification are numbered up to and including 4720-0089, 4723-0451, 4726-0572 and 4776-0032; all 4773-series chassis are suitable for the rear power take-off.

The centre power take-off is the same as the 80 type, and the rear power take-off is also the same except for longer propshafts. All rear power take-off output shafts have six splines and may be used to drive a drum for belt-driven machinery. A capstan winch may be fitted at the front of the vehicle and driven from the nose of the crankshaft. This is identical to the type supplied for 80-inch models in all essentials, but differs in minor details such as the mounting plate.

An engine oil cooler is usually fitted with the power take-offs. The cooler unit itself is the same as the 80 type, but the pipework differs. In addition, the oil cooler requires a special oil pump, sump, radiator and radiator cowl; a 12-blade engine fan is also usually fitted. The oil cooler should always be accompanied by an oil temperature gauge, mounted on its own bracket which bolts to the dashboard. On fire engines, this gauge is mounted on the pump control panel at the rear of the vehicle.

Clearly visible are the lockers in the front wings of this Tempo 86-inch model in service with the West German Bundesgrenzschutz. *The specification of these vehicles also included unique doors and back bodies.*

TOWING EQUIPMENT

Two different tow jaws were available for the 86s and 107s, one with parallel jaws and a two-bolt fixing while the other had a curved mouth and a four-bolt fixing. The same three types of tow plate offered for the 80s continued to be available. When towing equipment was fitted to 107 Station Wagons, different bolts were used to suit the different rear cross-member. When vehicles were used with a Brockhouse trailer (see page 126), they were fitted with the special 2-inch tow ball supplied with the trailer.

It was also possible to order lifting and towing rings for the front bumper of the 86s and 107s from the beginning of the 1955 model year. These should always be fitted in pairs.

MISCELLANEOUS EXTRAS

Other extras available included a radio set and aerial, floor mats, front and rear mud flaps and a 'cool-ride' seat pad. In addition, dealers and distributors could supply the 15cwt Brockhouse trailer (see page 126).

APPENDICES

IDENTIFICATION, DATING AND PRODUCTION FIGURES

The chassis number of both 86-inch and 107-inch Land-Rovers is stamped into the transfer box instruction plate fitted to the bulkhead on the passenger compartment side just above the gearbox cover. It is also stamped on the left-hand rear spring hanger on the chassis.

The engine number is stamped on the left-hand

side of the cylinder block at the front, just beside the exhaust manifold. The gearbox number is on the right-hand side of the gearbox casing. The axle number is on the top of the axle casing, on the left-hand side, for both front and rear axles.

Chassis Numbers

1954 models (86-inch)
4710-0001 to 4710-2861 (all models, home), 4713-0001 to 4713-5125 (all models, LHD), 4716-0001 to 4716-3434 (all models, RHD export), 4763-0001 to 4763-0564 (CKD all models, LHD), 4766-0001 to 4766-3096 (CKD all models, RHD)

1954 models (107-inch)
4720-0001 to 4720-0441 (all models, home), 4723-0001 to 4723-1245 (all models, LHD), 4726-0001 to 4726-1674 (all models, RHD export), 4773-0001 to 4773-0114 (CKD all models, LHD), 4776-0001 to 4776-0346 (CKD all models, RHD)

1955 models (86-inch)
5710-0001 to 5710-8185 (all models, home), 5713-0001 to 5713-5760 (all models, LHD), 5716-0001 to 5713-3537 (all models, RHD export), 5763-0001 to 5763-0482 (CKD all models, LHD), 5766-0001 to 5766-2250 (CKD all models, RHD)

1955 models (107-inch)
5720-0001 to 5720-1205 (all models, home), 5723-0001 to 5723-2120 (all models, LHD), 5726-0001 to 5726-3863 (all models, RHD export), 5773-0001 to 5773-0066 (CKD all models, LHD), 5776-0001 to 5776-1436 (CKD all models, RHD)

1956 models (86-inch)
1706-00001 to 1706-04807 (basic vehicle, home), 1736-00001 to 1706-04433 (basic vehicle, LHD), 1746-00001 to 1706-01000 (CKD basic vehicle, LHD), 1766-00001 to 1766-02441 (basic vehicle, RHD export), 1776-00001 to 1776-01367 (CKD basic vehicle, RHD)

1956 models (107-inch)
2706-00001 to 2706-00948 (basic vehicle, home), 2736-00001 to 2736-02399 (basic vehicle, LHD), 2746-00001 to 2746-00246 (CKD basic vehicle, LHD), 2766-00001 to 2766-03054 (basic vehicle, RHD export), 2776-00001 to 2776-01188 (CKD basic vehicle, RHD), 8706-00001 to 8706-00066 (Station Wagon, home), 8736-00001 to 8736-00632 (Station Wagon, LHD), 8746-00001 to 8746-00006 (CKD Station Wagon, LHD), 8766-00001 to 8766-00550 (Station Wagon, RHD export), 8776-00001 to 8776-00012 (CKD Station Wagon, LHD)

1957 models (107-inch)
1317-00001 to 1317-00053 (Station Wagon, home), 1327-00001 to 1327-01024 (Station Wagon, RHD export), 1337-00001 to 1337-00024 (CKD Station Wagon, RHD), 1347-00001 to 1347-01283 (Station Wagon, LHD), 1357-00001 to 1357-00036 (CKD Station Wagon, LHD)

1958 models (107-inch)
1318-00001 to 1318-00120 (Station Wagon, home), 1328-00001 to 1328-01541 (Station Wagon, RHD export), 1338-00001 to 1338-00036 (CKD Station Wagon, RHD), 1348-00001 to 1348-01618 (Station Wagon, LHD). No records exist for 1358-series CKD Station Wagons with LHD.

Note In these lists, the identifying prefix and vehicle serial number are separated by a dash to aid clarity. This dash is not found on the actual vehicles.

Engine Numbers

1954 models
4710-0001 (RHD), 4713-0001 (LHD)

1955 models
5710-0001 (RHD), 5711-0001 (RHD), 5713-0001 (LHD), 5714-0001 (LHD)

1956 models
1706-00001 (RHD), 1736-00001 (LHD)

1957 models
1117-00001 (RHD), 1147-00001 (LHD)

1958 models
1118-00001 (RHD), 1148-00001 (LHD)

Note In these tables, the identifying prefix and engine serial number are separated by a dash to aid clarity. This dash is not found on the actual engines. Commencing numbers only are given.

Factory reconditioned engines Engines reconditioned by Rover were renumbered. The reconditioning plate has the part number, which may be identified as follows:

245585 (1954, siamese-bore 2-litre)
248359 (1955, spread-bore 2-litre, with 1 11/16in diameter gudgeon pins)
269216 (1956-58, as above, but 7/8in gudgeon pins)

This part number is followed by a serial number and some identifying codes. A typical number would be S0011/20/10. This breaks down as follows:

S Engine reconditioned at Solihull; L indicates an engine reconditioned at the London service depot in Seagrave Road; K is also found and is not yet explained.
0011 Serial number, in this case the 11th of its type.
20 The increase in bore size in thousandths of an inch (90 indicates liners fitted with standard bore; 91 with 0.010in bore increase; 92 with 0.020in increase).
10 The undersize of the reground crank in thousandths of an inch.

Gearbox Numbers

1954 models
4710-0001 (RHD), 4713-0001 (LHD)

1955 models
5710-0001 (RHD), 5711-0001 (RHD), 5713-0001 (LHD), 5714-0001 (LHD)

1956 models
1706-00001 (RHD), 1736-00001 (LHD)

1957 models
1117-00001 (RHD), 1147-00001 (LHD)

1958 models
1118-00001 (RHD), 1148-00001 (LHD)

Note In these tables, the identifying prefix and gearbox serial number are separated by a dash to aid clarity. This dash is not found on the actual gearboxes.

Axle Numbers

1954 models
Front axle: 4710-00001 (RHD, 86in and 107in with 10in brakes); 4713-00001 (LHD, 86in and 107in with 10in brakes); 4720-00001 (RHD, 107in with 11in brakes); 4723-00001 (LHD, 107in with 11in brakes). Rear axle: 4710-00001 (86in and 107in with 10in brakes); 4720-00001 (107in with 11in brakes)

1955 models
Front axle: 5710-00001 (RHD, 86in); 5711-00001 (RHD, 86in); 5713-00001 (LHD, 86in); 5714-00001 (LHD, 86in); 5720-00001 (RHD, 107in); 5721-00001 (RHD, 107in); 5723-00001 (LHD, 107in); 5724-00001 (LHD, 107in); 1706-00001 (RHD, 86in); 1736-00001 (LHD, 86in); 2706-00001 (RHD, 107in); 2736-00001 (LHD, 107in). Rear axle: 5710-00001 (86in); 5711-00001 (86in); 5720-00001 (107in); 5721-00001 (107in); 1706-00001 (86in); 2706-00001 (107in)

1956 models
Front axle: 2706-00001 (RHD); 2736-00001 (LHD). Rear axle: 8706-00001

1957 models
Front axle: 1217-00001 (RHD); 1247-00001 (LHD). Rear axle: 1317-00001

1958 models
Front axle: 1218-00001 (RHD); 1248-00001 (LHD). Rear axle: 1318-00001

Note In these tables, the identifying prefix and axle serial number are separated by a dash to aid clarity. This dash is not found on the actual axles.

88-INCH & 109-INCH MODELS

A highly original diesel-engined 88-inch with hard top body: the wheelbase was extended by 2 inches to make room for the diesel engine introduced for the 1957 season. The driver's side mirror is clearly incorrect!

The 88-inch and 109-inch Land-Rovers were introduced in the autumn of 1956 and took over immediately from all 86 and 107 models except for the 107 Station Wagon. Even though they were in production for just two years, they were built in very large numbers, the total of 88-inch models being just short of 40,000 and the total of 109s falling a little under 24,000.

The extra two inches in the wheelbase made room for the new diesel engine which was introduced for the 1957 season, after the 88s and 109s had already been on sale for a year. The main reasons why the wheelbase was extended in advance of the engine becoming available were to minimise the production line disruption which major changes always cause, and to spread the cost of these changes.

All the first diesel Land-Rovers were sold in Britain, and the diesel engine did not become available for export until the beginning of the 1958 model year in autumn 1957.

CHASSIS

CHASSIS FRAME AND BUMPER

The chassis frames of the 88 and 109 Land-Rovers are essentially the same as those of the 86s and 107s, but their front cross-members are relocated an inch closer to the bumper. The extra two inches of wheelbase are created by mounting the front spring hanger brackets further forward. All chassis frames are painted black, and the front bumpers with their integral support brackets should be galvanised. The lifting handles on the rear cross-member should also have a galvanised finish.

Diesel models have two battery carriers at the front instead of just one. The one on the right-hand side also incorporates the air cleaner cradle, but is smaller than the type fitted to petrol-engined vehicles to suit the smaller (6-volt) battery. The carrier on the left is a unique fitting. Both carriers should be painted black to match the chassis frame.

The extra 2 inches in the wheelbase somehow help to make the 88-inch Land-Rover look more solid than the 86-inch which preceded it.

The front spring hanger brackets (right) are mounted further forward on 88-inch and 109-inch Land-Rovers than on the 86-inch and 107-inch models which they closely resemble. Detail of the rear axle (far right), spring, bump stop and brake pipes on a 1957 model 88-inch Land-Rover.

As on all earlier Series I Land-Rovers, the axle check straps are attached to the chassis by plates and set bolts, all of which should be painted black. The webbing straps themselves are the same as those on the 86s and 107s. However, when a fully-floating axle is fitted to either 88-inch or 109-inch models, only the right-hand check strap is the standard type. The left-hand strap differs, the 109 type being longer than the 88 type.

Springs and Dampers

Like the 86s and 107s, the 88s and 109s have 'handed' front road springs which are not interchangeable. Springs on 88-inch models have ten leaves, and those on 109-inch models have 11. In each case, the springs are identical to those on the later 86-inch and 107-inch models, and have a black painted finish.

Rear road springs are also 'handed' on both long- and short-wheelbase types. Those on the 88s have 11 leaves and are the same as the ones fitted to 86-inch Land-Rovers. However, starting with 1117-03274, which was built towards the end of the 1957 season, 88-inch fire tenders have eight-leaf rear springs.

There are three types of rear spring fitted to the 109-inch models. The first type has ten leaves, and is identical to that found on 107s. Only a few hundred vehicles have these, however, and from chassis number 1216-01602 (built some time around the beginning of 1956) the springs have 11 leaves; most 109s built in the 1956 calendar year have these. The third type, found on subsequent vehicles from chassis number 1217-00417, has eight leaves.

The dampers on 88s are the same as those on 86s, and those on 109s the same as their 107 equivalents. However, 88-inch diesel models fitted with heavy-duty rear springs have 109-type dampers all round. In all cases, the dampers are retained in the same way as on the later 86s and 107s.

AXLES

The front axle casing of the 88-inch and 109-inch Land-Rovers is the same as that fitted to 86-inch and 107-inch models, and to the later 80-inch models with 2½-inch wide road springs. As on these models, the differential housing is held to the axle casing by ten bolts with spring washers. In all cases, the axle casing is finished in black, and the crownwheel and pinion set once again provides a gear ratio of 4.7:1. Special conditions apply for the 4×2 88-inch models (see pages 124-125).

The swivel pin assemblies and hubs are exactly the same as on 86-inch and 107-inch models. In later years, Rover offered a kit to convert the swivel pins with their cone and spring steering dampers to a type which used a pin and thrust washer steering damper. The steering lock stop bolts are the same as on 86 and 107 models, three different types being available (one fixed and two adjustable). These are always fitted in matching pairs, and the longer ones are used on the 109 models and on 88s with the optional larger wheel and tyre combinations.

There are two different types of rear axle for the 88s and 109s, one a semi-floating type and the other a fully-floating type. The two types have different axle casings, and are easily distinguishable at a glance: the semi-floating type terminates in a recess at the wheel centre, while the fully-floating type protrudes through it. The fully-floating axles on 88s, and both types of 109 axle, also have a reinforcement under the left-hand side of the axle casing.

Semi-floating axles were standard on all 88s and on 109s built before April 1957. Later 1957-model 109s (1217-series chassis) and 1958-model 109s (1218-series chassis) had a fully-floating axle.

WHEELS AND TYRES

The 88s and 109s have the same standard wheels as the 80, 86 and 107 models. These wheels are date-stamped in the same way as earlier Land-Rover wheels, and are always painted to match the body colour unless to special order; however, the wheels on Grey 109s appear always to have been Blue. Split-rim wheels may be found on vehicles delivered to the military or to special order.

Tyre sizes were 6.00 × 16 on the 88s and 7.00 × 16 on the 109s, although the latter was also optional on the 88s. The range of tyres available from the factory was the same as for the 86s and 107s.

BRAKES

The 88s and 109s once again use Girling braking components, with drum brakes on the wheels and a mechanically operated drum-type parking brake on the transmission output shaft. The 88s have the same 10-inch diameter wheel brakes as the 86s, while the 109s have the same 11-inch wheel brakes as the final 107s, with twin leading-shoe types on the front axle.

The visual aspects of the wheel brakes are unchanged from the 86 and 107 models. However, the transmission brake on 109 diesel models has a circular vibration damper attached to it.

It is worth noting that many vehicles were fitted in service with Series II brake components, which have different wheel cylinders and different diameter brake pipes. This was done in later years as the correct items became scarcer and more expensive.

STEERING

The steering gear on the 88 and 109 Land-Rovers is Burman recirculating ball with a variable ratio. In the straight-ahead position that ratio is 15.6:1; on full lock the ratio increases to 23.8:1. The steering wheel requires 3.3 turns to take the wheels from one lock to the other. The principle of the steering rods and levers is unchanged from the earlier models, but the steering box and steering column differ.

The steering wheel is the same as the 86 and 107 type. However, it has a plain central boss in black painted metal. The horn push is relocated on a bracket clamped to the steering column. The bracket should be painted black and the horn push (Lucas part number 76205/B) should be dark brown or black Bakelite. The wire which runs from the back of the horn push is held to the steering column by a black rubber 'Christmas tree' cable cleat. The dipswitch is a press-type and is relocated on the floor; it should be left unpainted.

As on the 86s and 107s, the steering box is bolted to a support bracket on the chassis side rail, and this bracket should be painted black. The same type of flat rubber seal is used where the steering column passes through the bulkhead, and the same steering column support bracket and bulkhead reinforcing plate are found in the driving compartment.

ENGINE

PETROL ENGINE

The petrol engine fitted to the 88-inch and 109-inch Land Rovers is the same spread-bore 2-litre four-cylinder fitted to 86s and 107s after autumn 1954.

BLOCK, HEAD AND SUMP

These parts were unchanged. The block should be painted grey except on machined surfaces.

FUEL SYSTEM

The fuel system on petrol-engined 88-inch and 109-inch Land-Rovers was unchanged.

COOLING SYSTEM

The cooling system of petrol-powered 88s and 109s is generally similar to that of earlier models. However, the radiator cowl has a deeper rim around the circular cut-out for the fan; this is to allow for the

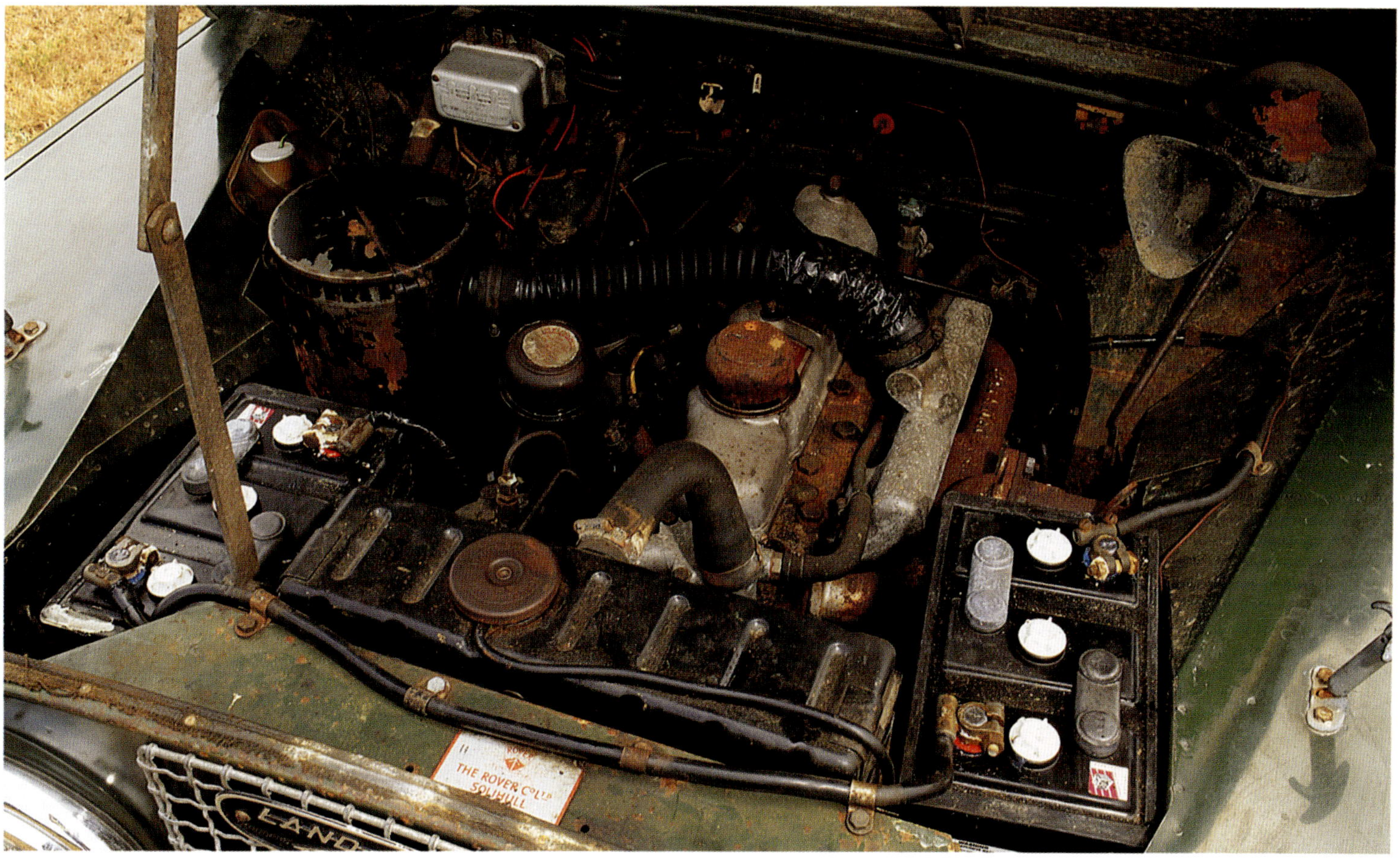

The 88-inch diesel engine bay looks very different from that of the older petrol-engined models. Apart from the engine itself, there are twin six-volt batteries. The forward extension of the bulkhead where it joins the inner wings is also curved rather than angular as on the 86s and 107s. The windscreen washer bottle is a later addition. This red Rover Company badge on the rearward extension of the grille panel was used on all 88s and 109s.

radiator being an inch further forward in the chassis than on earlier models. The oil recommendation plate on the front panel above the radiator is the same as the type fitted to 86s and 107s. Top and bottom hoses are longer than on the 86s and 107s to suit the repositioned radiator.

Diesel Engine

The 2-litre diesel engine is very different in conception from the 2-litre petrol type. It has a cast iron cylinder head as well as a cast iron block, and the block incorporates wet liners. Instead of the petrol engine's overhead inlet and side exhaust valves, there are overhead valves operated by pushrods. These pushrods are activated by a chain-driven camshaft. Long-life roller tappets are used instead of the pad-type tappets in the petrol engine.

When the Series II Land-Rovers were announced in 1958, it became clear that part of the original design brief had been to create an engine which was adaptable to petrol power – and the 2¼-litre petrol engine first seen in the Series IIs was a large-bore cousin to the 2-litre diesel.

Block, Head and Sump (Diesel)

The cylinder block and flywheel housing of the diesel engine should be painted grey, while the cylinder head should be left in bare metal. The sump, the engine mounting brackets, the oil filler pipe, its side cover and bracket, and the bracket holding the fuel filter to the cylinder head should all be painted black. The sump drain plug should have an unpainted brass finish.

The inlet manifold is made of alloy and should not be painted. The same goes for the front cover, which will of course have a brighter appearance than the cast iron block, but it should not be polished. However, the crankshaft and water pump pulleys should both be painted black, as should the fan. The body of the Lucas C45 PV5 dynamo should also be black, but its mounting bracket and strap are bare metal. The starter motor is also from Lucas – type M45G with part number 26147A – and both this and its solenoid should have a black finish.

At the top of the engine, the aluminium alloy rocker cover at the top of the engine should also be unpainted and not polished, and it should have a red instruction plate (with details of the compression ratio and of Hot and Cold tappet clearances) held to it by drive screws. The three nuts which hold the rocker cover down should also be unpainted, with the black of the rubber sealing washers just visible around their bases. The domed AC breather filter (AC part number 7223381) fitted to the rocker cover should be painted black.

The oil filter housing on the engine has a bare metal finish. The oil filter is a disposable-element type, with a cylindrical steel casing which screws into the housing and protects the filter element. This casing is part of the complete oil filter assembly (AC part number 1531477) and has a black finish.

The exhaust manifold normally took on a characteristic rusty appearance after a few months' use, but when new it had an unpainted cast iron finish. Modern heat-resistant paint can recreate the original finish quite successfully.

FUEL SYSTEM (DIESEL)

The diesel 88s and 109s have a different fuel tank from the petrol models. Although visually similar to the petrol type, it incorporates a fuel return pipe and a different gauge unit. Like the petrol type, it should be finished in black.

There are two types of fuel pump, both incorporating a glass sediment trap. Both are of AC manufacture, the earlier one bearing AC part number 7950285 and the later being 7950445. Both should have a bare metal finish.

The fuel filter is mounted to the top left of the engine, and there is a second one on the left-hand side of the bulkhead on export models (it was also optional on home market models). These filters have unpainted tops but black-painted bowls; the top sections also bear the maker's name (CAV). The first 460 diesel engines (which were presumably fitted to both 88 and 109 chassis) actually had a different fuel filter from later examples, but it is not clear how it differed.

At the top left of the engine, towards the back, is the distribution pump. Its cylindrical top section should be black; the rest of the pump has a bare metal finish. The fuel pipes to and from the distribution pump should be unpainted. Alongside the distribution pump, the two-piece support bracket for the injector pipe damper shroud should be black.

COOLING SYSTEM (DIESEL)

The cooling system fitted to diesel 88s and 109s incorporates a radiator which is different from the petrol type and has its bottom outlet on the opposite side. Rover offered pressure caps of 9lb and 10lb per square inch rating as alternatives. Two types of radiator cowl are fitted, each of them different from the equivalent petrol type. One was introduced later than the other, but they may have been fitted interchangeably at some stage during 88 and 109 production. Top and bottom hoses are also different from their petrol equivalents.

EXHAUST SYSTEM (ALL MODELS)

The 88-inch and 109-inch Land Rovers have exactly the same three-piece exhaust system as their 86-inch and 107-inch predecessors. Once again, the rear silencer is 'handed' for right-hand drive and left-hand drive. There is no difference between the systems fitted to petrol- and diesel-engined models.

TRANSMISSION

As on earlier models, the 88s and 109s have a rod-operated single dry-plate clutch and a four-speed primary gearbox with synchromesh on third and top only. The transfer box again gives low and high ratios, and drive to the front axle may be disengaged for road use.

CLUTCH AND BELLHOUSING

The flywheel housings differ between petrol and diesel engines. The clutch used with both engines is essentially the same Borg and Beck type, but the diesel item has stronger springs.

Petrol models have the same bellhousing as the final 86s and 107s. However, two types of bellhousing are fitted to the diesels, both of them different from the petrol types. The first type is found with engines numbered up to and including 1168-00378, 1198-00013, 1268-00147 and 1298-00017. During the 1958 model year, a deeper bellhousing was fitted to reduce vibration and noise, and this is found on all subsequent diesel engines. All bellhousings were left unpainted.

PRIMARY GEARBOX AND CONTROLS

The casing of the primary gearbox on all 88s and 109s is the same as that of the last 86s and 107s. This casing is unpainted and has a brass drain plug in its underside. The dipstick is the 86 and 107 type. The gearchange lever and its knob are also the same as on 86s and 107s.

TRANSFER BOX AND CONTROLS

All details of the transfer box and its control levers are the same as on 86 and 107 models. Differences unique to the special 4×2 88-inch models are discussed on pages 124-125.

PROPELLER SHAFTS

The front propshaft on both 88 and 109 Land-Rovers is longer than the one fitted to earlier models, to allow for the repositioned front axle. The rear propshaft on the 88 is the same as on the 86, and that on the 109 the same as on the 107. Like earlier types, all of them have splined sliding joints and are finished in black.

ELECTRICAL COMPONENTS

Most of the components in the electrical system of the 88s and 109s are of Lucas manufacture. Petrol models have a 12-volt system with a single battery, but diesels have two 6-volt batteries. When the vehicles were new, all batteries would have had a black rubber casing, and the battery leads would have had clamp-type terminal connections. The earthing strap should be braided wire with no outer sheath.

As on earlier Land-Rovers, the wiring harness has an outer casing of black cotton braid with a yellow stripe, while the cables inside are braided and lacquered. Harnesses for 88s and 109s differ; harnesses for petrol and diesel variants have further differences; and there are other detail variations.

The voltage control box on petrol models is the same Lucas item (part number 37138A) found on

The voltage control box on the diesel-engined models was quite different from the one used on petrol-engined Land-Rovers.

the 86s and 107s. Diesel models, however, have a different type, with Lucas part number 37189. The fuse box is the same on both petrol and diesel models, and is the type also used on 86s and 107s. Diesel models also have a glow-plug resistor bolted to the bulkhead.

Petrol models have the same dynamo as the 86s and 107s, but the diesels have a more powerful Lucas C45 PV5 type. Petrol models all have an M418G type G76 starter motor with Lucas part number 255330, but the diesels have an M45G type with separate solenoid.

The ignition system on petrol models has the same Lucas side-entry distributor found on 86s and 107s. The coil is once again a Lucas B12, mounted with its top towards the centre of the vehicle. The spark plugs and suppressers are also the same as on 86s and 107s.

The horn is bolted to the left-hand bonnet hinge under the bonnet. All 88s and 109s have the same type, a wind-tone horn made by Clearhooter. Both 88 and 109 once again had only a single windscreen wiper unless one was specified for the passenger's side at extra cost. The Lucas motor is the same as that fitted to late 86s and 107s, and bolts to the inside of the windscreen frame in the familiar way.

LIGHTING

Lighting arrangements on the 88 and 109 models were hardly any less complicated than on previous Land Rovers. Although only one basic type of headlight was used (with variations to suit different markets), there were sidelight variations and several different rear lighting arrangements.

Headlamps on the 88s and 109s are 7-inch Lucas F700 units. Their outer trim rings should be chromed. Sidelights are mounted in the wing fronts, as on 86 and 107 models, and are the same Lucas type 489. However, 88-inch Station Wagons have a Lucas type 488 lamp which doubles as a flashing turn indicator.

At the rear, the stop-and-tail lamps are round Lucas items, type number 518. However, during the 1957 model year several vehicles were fitted with Sparto lamps or Della Red Beacons. These two types were probably fitted because of a shortage of the Lucas components, and it is not clear how many vehicles were affected, or what their chassis numbers were. Both the Sparto and Della lamps have a large all-red plastic body, a die-cast alloy base and a single bulb with twin filaments; the stop lamp is automatically cancelled when the flasher comes into operation. All types of rear lamp are accompanied by stand-alone circular reflector plates with a diameter of 2¼ inches, like those on the final 86s and 107s.

Many 88 and 109 Land-Rovers have been fitted with flashing turn indicator lamps, but relatively few would have had them from new. Semaphore arms were still available as an option for these vehicles and were certainly being fitted as late as 1957 in Britain, where the changeover to flashers was quite slow. Nevertheless, flashers were optional on the 88s and 109s, and standard on 88 Station Wagons.

The Rover-approved flashers operated through the front sidelamps and the rear stop lamps, and were operated by a switch mounted on an arm on the steering column which incorporated a repeater lamp. In later years, Rover approved the replacement of the sidelamp with an amber flasher lamp, and the relocation of the sidelamp inboard of the flasher. A second additional amber lamp would then also be fitted at the rear. On Station Wagons and hard top models, this was fitted on the top of the rear body; on other models it was fitted to the rear panels on either side of the tailgate.

Some 1957-model 88s and 109s were fitted with Della Red Beacon rear lamps, like this one. Note the tailgate fixings, which differ from those on earlier models.

BODY

BULKHEAD AND WINDSCREEN

The bulkhead used on the 88 and 109 Land Rovers is essentially the same as that on the 86 and 107 models, but has an extra reinforcing plate spot-welded to the top of the bellhousing cut-out. The forward extensions of the bulkhead also have radiused corners around the cut-out, where the 86 and 107 bulkheads have angular reinforcing plates. The 88 and 109 bulkheads also have a prominent 'shelf' running across their upper section and rectangular cut-outs for ventilator flaps below the top rail. There are welded tube housings for the door hinges, and the toebox floor sections are finished off level with the main panel. The large, shaped sealing rubber which runs across the top of the dashboard is the same as on the 86s and 107s.

The windscreen frame of the 88 and 109 models is also the same two-pane type in galvanised steel as that on the 86s and 107s. Special glass was used on vehicles exported to France, Algeria and the USA, and was probably laminated. The windscreen pivot arrangement is identical to that on the 86 and 107 Land-Rovers, and the top frame has the same angle brackets for hood, truck cab or hard top fixings. Windscreen clamp arrangements are also the same. On 88-inch soft top models, there is a pivot arm attached to a bracket on the top rail above each of the windscreen panes; these arms support the windscreen when it is folded down across the bonnet, exactly as on the 86-inch models.

Wings, Bonnet and Grille Panel

The front wings are generally similar to those fitted to the 86-inch and 107-inch models, but are one inch longer. The wheelarch cut-out is also approximately two inches further forward in the wing, so that the hole for the wing mounting bracket behind the wheelarch appears to be further back than on the 86 and 107 type (in fact, it is in the same position relative to the bulkhead). In addition, a reinforcing plate is spot-welded on the inner surface of the wing behind the rubber door buffer, and the traces of these welds visible on the outside are the easiest recognition feature of an 88 or 109 wing.

These wings consist of three separate pressings. The inner wing and top panel are one pressing, the outer wing is the second, and a front closing panel is screwed to them. This front panel has a scalloped indentation for the sidelight. Both wings may be drilled to take wing mirrors, but normally only one mirror was fitted and the redundant hole was filled with a bolt. This has a plain washer visible on the top surface of the wing, and the nut on the underside is kept tight by a spring washer.

The grille panel on 88-inch and 109-inch Land-Rovers is quite different from earlier types. It is made of steel instead of alloy, and is a simplified pressing with only three apertures. There are two circular ones for the headlamps and one large rectangular one between them. There are also two cut-outs at the lower corners of the panel. As on earlier models, a strip of sand-coloured webbing secured to the top edge of the panel by 12 bifurcated rivets serves as a bonnet rest.

The wire mesh grille has the same inverted T-shape as on the final 80s, the 86s and 107s. As before, it is clipped to the grille panel at the bottom and bolted to it at the top. The two bolts which hold the grille in place also locate the oval Land-Rover badge, which is the same 7$\frac{3}{16}$ inch wide type found on the 86s and 107s. On Station Wagons, these bolts also hold a second plate badge, which hangs below the oval and reads 'Four Wheel Drive Station Wagon'.

The horn was always attached to the underside of the bonnet panel on 88s and 109s, and the scissors-type bonnet prop changed sides on a diesel.

As on earlier models, the fuel tank was under the right-hand seat. This one is on a diesel model. The yellow paint on the filler cap is a standard British military identification for diesel-powered vehicles (petrol types have red-painted caps), but it is not clear whether this Land-Rover has a military history. Note the brake fluid reservoir alongside the fuel tank.

The bonnet panel is a single curved piece of Birmabright alloy, with two hinges at the bulkhead end. Both panel and hinges are different from their counterparts on 86 and 107 Land-Rovers, the panel being an inch longer. The 88-inch Station Wagons have their spare wheels stowed on the bonnet, and this fitting was optionally available for other models. The bonnet-top spare wheel stowage kit consists of a strengthening dome fitted on the outside of the panel. As on 86 and 107 Land-Rovers, the bonnet prop rod on all models is a scissors type, consisting of two flat metal arms. One end is attached to the underside of the bonnet, and the other to the right-hand side of the grille panel, inside the headlamp aperture.

Seat Box and Cab Floor

All the panels in this area are exactly the same as their equivalents on the 86 and the 107 models, and are once again painted in the main body colour. Rubber gaiters for the gear lever, transfer box control and handbrake are again identical to the 86 and 107 items.

Sidescreens on the 88s and 109s had more substantial fixings than those on earlier models.

Doors and Sidescreens

The doors of the 88 and 109 Land Rovers are similar to those on the 86 and 107 models. They come in two sections, the main door reaching up to waist height only and a sidescreen being bolted in place to form the upper part of the door. These sidescreens were standard equipment on all models.

Galvanised door cappings and hinges are the same as those on the 86 and 107 models. The door seals are again carried on the bodywork, and the sidescreens bolt through the tops of the doors in exactly the same way as on earlier models.

The sidescreens themselves are superficially similar to those on the final 86s and 107s and are physically interchangeable with them, but they are not the same. As before, the window frames are made of steel with a galvanised finish. On the 86 and 107 models, the frame is quite narrow here and leaves the inner edge of the glazing strip exposed; the 88 and 109 type is much wider and covers the inner edge of the glazing strip. In addition, the 88 and 109 sidescreens have two drain holes for the glazing strip channel drilled above the top corners of the rectangular alloy panel which forms the bottom half of the sidescreen. This panel should be painted in the body colour, as it is on earlier models.

Between sidescreen and door top is a weather strip, retained to the underside of the sidescreen by spring clips. The hinges retaining the sidescreen to the bulkhead are the same as those on the final 86s and 107s.

Back Body and Tailboard

The back body of the 88-inch Land Rovers is identical to that fitted to the superseded 86-inch models, and the back body of the early 109-inch models is identical to that of the 107-inch types except for the rear lamp drillings. Late in 1957, however, the front pair of hood stick sockets on the 109 were changed for a different type.

The tailboards on the 88 and 109 models are also the same as those on the 86s and 107s, the 109's being taller than that on the short-wheelbase model.

All 88s and 109s exported to North America and Australia have their number plates on a mounting bracket in the centre of the tailboard rather than on the right-hand rear body panel.

Paint Colours (Bodies)

The principal colour for the 88-inch and 109-inch Land Rovers was once again Green. However, the Grey, Blue and Beige which had been available on earlier models remained on offer. All four colours were available for both utilities and Station Wagons on both wheelbases. Hard tops are normally finished in Ivory. The paint codes and formulae are the same as for the 86 and 107 models (see page 78).

Canvas, Cab and Hard Top

Hood and Hood Supports

As on the 86-inch models, the hood for the 88-inch was always a full-length type. Similarly, 109-inch models for temperate climates had a metal truck cab like their 107-inch predecessors, and therefore came with a tilt cover over the load-bed rather than a full-length hood.

Hood sticks and other elements supporting the canvas on both 88-inch and 109-inch Land-Rovers are exactly the same as on the 86-inch and 107-inch models. The hood sticks fit into sockets in the cappings at each corner of the body in exactly the same way, and are held in place by the same type of simple clamp. The 109-inch models have vertical support rods for the intermediate roof bar which are fixed to the body side cappings by screws and nuts, again exactly as on the 107s.

The canvas of the hood on 88-inch models is once again khaki-coloured, with straps made of khaki webbing. On the 109s, the tilt covers are in blue or green with matching webbing straps, the colour choice depending on the body colour. The hoods of 88-inch models are interchangeable with those of the 86-inch types, although late 88s do have plastic windows instead of the celluloid type fitted to early examples; the date of the change is not clear. However, 109 tilt covers are not interchangeable with 107 types: where the 107 tilt has a full front curtain, the 109 type does not, and fixes to mounting flanges on the rear of the cab. Late 109 tilts have a single window in their front and rear curtains instead of two; export types also have a single side window in place of the earlier two.

Both 88-inch hood and 109-inch tilt are held to the hood sticks by straps and to the body sides and rear by rope. The 109 tilt, of course, also attaches to the rear of the truck cab. Both 88 hood and 109 tilt can be fitted like their predecessors with additional webbing straps to allow the side curtains to be rolled up and fixed in the open position.

TRUCK CAB

The truck cab was once again an optional extra on the short-wheelbase models but standard on the long-wheelbase pick-ups. It is the same as the type fitted to 86s and 107s, except that the rear panel has extra flanges to accept the tilt fixings (these flanges are present but redundant on 88-inch models with the truck cab). On later 1957 and all 1958 109s, there are fixed brackets instead of adjustable ones to hold the roof panel to the windscreen frame. The first vehicles with the fixed brackets are 1217-00362, 1227-01780 and 1247-01285.

HARD TOP

Hard tops were available only for the 88-inch models, although a few 109s were probably built to special order with truck cabs and separate enclosed rear bodies.

The hard top on the 88s is identical to its equivalent on the 86s. A keylock option was available for the upper tailgate, and this came either as part of a set which included locks for the two cab doors or as a separate item. A single running change was made during production, and this probably coincided with the similar change made for the truck cab: with effect from chassis numbers 1117-02593, 1127-01409 and 1147-02376, fixed brackets replaced the adjustable type holding the roof canopy to the windscreen frame.

The hard top body on this 88 follows the same principles as earlier hardtops, with a top-hinged upper tailgate. The amber flasher lamps are not original equipment, and the red reflectors were probably originally located where the flashers now sit.

The hard top bolts down to the sockets provided for the hood sticks at front (above left) and rear (left).

INTERIOR

DASHBOARD

The instrument panel and bulkhead controls of the 88 and 109 models are exactly the same as those of the 86s and 107s, except when a diesel engine is fitted. On diesel models, the instrument panel has an extra warning light in the centre for low fuel level. The vehicles also operate on a two-key system, the first being inserted into the 'electrical services' or lighting switch on the main instrument panel, and the second going into a key-operated starter switch which replaces the petrol models' starter knob under the instrument panel.

This starter switch also initiates the engine's glow plugs when necessary, and is a Lucas type S60 (part number 31629E). Alongside it is the black knob of the 'Engine Stop' control, which is connected by a cable to the distribution pump. Diesel 88s and 109s, of course, do not have a choke knob, and equally do not have the bracketry for this on their bulkheads.

HANDBRAKE

The handbrake lever on all LHD 88s and 109s is the same as that found on 86s and 107s. Early RHD 88s and 109s have the same lever as 86s and 107s, but later ones have a slightly different type. As before, the shaft of the handbrake should be painted black.

The cab area of this diesel 88 is substantially correct, although the gear lever is the cranked type from a Series II model; it should be the same as on the 86s and 107s. Note the engine speed governor control quadrant, the auxiliary switches alongside the steering column, the substantial hinges for the scuttle ventilator, the late wiper motors and the black Smith's heater. The headlamp dipswitch is mounted on the floor in the driver's footwell.

The seats on the 88s and 109s were upholstered in a darker green than on earlier vehicles, and the colour fades to almost black with age.

Pedals

The clutch and brake pedals on all 88s and 109s are identical to their 86 and 107 counterparts. The accelerator pedal on petrol models is also the same as the earlier type; on diesel models, however, the linkages differ even though the actual pedal is the same.

Once again, the pedals should all be black. Rubber pads were an extra-cost option for the brake and clutch pedals, and are the same as those available for 80s, 86s and 107s.

Seats

The seats in the driving compartment of the 88 and 109 Land-Rovers are exactly the same as those in the 86s and 107s.

The De Luxe Cab

The De Luxe cab appears to have remained available for 88s and 109s. Some examples – possibly all – have a bench seat with a higher back than the standard seats. The cushion of this seat is in two sections, one covering the passenger and centre seats and the other the seat over the fuel tank. Other details of the De Luxe cab appear to have been unchanged.

Heater

The recirculating heater available as an optional extra on petrol-engined 88s and 109s was the same Smith's 620 type as had been supplied for the 86s and 107s. The same options of a second cab heater and a rear heater were also available.

The heater fitted to diesel models is a different recirculating type, although similar in appearance. It uses the same demister tubes and nozzles and the same dashboard-mounted blower switch. However, the water inlet and outlet pipes differ, and both the tap on the rear of the heater and the return pipe adapter on the thermostat housing are different from their equivalents on the petrol models.

A fresh-air heater was also made available for LHD petrol models, probably quite late in production. This consists of a large heater box attached to the bulkhead inside the cab, with flexible hoses running to two demister nozzles screwed to the windscreen bottom rail. A duct then runs through the bulkhead on the passenger side to a blower fan housing on the engine side of the bulkhead. This in turn draws air through a long duct attached to the inner wing, which terminates in an inlet with a mesh covering on the inward-facing surface of the wing ahead of the radiator grille.

STATION WAGONS

THE 88-INCH STATION WAGON

The 88-inch Station Wagon shares all its main features with the 86-inch model. Production volumes are not known because the vehicle shared its chassis number sequences with the standard utility models on the same wheelbase. There is no 109-inch Station Wagon, because the 107-inch type remained in production after the 109-inch chassis was introduced in 1957.

EXPORT VARIATIONS

There were fewer special export variations of the 88-inch and 109-inch Land-Rovers than of previous models, although CKD vehicles may have accounted for a multitude of sins against the 'standard' specification.

LAND-ROVERS FOR THE USA

Those 88s and 109s which were shipped to the USA have special lighting arrangements, with flashing turn indicators exactly like those on the later 86s and 107s shipped to this territory. The rear number plate is also centrally mounted on the tailboard, with its own separate illumination. In addition, the windscreen glass on these vehicles appears to have been laminated.

LAND-ROVERS FOR CANADA

Once again, Rover's preoccupation on Land-Rovers shipped to Canada was with keeping out the cold. Most vehicles probably had a heater, which in some cases must have been the special LHD-only type with its blower fan on the engine side of the bulkhead.

Single-piece door seals are another characteristic of Canadian models, and there is the same special interior trim as fitted to 86s and 107s for this market.

LAND-ROVERS FOR AUSTRALIA

Australian vehicles share with US-model Land-Rovers the centrally-mounted rear number plate and its special illumination.

OPTIONS AND ACCESSORIES

TOOLS

Like their predecessors, the 88 and 109 Land-Rovers came with major tools and a set of small hand tools. These are identical to those supplied with the 86s and 107s, except that diesel-engined models have different spanners. There are three of these: the first has 7/16 and 1/2-inch AF sizes, the second has 9/16 and 5/8 sizes, and the third is a single-ended spanner with a 5/16 AF size to fit the distributor pump bleed screw.

POWER TAKE-OFFS

As with all earlier Land-Rovers, the 88s and 109s can be fitted with power take-offs in the centre and at the rear, and the nose of the crankshaft can be used to drive a capstan winch mounted at the front.

This winch is essentially the same as on earlier Land-Rovers except for a different mounting plate to suit the smaller gap between the bumper and the front cross-member. The drive linkages to the diesel engine are also different from those to the petrol engine, the diesel type having a different length of shaft and a different dog-clutch. With effect from chassis numbers 1117-03625, 1127-02419 and 1147-03925, Rover specified stronger front road springs for petrol-engined 88s equipped with this winch.

As before, the rear power take-off may also be used to drive a drum. The centre power take-off is the same as the one fitted to all earlier models. An engine oil cooler is usually fitted with the power take-offs, and on both petrol and diesel models the cooler unit itself is the same as on earlier models. However, pipework differs between the two types of engine. An oil temperature gauge was always supplied with the oil cooler, and this fits on a bracket in the same way as on 86s and 107s.

TOWING EQUIPMENT

The 88s and 109s could be fitted with the same two different types of tow jaw and the same three different types of tow plate as the 86s and 107s. The same lifting and towing rings could also be fitted in pairs to the front bumper.

MISCELLANEOUS EXTRAS

The optional extras available for 88 and 109 models were the same as those for the 86s and 107s.

Detail of the optional Smith's heater fitted to a diesel 88. The heater fitted to petrol-engined models was similar in appearance but differed in the detail of its fittings.

APPENDICES

IDENTIFICATION, DATING AND PRODUCTION FIGURES

The chassis number of 88-inch and 109-inch Land Rovers is stamped into the transfer box instruction plate fitted to the bulkhead on the passenger compartment side just above the gearbox cover. It is also stamped on the right-hand front spring hanger on the chassis, on the inside of the leg.

The engine number is stamped on the left-hand side of the cylinder block at the front, just beside the exhaust manifold. The gearbox number is on the right-hand side of the gearbox casing. The axle number is on the top of the axle casing, on the left-hand side, for both front and rear axles.

CHASSIS NUMBERS

1956 models (88-inch)
1116-04808 to 1116-05472 (all models, home), 1126-02442 to 1126-02800 (all models, RHD export), 1136-01368 to 1136-01488 (CKD all models, RHD), 1146-04434 to 1146-05372 (all models, LHD), 1156-01001 to 1156-01186 (CKD all models, LHD), 1166-00001 to 1166-00006 (Diesel prototypes). Note: serial numbers on 1956 models continued the sequences initiated by 1956-model 86s, but with different identifying prefixes.

1956 models (109-inch)
1216-00949 to 1216-01227 (basic models, home), 1226-03055 [one only] (basic model, RHD export), 1236-01189 to 1236-01440 (CKD basic models, RHD), 1246-02400 to 1246-03001 (basic models, LHD), 1256-00247 to 1256-00264 (CKD basic models, LHD), 1266-00001 [one only] (Diesel prototype). Note: serial numbers on 1956 models continued the sequences initiated by 1956-model 107s, but with different identifying prefixes.

1957 models (88-inch)
1117-00001 to 1117-03951 (all models, home, petrol), 1127-00001 to 1127-02957 (all models, RHD export, petrol), 1137-00001 to 1137-01798 (CKD all models, RHD, petrol), 1147-00001 to 1147-04526 (all models, LHD, petrol), 1157-00001 to 1157-00745 (CKD all models, LHD, petrol), 1167-00001 to 1167-00298 (all models, home, diesel). No records exist of any vehicles built in the 1177-, 1187-, 1197- or 1207-series.

1957 models (109-inch)
1217-00001 to 1217-00719 (basic models, home, petrol), 1227-00001 to 1227-03850 (basic models, RHD export, petrol), 1237-00001 to 1237-01281 (CKD basic models, RHD, petrol), 1247-00001 to 1247-02581 (basic models, LHD, petrol), 1257-00001 to 1257-00044 (CKD basic models, LHD, petrol), 1267-00001 to 1267-00153 (basic models, home, diesel). No records exist of any vehicles built in the 1277-, 1287-, 1297- or 1307- series.

1958 models (88-inch)
1118-00001 to 1118-01912 (all models, home, petrol), 1128-00001 to 1128-01702 (all models, RHD export, petrol), 1138-00001 to 1138-01296 (CKD all models, RHD, petrol), 1148-00001 to 1148-02230 (all models, LHD, petrol), 1158-00001 to 1158-00198 (CKD all models, LHD, petrol), 1168-00001 to 1168-01488 (all models, home, diesel), 1178-00001 to 1178-00176 (all models, RHD export, diesel), 1188-00001 to 1188-00048 (CKD all models, RHD, diesel), 1198-00001 to 1198-00283 (all models, LHD, diesel), 1208-00001 to 1208-00060 (CKD all models, LHD, diesel)

1958 models (109-inch)
1218-00001 to 1218-00435 (basic models, home, petrol), 1228-00001 to 1228-02450 (basic models, RHD export, petrol), 1238-00001 to 1238-01125 (CKD basic models, RHD, petrol), 1248-00001 to 1248-01371 (basic models, LHD, petrol), 1258-00001 to 1258-00024 (CKD basic models, LHD, petrol), 1268-00001 to 1268-00457 (basic models, home, diesel), 1278-00001 to 1278-00309 (basic models, RHD export, diesel), 1288-00001 to 1288-00075 (CKD basic models, RHD, diesel), 1298-00001 to 1298-00093 (basic models, LHD, diesel), 1308-00001 to 1308-00012 (CKD basic models, LHD, diesel)

Note In these tables, the identifying prefix and vehicle serial number are separated by a dash to aid clarity. This dash is not found on the actual vehicles.

ENGINE NUMBERS

1956 models
1706-00001 (RHD), 1736-00001 (LHD)

1957 models
1117-00001 (RHD, petrol), 1147-00001 (LHD, petrol), 1167-00001 (RHD, 88in diesel), 1197-00001 (LHD, 88in diesel), 1267-00001 (RHD, 109in diesel), 1297-00001 (LHD, 109in diesel)

1958 models
1118-00001 (RHD, petrol), 1148-00001 (LHD, petrol), 1168-00001 (RHD, 88in diesel), 1198-00001 (LHD, 88in diesel), 1268-00001 (RHD, 109in diesel), 1298-00001 (LHD, 109in diesel)

Note In these tables, the identifying prefix and engine serial number are separated by a dash to aid clarity. This dash is not found on the actual engines. Commencing numbers only are given.

Factory reconditioned engines Engines reconditioned by Rover were renumbered. The reconditioning plate carries the part number, which for the 2-litre petrol engines fitted to 88s and 109s is 269216. No details of reconditioned diesel engines are available.

This part number is followed by a serial number and some identifying codes. A typical number would be S0011/20/10. This breaks down as follows:

S	Engine reconditioned at Solihull; L indicates an engine reconditioned at the London service depot in Seagrave Road; K is also found and is not yet explained.
0011	Serial number, in this case the 11th of its type.
20	The increase in bore size in thousandths of an inch (90 indicates liners fitted with standard bore; 91 with 0.010in bore increase; 92 with 0.020in increase).
10	The undersize of the reground crank in thousandths of an inch.

GEARBOX NUMBERS

1956 models
1706-00001 (RHD), 1736-00001 (LHD)

1957 models
1117-00001 (RHD, petrol), 1147-00001 (LHD, petrol), 1167-00001 (RHD, 88in diesel), 1197-00001 (LHD, 88in diesel), 1267-00001 (RHD, 109in diesel), 1297-00001 (LHD, 109in diesel)

1958 models
1118-00001 (RHD, petrol), 1148-00001 (LHD, petrol), 1168-00001 (RHD, 88in diesel), 1198-00001 (LHD, 88in diesel), 1268-00001 (RHD, 109in diesel), 1298-00001 (LHD, 109in diesel)

Note In these tables, the identifying prefix and gearbox serial number are separated by a dash to aid clarity. This dash is not found on the actual gearboxes.

AXLE NUMBERS

1956 models
Front axle: 1706-00001 (RHD, 88in); 1736-00001 (LHD, 88in); 2706-00001 (RHD, 109in); 2736-00001 (LHD, 109in). Rear axle: 1706-00001 (88in); 2706-00001 (109in).

1957 models
Front axle: 1117-00001 (RHD, 88in); 1147-00001 (LHD, 88in); 1217-00001 (RHD, 109in); 1247-00001 (LHD, 109in). Rear axle: 1117-00001 (88in, semi-floating type); 1117-80001 (88in, fully-floating type); 1217-00001 (109in).

1958 models
Front axle: 1118-00001 (RHD, 88in); 1148-00001 (LHD, 88in); 1218-00001 (RHD, 109in); 1248-00001 (LHD, 109in). Rear axle: 1118-00001 (88in, semi-floating type); 1118-80001 (88in, fully-floating type); 1218-00001 (109in).

Note In these tables, the identifying prefix and axle serial number are separated by a dash to aid clarity. This dash is not found on the actual axles.

FIRE ENGINES

All the fire engines on the 80-inch chassis were built at Rover's Solihull works. David Viewing, the owner of this 1953-model 2-litre, uses the vehicle primarily as a water tender for his steam traction engine, seen in the background.

Among the most attractive early Land-Rover variants are the Fire Engines that were built on the 80-inch, 86-inch and 88-inch chassis. Although not every Fire Brigade needed a small and easily manoeuvrable fire tender, capable of operating in restricted spaces that larger appliances could not reach, many of these Land-Rovers were sold to works fire services or small airfields, where they acted as first-response vehicles.

Whereas Rover sub-contracted the construction of later Fire Engines to specialist manufacturers through what became known as its Special Projects Department, the Series I models were actually built at the Rover factory. It was never a very satisfactory arrangement: most Chief Fire Officers wanted fire appliances built to meet their own requirements, and Rover found it very hard to establish a basic specification that would suit everybody.

Some Land-Rover Fire Engines, therefore, probably differed from the standard specification when they were built, while others were modified by their owners either when new or during service. As a result, it is likely that no two examples are exactly the same, and – as with former military Land-Rovers – it is always advisable to research a vehicle's history thoroughly before attempting a restoration to original condition. The guidelines given here cover the basic specification only – the one Rover would have liked every customer to order.

THE 80-INCH FIRE ENGINE

Fire Engines were available on the 80-inch chassis from July or August 1949, but were never very numerous. Their basis is a standard 80-inch Land-Rover, without its tailboard and painted in Poppy Red instead of the standard green. The chassis should be painted to match and the seats should also be upholstered in red. A number of options for the ordinary 80s are fitted as standard. These are the centre power take-off, a spare wheel carrier on the bonnet, 7.00 × 16 tyres, an oil cooler, an engine governor (without its operating rod and ball joint), and a 15lb

Rear view of 1953-model 2-litre shows the characteristic red-painted chassis and red seat upholstery. Even the tilt cover on these early models was red, when specified. Note the brass piping between hose-reel and pump control panel.

radiator pressure cap. The oil gauge which normally accompanies the oil cooler is fitted to the fire pump control box rather than to the vehicle's dashboard.

In addition, all 80-inch Fire Engines have the uprated rear road springs which are also found on Welders and on the later Station Wagons. Some examples built after around June 1952 have a truck cab, which was an extra-cost option. The longitudinal reinforcing bars on the roofs of these cabs appear to have been galvanised, or at least unpainted, rather than painted red to match the rest of the vehicle. A three-seater canvas hood was probably available, but no examples have so far been discovered on 80-inch Fire Engines.

The 80-inch Fire Engine has a fire pump mounted on the rear towing plate. This is driven by the engine through the centre power take-off and through an additional set of gears in what Rover called an 'overdrive' gearbox mounted between the power take-off and the pump itself. The pump has two functions: it can draw water from the vehicle's on-board tank and pump this through the small-bore rubber hose which is carried in the load-bed; and it can also draw water from a fire hydrant connected to the mains supply and pump it through the first-aid hose or through hoses connected to two delivery outlets. The pump speed is regulated by an engine speed governor on a control panel at the rear of the vehicle that also contains water valves and gauges to monitor the operation of the pump.

The so-called overdrive gearbox is bolted to a carrier bracket mounted to the chassis behind the centre cross-member. A short propshaft with a sliding joint runs between the overdrive and the centre power take-off, and a longer propshaft takes the drive back to the fire pump. The gearbox has an eight-blade cooling fan mounted on its rear output flange; it is further protected by a heat shield clamped around the exhaust pipe.

The fire pump is a Pegson type 27H, with an aluminium body and a 200 gallons per minute rating. Its primary inlet faces the rear of the vehicle and is protected by a cap which should be held to the pump body by a chain. The suction hose coupling

suits a 3-inch suction hose and its thread has three turns to the inch; the whole meets British Standard specification number 336. The delivery hose outlets on the top of the pump take a standard British instantaneous coupling and a 2½-inch delivery hose. They are also protected by caps with chains which retain them to the pump body. The pump itself is mounted directly to the rear chassis cross-member by three long bolts, and also to an angled support plate by two further bolts. This support plate is in turn held to the towing plate by four bolts.

A bracing bar runs across the gap normally occupied by a tailboard, and this is bolted to the two rearward-facing body panels immediately below the galvanised capping. The body of the control box is mounted to this by four bolts, and on the right of the control box is a further water inlet with a protective cover that has a retaining chain. The rearward-sloping cover of the control box contains three dials and three black- or red-painted hand-wheel water control valves. A pipe runs from the top of the control panel to the right-hand inlet on the hose reel.

Each hand-wheel has its own label, printed red on an alloy plate and held to the control box by two rivets. Above the top left hand-wheel, the label normally reads 'Pressure pump to first aid hose'. Under the lower left hand-wheel it reads 'Suction tank to pump'; and above the hand-wheel on the right it reads 'Pressure hydrant to first aid hose'.

The three dials are each held to the control panel by three screws; the two large ones are mounted side by side above the small one. The left-hand large dial has a white face with red and black markings, and is a combined vacuum and pressure gauge, reading to 30 inches of vacuum and 100psi. The right-hand dial is a 200psi pressure gauge, and also has a white face, this time with all black markings. The small dial records the engine oil temperature (necessary when it is driving the pump through the power take-off) and has a black face with white markings.

On right-hand drive models, a rectangular number plate is fitted to the vertical rear face of the control box, and a number plate lamp (identical to the one fitted to US-market vehicles) is mounted above it. On left-hand drive fire engines, the number plate is in the standard position on the left-hand rear of the body and is illuminated as normal through a small clear lens under the rear lamp.

Below the control box, the engine speed governor quadrant is mounted on a support bracket which is bolted to the control box itself. The control knob should be in black Bakelite and the notched quadrant plate should be in bare metal; both are identical to the cab-mounted governor controls fitted to Land-Rovers with other power take-off applications. A sheathed control cable runs from the quadrant, alongside the right-hand chassis side member and up into the engine compartment, where it is then connected in the same way as the ordinary optional engine governor.

Inside the rear load-bed, the floor area is protected by a sheet of marine ply (although some vehicles may have had steel or other metal plates here). On this rests the 40-gallon galvanised steel first-aid water tank, with a large central filler cap and its own internal filter. The tank is prevented from chafing against the floor by a rubber mounting pad at each corner. It is held in place by four transverse metal straps bolted to the wheelarches at each end.

The hose-reel is mounted on a support frame consisting of a triangulated leg structure on each side held by four bolts to shaped metal support panels bolted to the wheelarches. A transverse bar braces this support structure at the bottom, and on it should be a clip for the hose nozzle. The whole of this support structure, and the large wheels at each end of the hose-reel, should be painted red to match the body. The hose itself is 120 feet long with a diameter of approximately 1¾ inches and an adjustable brass nozzle. It would normally have been made of black or red rubber.

The pump support plate should be bolted to the draw bar; note how the towball on this vehicle is fitted to an extension of that plate. It is not clear whether the fire pump was always painted red or was originally unpainted; sales brochures of the period show unpainted pumps, but individual users no doubt had their own preferences.

The control panel and its dial gauges are clearly seen, although there are no labels for the dials. They may never have been fitted to this vehicle, but some 80-inch fire engines certainly had them. To the right of the control panel is the governor control quadrant. The large filler aperture for the first-aid water tank is seen at top centre.

Detail of the reel, showing the manufacturer's name cast into one of the turnwheels.

At the front of the vehicle are hose cradles to allow a suction hose to be carried on top of the wings and above the grille panel. As different Fire Brigades specified different types of hose, Rover did not supply the hose itself. However, most Fire Brigades used these cradles to carry two interlocking lengths of hose, stowed in a U-shape around the bonnet-mounted spare wheel. Some Fire Engines allegedly carried wicker baskets to put over the end of the suction hose and act as a strainer when water was being picked up from ditches, although the basket again was not supplied by Rover!

The centre hose cradle bolts to the centre of the front bumper, and consists of a single upright with a U-shaped cradle at the top. Reinforcing plates are pop-riveted to the top of each front wing, and through these are bolted further hose cradles, one on each side. The cradles and front support bracket are normally galvanised. Each of the three cradles also has a strap to hold the suction hose in place. Each strap is held to the cradle by four rivets and has an instantaneous buckle.

Delivery hoses are normally stowed in the rear body, either on the wheelboxes or behind the fire pump. However, there is no standard type because individual Fire Brigades had their own preferences; Rover did not therefore supply these hoses. Nevertheless, the company did supply mechanical foam generators as an extra-cost option. These fit to either or both of the main delivery hoses and are Pyrene type MFG 5.

Even the background to the badges was red on Solihull-built fire engines like this one. The D-lamp has been turned through 90 degrees to make room for non-original flashing indicators.

THE 86-INCH FIRE ENGINE

The 86-inch Fire Engines made during the 1954 model year are essentially the same as the superseded 80-inch types, with minor modifications to suit the longer wheelbase. However, the 1955 and later models have a different type of fire pump without an additional gearbox in the driveline, and a different control box.

Like the 80-inch Fire Engine, the 86-inch model is essentially a standard basic Land-Rover with a few modifications. All body panels normally painted green, blue or beige are finished in Poppy Red, the seats are upholstered in red, and the body has no tailboard. The chassis, axles and running gear are also painted red, although the fuel tank should be black. A centre power take-off is standard, together with a spare wheel carrier on the bonnet, 7.00 × 16 tyres, an oil cooler (with a different oil gauge), and a modified engine governor. The rear road springs are the standard type (in contrast to the 80 and 88 models). The truck cab was optional on 1954 models but is found on all subsequent examples, while 1955 and later models have door check straps not found on the 1954 models.

This 86-inch fire engine is a 1954 model owned by Andrew Ings. Although the chassis is red, the badges have black backgrounds. The Pegson fire pump is unpainted, and is surrounded by a protection bar which was either a special-order feature or a modification made by the original purchaser. The stowage compartments have metal covers, although sales brochures suggest that canvas covers were the standard issue. Variations like this, probably included at the insistence of the original purchaser, must have been a nightmare for Rover and were one reason why the company later farmed out fire engine production to specialist companies.

On 1954 models, the water tank, overdrive gearbox and control box are the same as on 80-inch models. The fire pump is again a Pegson type, but is not the same as on the 80s. These early 86s also have differences in the hose-reel support brackets and have hose lockers on their rear body sides. These items are the same as on 1955 and later 86-inch fire engines. In addition, the propshaft between overdrive gearbox and fire pump is longer than on the 80-inch Fire Engine, to suit the longer wheelbase.

The fire pump on 1955 and later models is made by KSB and is easily distinguishable from the earlier Pegson type: it has a large 'A' cast into its front face and a brass priming handle on the right-hand side of the pump casing. It is a twin-impeller pump, driven directly from the centre power take-off by a single propshaft, and its associated governor limits engine speed to 2850rpm. It has two integral mounting feet, through which it is bolted to a support bracket that extends the rear towplate.

The pump's suction inlet faces the rear of the vehicle and is protected by a cap with a retaining

John Taylor's 1957 88-inch version appears to have been ordered as an airfield fire tender, which would explain why it carries no ladders. An additional hand-held spotlight is fitted behind the windscreen. With the main hoses removed (right), the brackets holding them to the front wing can be seen clearly. There is the usual protection plate on the wing, although on this 88 it is metal rather than rubber-faced. The metal rectangle fitted into slots on the wing probably originally carried the name of the station to which the vehicle was attached, or else the name of the operating company.

chain which attaches it to the pump body. The coupling suits a 3-inch suction hose and its thread has three turns to the inch; the whole meets British Standard specification number 336. The two delivery hose outlets on the top of the pump are suitable for a 2½-inch hose with a standard British instantaneous coupling. Like the suction hose coupling, they have protective caps with retaining chains.

The tailboard aperture is braced by an unpainted square strut which is bolted to the two rearward-facing body panels immediately below the galvanised capping. To the upper face of this bar is bolted a roller guide for the first-aid hose, and this should also have a galvanised finish. The bracing strut also serves as the support for the control box.

The control box for the KSB pump is quite different from the type fitted with the Pegson pump. It is narrower, with all three dials fitted on the right-hand side and just two red-painted turn-wheels for the water valves on the left-hand side. It has no hydrant inlet on its right-hand side and leaves room for the number plate to be fitted in its standard place on right-hand drive vehicles.

The labels for the water valves may be alloy plates printed in red or black plastic type with white engraved capitals. Both types are attached by two screws. The lower one is usually below the lower turn-wheel; the upper one may be either above or below the upper turn-wheel. The upper one normally reads 'Suction tank to pump' and the lower one 'Pressure pump to first aid hose'.

The dials are attached to the control panel by three screws each. The upper large dial is a combined vacuum and pressure gauge with a white face, reading to 30 inches of vacuum and 100psi. The middle dial, which has the same diameter and again has a white face, is a 200psi pressure gauge. The small dial at the bottom has a black face with white lettering and gives the engine oil temperature.

Below the control box is the engine speed governor quadrant, fitted on a support bracket bolted to the control box itself. In appearance, it is the same as the earlier type, although a slightly different assembly is in fact used.

The 40-gallon galvanised steel first-aid water tank is not the same component as in the 80-inch models, although it is generally similar in appearance. Like the earlier type, it rests on four rubber mounting pads. There are two transverse straps to hold it in

place, each split into two unequal segments and bolted together in the middle. The shorter piece of each strap should be on the left and the longer on the right; their outer ends are bolted to the wheelarches. Both straps and tank should be painted red.

The hose-reel is the same as the 80-inch type, but its support arrangements differ. On each side, a foot plate is bolted to the wheelarch box; on 1954 models, a water pipe emerges through the right-hand foot plate and connects with the hose through a tee-piece on the end of the reel. A stiffener plate runs between the two foot plates. The reel itself is then mounted between a pair of tubular structures which are bolted to the foot plates. All these items, and the large wheels at each end of the hose-reel, should be painted red. The hose itself is 120 feet long with an adjustable brass nozzle. The original hoses were probably all made of red rubber.

There are three hose cradles at the front of the vehicle. Those on the wing tops are the same as their equivalents on the 80-inch models, and are bolted through the same stiffener plates riveted to the wing tops. However, the front cradle differs by providing two supports for the hose rather than one. As on the 80s, it is bolted to the front bumper and should have a galvanised finish. Each cradle has a single strap to hold the hose in place; and, as before, different Fire Brigades specified different types of hose, normally carried as two interlocking lengths and stowed in a U-shape around the bonnet-mounted spare wheel.

All 86-inch Fire Engines, including the 1954 models, have hose boxes above the rear wheelboxes, to provide covered stowage for the delivery hoses which remain exposed on 80-inch models. These hose boxes consist of three steel hoops, steel side-

This fire tender was still under restoration when photographed: the pump control panel is obviously lacking its dial gauges and turnwheels, while the hose and its reel have yet to be fitted. Clearly visible within the specially-made rear body are the filler for the first-aid water tank and the galvanised guide for the fire hose. The chassis is painted black rather than red. The later type of fire pump (left) is fitted and remains unpainted.

Door stays were not part of the standard specification, but were clearly ordered for this vehicle.

Even though brackets and rubber buffers for a centre seat were fitted, this fire engine (right) appears always to have had just two seats in its truck cab. Interesting dashboard details (below) are the hand-held spotlight and (just visible) the black Smith's heater.

plates and a steel back-plate, and they are bolted to the body. There is a canvas cover for each one, attached to the hose box at the top by a riveted metal strip. Each cover is held in the closed position by a pair of sprung hooks, and there are matching studs on the body sides over which the hooks fit. The canvas covers should be in a natural canvas colour.

As on the 80-inch Fire Engines, mechanical foam generators were an extra-cost option supplied by Rover. Those used on 86-inch models are the same Pyrene type MFG 5.

THE 88-INCH FIRE ENGINE

The Rover-built Fire Engines on the 88-inch Land Rover chassis are essentially the same as the last of their 86-inch predecessors. They are all petrol-powered; Rover did not offer a diesel Fire Engine at this stage.

The rear springs on Fire Engines subsequent to chassis number 1116-05331 are those of the 109 rather than the standard 88 type. As this chassis was built quite early in 88 production, it is likely that there were no 88-inch Fire Engines with the rear springs of the standard model.

MILITARY LAND-ROVERS

Registered as 09 BC 02 when recruited into British Army service in 1950, Ken Wheelwright's 80-inch model is now registered on the civilian plate 438 DEL. It was built for the first big British military order, placed on 2 May 1949 and calling for a total of 1878 Land-Rovers.

Land-Rovers were ordered by the military authorities of countries all over the world during the lifetime of the Series I models, and many of those vehicles were built to specifications which differed from the standard civilian one. It is simply not possible to give full details of every different variety of military Series I, nor is it likely that full details could ever be obtainable in some of the more obscure cases.

Not every owner of an ex-military Land-Rover wants to restore it to military service condition, in any case. Many enthusiasts are quite content to 'restore' such vehicles to civilian specification, which inevitably results in some compromises. However, for owners who wish to restore a former British military Series I to in-service condition, the guidelines which follow may prove helpful. In addition, there is some more detailed material on two special British military variants – the Rolls-Royce-engined 81-inch and the 4×2 88-inch models.

The British Armed Forces used Land-Rovers for a wide variety of purposes, and equipped them in a wide variety of ways. The precise specification of a former military Land-Rover therefore has to be researched individually – and may never be satisfactorily established. Without details of the original military registration number (found on a bulkhead-mounted plate, if the plate is still present), it is next to impossible to research an authentic restoration. With that number, the first stage is to contact the Military Transport Museum at Beverley, Yorkshire, to see if a record of the vehicle exists.

This record will not provide much, but it will at least be a start. The next stage is to proceed through regimental and unit records (if they exist), in the hope of finding some reference to the vehicle or to one like it. This kind of research cannot be done quickly. Sometimes, additional clues will be provided by military insignia on the vehicle's body panels beneath a later coat of paint; very occasionally, a picture of the vehicle in service may surface; but often all that remains of additional fittings long since removed will be unexplained holes and brackets on the body.

For those who are serious about restoring a former British military Series I, it is also advisable to join the Ex-Military Land Rover Association. In early 1996, this society could be contacted through Nick Percival, at Birch Cottage, 7 Newbury Lane, Silsoe, Bedfordshire MK45 4ET.

The starting point of any authentic restoration of a British military vehicle must be this identification plate (right). In this case screwed to the bulkhead, it carries the vehicle's chassis number, original W.D. (War Department) registration, and details of the contract under which it was ordered. British military 80-inch models normally had the optional scuttle ventilator (far right) fitted. The crude 'lock', secured by a wing nut, is clearly visible.

A grab handle (right) was fitted to either side of the rear body on British military 80s. It helped soldiers climb in and out – and stopped them from falling out if they were sitting in the back! Most British military 80-inch Land-Rovers were fitted with split-rim wheels (far right).

THE MILITARY 80-INCH

The British military authorities soon took an interest in the Land-Rover. As early as June 1948, the Fighting Vehicles Research and Development Establishment at Chertsey started an evaluation of two pre-production examples, and this resulted in an order for 20 vehicles. For this batch, Rover changed from the production light green body paint to a darker green more appropriate to military requirements, although the vehicles still had silver-painted chassis. These first 20 military Land-Rovers were delivered in December 1948 and had chassis numbers R86-0751 to R86-0770; their military (bonnet) numbers were M6279781 to M6279800. Eighteen were delivered with 6.00 × 16 tyres, and two with 7.00 × 16s.

In May 1949 came a second order, this one for 1878 vehicles. Delivery started during June 1949 at a rate of 50 Land-Rovers a week, and continued into 1950. For these vehicles, Rover changed to Bronze Green paint, and it appears that the new colour was standardised on civilian models at the same time. These Land-Rovers were given the new style of military registrations, being numbered from 00 BC 01 to 08 BC 78. Several further orders followed.

All 80s which served with the British armed forces carried a metal identification plate with details of the military contract number and – more important – the vehicle's military registration. This plate may now be missing, and its original location betrayed only by the presence of four screw holes. On early examples, this identification plate is on the engine side of the bulkhead; sometimes it was fitted to the front inner wing; and it is on top of the left-hand dumb-iron on 2-litre models and possibly on some later 1.6-litre types. Some vehicles will betray part of their history in the form of workshop repair details stencilled in white on the underside of the bonnet or on a front inner wing.

British military 80s all had a special wiring harness, covered with stiff black coarse braid which had been treated, or 'tropicalised'. Lighting arrangements were also special to these vehicles. To aid convoy driving without lights in the dark, the rear face of the rear differential was painted white and a light mounted on the rear cross-member was arranged to shine on it so that the vehicle would be visible from behind. Some examples had an extra dashboard switch which disabled the brake lights, and some had

the horn transferred to a push-switch on the dashboard; in these cases, the wheel centre was removed and replaced with a block of polished wood. For trailer lighting, there was a small two-pin or three-pin trailer socket on the right of the rear cross-member. This had a rubber protective plug cover held to it by a safety chain.

Other identifying features include the letters 'OEP 220' stencilled or sometimes hand-painted on the rear differential housing (OEP stands for Oil Extreme Pressure and the figure was an aid to using the correct lubricant during servicing). Many military Land-Rovers had 6.50 × 16 tyres (commonly Dunlop Trakgrip T29s), and there were also special military wheels for use with snow chains, which had fixing lugs for the chains welded around their rims.

The military often reinforced components to improve their resistance to hard use, and it is quite common to find additional stiffening under the load floor of a former British military Land-Rover. From 1950, an extra strengthening plate was added to the bulkhead on the cab side at the steering box mounting – a modification that was also recommended by Rover as a service modification in cases of cracked bulkheads. A small number of 80-inch models used by the Royal Marines on board aircraft carriers also had galvanised chassis to improve their resistance to the corrosive effects of sea water.

Looking almost standard from a distance, 539 KVA is one of the 33 vehicles fitted with Rolls-Royce engines for the British Army in 1949. Outward indications that a Rolls-Royce engine is fitted are the bonnet panel standing proud of the grille panel and the radiator filler cap protruding through it. The two plates on this vehicle's bulkhead tell volumes about its history. The contract for the engine conversion was separate from the original contract for the purchase of the vehicles.

Lastly, many British military Land-Rovers also ended up with green paint on components which left the factory unpainted or in another colour; it appears to have been regular military practice to slap a coat of paint on anything that did not move when the vehicles came in for major overhauls!

A well-filled engine bay, with the huge air cleaner of the Rolls-Royce B40 engine dominating. There is some doubt that the air cleaner, elbow and pipe are correct for this vehicle, although they are very similar to the items originally specified. The rubber buffers on the wing tops help to hold the bonnet clear of the taller than standard radiator. Note the additional holes in the bulkhead for various cables and controls.

THE 81-INCH WITH ROLLS-ROYCE ENGINE

In the late 1940s, the British Army was keen to rationalise the vast assortment of motor vehicles it had acquired during World War II. As part of this rationalisation, it proposed to order the majority of its new petrol-engined vehicles with variants of the Rolls-Royce B-series engine. This engine was used in six-cylinder form in contemporary Rolls-Royce and Bentley saloons (when it was called the B60), there was an eight-cylinder version for the limousines (the B80), and a four-cylinder variant (the B40) had also been developed. A major attraction of the B-series range was that around 90% of the wearing parts were common to the four-, six- and eight-cylinder versions of the engine, which would greatly simplify supply logistics in the field.

After making its major order for 1878 Land-Rovers in May 1949, the British Army decided to investigate whether the B40 engine could be fitted in place of the 1595cc Rover engine. Towards the end of the year, a trial batch of 33 B40-engined Land-Rovers was therefore ordered through the Ministry of Supply. These were to be converted from standard specification by Hudson Motors Ltd of Chiswick, London.

As the Army was keen to press on with trials as soon as possible, the 33 vehicles were taken from those already being delivered under the May 1949 contract, and a further contract for 33 vehicles was signed to make up the deficit of standard types. The chassis numbers of the vehicles converted all fell within the ranges R866-7261 to R866-7807 and 0610-0091 to 0610-07434. The original military registration numbers were in the range 00 BC 01 to 18 BC 78.

The trials were conducted in the spring of 1950 at the Fighting Vehicle Research Department proving grounds at Chobham in Surrey. Among the vehicles used for comparison was a standard 1595cc Land-Rover, which proved superior to all the other vehicles on test. Other problems with fitting B-series engines across the range of military vehicles were already becoming apparent, and, as a result, no more was heard of the idea for a B40-engined Land-Rover. At least one example was subsequently converted into a Review Vehicle, but the majority retained the standard Land-Rover body configuration until they were sold onto the civilian market, mostly in the early 1960s.

The engine in these vehicles is a Rolls-Royce B40 MkIIB, with iron block and cast aluminium cylinder head, and is predominantly painted black. It has a capacity of 2.8 litres (2838cc), a compression ratio of 6.4:1 and a power output of 82bhp at 3500rpm. As on the Rover engine, there are overhead inlet valves and side exhaust valves, the former operated by pushrods and the latter driven directly by the camshaft. The carburettor is a Solex side-draught type. The MkIIB engine differs from the MkIIA fitted in the Austin Champ in two important respects: the Champ engine has both its water pump and a harmonic vibration damper on the crankshaft nose, whereas the Land-Rover variant has the water pump mounted conventionally and lacks the vibration damper.

The B40 engine has special engine mountings, and in consequence the chassis number is not stamped into the foot of the left-hand mounting but rather on the left-hand dumb-iron. There is a special chassis-mounted cradle for the air cleaner, a large cast aluminium item, for which room is created by a cut-out in the right-hand inner wing panel. This cut-out is closed by a shaped metal section which is riveted in place. As the B40's bellhousing is larger than the Rover type, the bulkhead and transmission cover are both modified to suit.

In order to make room for the larger engine in the Land-Rover chassis, several items had to be modified. The gearbox cross-member is unique and runs under the main chassis rail on the left-hand side in order to leave room for the starter motor. The battery is relocated in the seat-box and its original mounting removed. The webs of the front differential are cut away, and the camber of the left-hand road spring is increased.

As the engine also sits higher in the chassis than the standard Rover type, the front bumper is modified and mounted higher up, so that its starting handle hole lines up with the starter dog on the engine crankshaft pulley. There is an additional hole in the cross-member ahead of the engine to allow this handle to pass through.

A larger radiator is also fitted, with special top and side panels riveted in place. The headlamp mounting brackets are also repositioned to suit. The bonnet panel has a circular cut-out at the front to clear the radiator cap, and closes on rubber blocks on the inner wings and grille panel to give clearance above the engine.

The clutch is replaced by a larger 10-inch diame-

The Rolls-Royce-engined 81-inch models have a substantially larger bellhousing cover (above). The accelerator cross-shaft was repositioned on the driver's side of the bulkhead (left).

The battery was relocated under the passenger seat.

The front bumper was repositioned higher up, on special brackets.

John Banham's 88-inch model has been restored with the colours and insignia it wore when in service with British forces in the Middle East. The Army knew this desert camouflage colour as Stone. Note the yellow disc on the front wing (a bridging classification sign that would have been used to carry a weight classification when the vehicle was operational) and special military headlamps.

ter item, and its linkage is repositioned. The transfer box is physically much larger than the standard type, and incorporates different ratios. It is located slightly further back than standard, and a unique front propeller shaft mates up to it. The handbrake linkage is also relocated to suit. The rear axle is an inch further back (hence the 81-inch wheelbase), and the rearmost spring hangers (but not the forward hangers for the rear springs), damper mountings, bump-rubber mountings and check-strap mountings are all repositioned to suit.

There are also small modifications to the interior. The oil warning light is deleted and an oil pressure gauge replaces the petrol gauge; the petrol gauge is then remotely mounted to the right-hand side of the instrument binnacle. There is also a unique accelerator pedal, with a steel roller. Its linkage is all on the cab side of the bulkhead instead of the engine side as on standard models.

The Rolls-Royce-engined Land-Rovers sit slightly lower on their springs than do standard models. This is caused by the greater weight of the engine at the front, and is matched by the flatter rear springs with their ends mounted an inch further apart than normal.

As many parts are unique to the 81-inch Land-Rover, restoration of one of these vehicles to authentic original condition is likely to prove very challenging indeed!

THE MILITARY 86-INCH AND 107-INCH

The 86-inch took over an expanding military market from the 80-inch Land-Rover. In British military service, it was known as a Rover Mk3 and was normally fitted with a full tilt. Some examples were fitted with 24-volt electrical systems and were known as FFR (Fitted For Radio) types; others were given more temporary communications equipment powered by additional batteries and were known as FFW (Fitted For Wireless) types. The 107 was altogether less successful as a military vehicle, but a few were taken by the British Army, where they were known as the Rover Mk4. None of them were General Service vehicles; probably just one Station

Engines rebuilt or overhauled in British military service were usually painted in light green all over.

Camouflage paint on everything! The military favoured their own style of towing jaw (far left) and the trailer socket was protected by a large cover on a chain (left).

Wagon entered service in 1955, and this was followed over the next two years by around 20 chassis with special ambulance bodywork by Bonallack.

The problems associated with restoring a military 86 or 107 are exactly the same as the ones outlined in the section on 80s: without a detailed record of the vehicle's service history, preferably with photographs to back it up, it is impossible to carry out an authentic restoration.

Military identification plates on 86-inch models are found on the top left of the bulkhead on the cab side, and should be the starting point of any restoration. The left-hand inner wing may also bear a military repair plate which can provide useful information about a vehicle's history.

Certain features were common to many British military 86s. Tyres were often Dunlop T29A or Avon Cross-Country in 6.50 × 16 size. Many vehicles had a black circular Lucas switch on the dashboard which killed the vehicle's main lights and illu-

Leather gaiters (right) protected the hub swivels. Special sand tyres (far right) were a feature of vehicles used in desert conditions.

Special military features are the ignition-and-lighting switch (right) and the convoy lights switch partially visible at the right. The white-painted rear differential housing (far right) could be illuminated for black-out convoy driving by the under-chassis lamp seen in the foreground. By the time of this military 88, split-rim wheels were no longer part of the normal specification.

Removable seat covers like these were a feature of vehicles used in the desert.

Paint on everything again, including the gaiter for the transfer box gear lever. Most British military Series I Land-Rovers seem to have carried a brass fire extinguisher in the position shown.

minated its convoy lights; this was accompanied, of course, by a special additional wiring harness. The left-hand rear body panel often carried a large Warner trailer socket with a knurled screw-off cover with safety chain. When not in use, this cover was screwed onto a 'keep' in the shape of a threaded boss to the left of the socket. A black plastic adapter was also available for this socket, so that it could be used with the earlier bayonet-type trailer plug.

THE MILITARY 88-INCH AND 109-INCH

The 88-inch Land-Rover continued to be popular with military authorities, although relatively few 109s entered military service. In British military service, the 88 was known as a Rover Mk5; the designation of Rover Mk6 was probably reserved for the 109, but there is no evidence that any were delivered to the British Armed Services.

Rob Ivins' 88-inch 4×2 model looks perfectly standard externally but the front axle is an undriven tubular type.

THE 4×2 MODELS

One particularly interesting and relatively numerous variant of the 88-inch Land-Rover is the 4×2 model built for the British Army in 1958. The requirement was for a vehicle for purely administrative use, and Rover successfully tendered a bid for a two-wheel drive version of the Land-Rover. While the idea of deleting the Land-Rover's most important feature of four-wheel drive may sound rather eccentric, it probably made good sense to the Army because these two-wheel drive Land-Rovers would share spare parts with the 4×4 variants already in service, thus simplifying maintenance arrangements.

A total of 655 4×2 petrol-engined Land-Rovers was ordered under contract number 6/Veh/26222 on 1 November 1957, and the vehicles were registered as 01 CE 89 to 08 CE 63 when they entered service in 1958. The vehicles were not given special

Inward-facing rear bench seats, grab rails, and a military-style trailer socket are all visible. The rear lamps are Della Red Beacons.

The front output housing of the transfer gearbox (right) is simply blanked off by a domed plate on the 4×2 models. Examples of the two-pin and three-pin military trailer sockets (far right). The three-pin type has a rubber cover attached to it by a chain.

chassis numbers by Rover, but were numbered within the 1118-series of right-hand drive home market petrol 88s, probably starting with 1118-01726. As a result, the presence of the contract number and the original military registration on an identification plate may now be the only confirmation of a vehicle's identity, particularly because many examples have been converted to 'standard' 4×4 configuration in more recent years.

The Army was sufficiently convinced of the merits of the 4×2 Land-Rovers to order a further batch of 275 in August 1958, this time Series II models. However, in practice they do not seem to have been very successful, and some were probably converted to 4×4 while in Army service. Most of the Series I 4×2s seem to have been handed over to the Ministry of Public Works in 1963, and they were re-registered with reversed FUV numbers in May that year (the lowest number known is 25 FUV, the highest 764 FUV). Some were possibly converted to 4×4 configuration during their Ministry of Public Works careers, and yet others have been converted since they came onto the civilian market. Vehicles in original form are rarer than they used to be...

As originally delivered to the Army, the whole batch of 'Car, CL, Utility, Light, 4×4 Rover Mk.5' had seven-seater tilts and were painted green. They were fitted with bench rear seats, grab handles on the rear body cappings, and came without heaters. The front output was deleted from the transfer box, and in place of the usual housing there was a blanking plate with a domed centre to clear the splined output shaft which remained inside. Neither High-Low nor four-wheel drive selector lever was fitted, and the holes in the floor panels for them were plated over. The front axle was a simple tubular type without half-shafts but with the standard Land-Rover swivel housings at its ends.

BROCKHOUSE TRAILER

Andrew Ings' example of a later Brockhouse trailer demonstrates the distinctive shape, with curved mudguards outside the rectangular body.

During 1949, Rover added to the list of Land-Rover accessories a 15cwt trailer, built by J. Brockhouse & Co Ltd of West Bromwich and specifically designed to be used with the Land-Rover. The earliest known examples of the Brockhouse trailer were probably built in April 1949 or thereabouts, but Rover seem not to have advertised its availability until November that year. The trailer remained available right through to 1965, and is today one of the most sought-after of Land-Rover accessories. However, it is relatively rare, mainly because its all-steel body lacks drainage and is extremely prone to corrosion.

The trailer was designed to have exactly the same track as the Land-Rover so that it would more easily follow the vehicle in rough terrain, and it was also designed to use Land-Rover wheels and tyres, so that valuable space was not wasted by the need to carry an extra spare. The lights fitted were also common to the contemporary Land-Rover.

BASIC CONSTRUCTION

The trailer sides and ends are made of 18swg steel, swaged to provide additional strength. These swages have a very distinctive form, being diagonal behind and in front of the wheel and cross-shaped with a circular centre pressing on the front and rear panels. The tailboard swings on pivot pins at the top to allow tipping, and is held closed by retaining pins on chains. Cut-outs in the top edge of the sides and tailboard expose a rod which runs around the top, and to which the canvas cover can be lashed. The trailer floor is of 16swg steel. A domed steel wing is bolted to each side panel.

The trailer's axle is a 1½-inch square bar type made of mild steel. It has drop-forged steel hubs with roller bearings and 8-inch twin-shoe drum brakes operated by rods linked to an over-run mechanism (and to a handbrake lever) on the draw bar. The road springs are two inches wide and have seven leaves each; they are anchored at the front and shackled at the rear.

The draw bar carries the pull pin and the housing in which it slides to operate the over-run brakes. It also carries a handbrake lever and an adjustable drop leg. The hitch is a Brockhouse patent type designed to fit a 2-inch ball, and an appropriate towball was supplied with the trailer for bolting to the rear cross-member of the towing Land-Rover. It is worth noting that this 2-inch ball is larger than the current standard towball size of 50mm. It is also perfectly spherical, whereas the standard 50mm ball has a flattened top surface.

The body and 'chassis' of the trailer should be painted green to match the towing vehicle. There is no evidence that any trailers were painted in the Light Green applied to early 80-inch Land-Rovers.

Each trailer has a serial number on the maker's plate attached to the draw bar. It seems likely that all Brockhouse trailers shared a common number sequence, but that the different types were identified by different prefixes; that on the Land-Rover trailers is BT8. The earliest known trailer is numbered BT8-4260, and the last but one BT8-16666; the final trailer appears to have had a special number which does not fit into the regular sequence.

The design of the trailer did not change greatly over the 15 years of its production, but the tow hitch design was changed in mid-1955. Trailers built

Brass plates on the trailer draw bar give details of the manufacturer and carry the trailer's identification number.

All Brockhouse trailers had a drop-down tailgate. Note details of the pressings in the body sides and mudguard fixings. The lights – contemporary Land-Rover 'pork-pie' items – were fitted on plates which stood proud of the body.

before this are generally known as 'early' types, and those built afterwards as 'late' types.

EARLY TRAILERS

The early trailers have a very distinctive tow hitch and handbrake. The hitch has an oval release handle and its mounting is held to the draw bar by four bolts which pass through separate cylinders cast into the edges of the mounting. The handbrake has a narrow grip. Other details are a hexagon-headed screw in each hub grease cap, grease nipples in the ends of the spring eye pins, and shaped cast spring shackle plates.

The tailboard of those trailers supplied for use in Britain should have a rectangular number plate and a square plate with the letter 'T' in white with reflective red studs. The rear lights are carried on brackets attached to the body sides, and trailers built between 1949-54 have the same D-lamps as the contemporary Land-Rover. Those built in 1955 have small round reflectors as well.

A running change was made after trailer BT8-9301, when minor changes were made to the brake shoes and backplates.

The trailer's leaf springs and square-section beam axle, together with the fixed rear leg.

Detail of the tailboard fixing chain and of the support rod running along the top of the trailer sides.

LATE TRAILERS

With effect from trailer BT8/12325, which was built in July 1955, there was a different draw bar with a different pull pin and housing. The handle of the tow hitch is a simple bar with a serrated lower edge, and the four bolts securing the hitch to the draw bar are no longer in separate housings. The handbrake grip has a serrated lower edge and there is a securing loop attached to it.

The road springs have plain shackle plates and there are no nipples in the spring pins, although some trailers have grease nipples in the spring eye itself. The hub grease caps are simple push-in types, without a screw fixing. Lighting arrangements are also different from the earlier trailers, with circular stop/tail lamps and red reflectors on brackets attached to the body sides at the rear. In addition, most are also fitted with circular flasher lamps; when these are present, the plug for the socket on the Land-Rover's rear cross-member should be a four-pin type instead of the earlier three-pin type. Lastly, examples sold in Britain have a triangular trailer warning plate on the tailboard.

SPECIAL VARIATIONS

Many trailers were undoubtedly sold to private customers, but a quantity were also supplied to the Ministry of Supply for military use, and many also went to the Civil Defence organisation. Some of these were used by Field Cable Party units to lay emergency telephone lines, when they were fitted with a cable reel. The support frame for this appears to have been bolted through the floor to a threaded pad on an additional cross-member; the chassis uprights were also drilled to take a tilt frame. In some cases, additional internal divisions or lockers may have been fitted to these trailers, and additional grab-handles and clips for tools may have been fitted to the outside panels.

It is possible that there were other variations. One trailer known to exist has a detachable front panel as well as a detachable rear one.

LAND-ROVER CLUBS

There are Land-Rover clubs all over the world who will welcome the Series I enthusiast, and up-to-date lists of these are printed in several 4×4 magazines. A full list can be obtained by writing to the Association of Rover Clubs, whose contact address in 1996 was:

Andrew Stavordale
65 Longmead Avenue
Hazel Grove
Stockport SK7 5PJ
UK

However, the majority of ARC-affiliated clubs are primarily concerned with using Land-Rovers, and their many events tend to centre on such things as caravanning and off-road trialling. There are just two clubs devoted to the Series I Land-Rovers as vehicles, and the type of information likely to be needed by a restorer will probably be most readily available here. These clubs are listed below with their 1996 contact addresses; please note, however, that club officials are volunteers and that contact addresses do change from time to time. Please remember, too, that a stamped addressed envelope sent with any letter you address to club officials is a courtesy which is best not overlooked.

THE LAND-ROVER REGISTER (1947-51)
This long-established club focuses on the 1.6-litre models and on the pre-production vehicles. It has an 'approved' list of reproduction parts suppliers, which is a very valuable aid to correct restoration of an early vehicle. Its contact address in early 1996 was:

Richard Lines
Ricoli
Conisholme Road
North Somercotes
Louth
Lincolnshire LN11 7PS
UK

THE LAND-ROVER SERIES ONE CLUB
This club welcomes the owners of all Series I models, from the first 80s to the final 109s and 107 Station Wagons. Its contact address in early 1996 was:

David Bowyer
East Foldhay
Zeal Monachorum
Crediton
Devon EX17 6DH
UK